The History of the Family

NEW PERSPECTIVES ON THE PAST

General Editor
R. I. Moore

Advisory Editors
Gerald Aylmer
Tanya Luhrmann
David Turley
Patrick Wormald

PUBLISHED

David Arnold Famine
Patricia Crone Pre-Industrial Societies
Ernest Gellner Nations and Nationalism
Richard Hodges Primitive and Peasant Markets
Eugene Kamenka Bureaucracy
Edward Peters Torture
Jonathan Powis Aristocracy

IN PREPARATION

Richard Bonney Absolutism
Bernard Crick Representative Institutions
Ernest Gellner Reason and Rationalism
David Gress The Modern State
R. M. Hartwell Capitalism
Linda Levy Peck Patronage
Brent Shaw Bandits
David Turley Slavery
Chris Wickham and James Fentress Collective Memory

THE HISTORY OF THE FAMILY

James Casey

Basil Blackwell

Basil Blackwell Ltd
108 Cowley Road, Oxford, OX4 1JF, UK

Basil Blackwell Inc.
432 Park Avenue South, Suite 1503
New York, NY 10016, USA

British Library Cataloguing in Publication Data

Casey, James
  The history of the family. – (New perspectives
on the past)
  1. Families. Social aspects, to 1980
  I. Title II. Series
  306.8′5′09

  ISBN 0-631-14668-7
  ISBN 0-631-14669-5   pbk

Library of Congress Cataloging in Publication Data

Casey, James, 1944–
    The history of the family/James Casey.
        p. cm. – (New perspectives on the past)
  Bibliography: p.
  Includes index.

  ISBN 0-631-14668-7
  ISBN 0-631-14669-5 (pbk.)
      1. Family – History. 2. Family – Europe – History. I. Title.
  II. Series.
  HQ503.C37   1989
  306.8′5′09–dc19
  88-34189
  CIP

Typeset in 10 on 12pt Plantin
by Graphicraft Typesetter Ltd., Hong Kong
Printed in Great Britain by
Billing & Sons Ltd., Worcester

To my mother and the memory of my father

Contents

Acknowledgements

This book was born of an interest awakened by the European Social History course at the University of East Anglia. To my former colleague on the programme, Morley Cooper, I owe my awareness of the family as a sociological and historical problem. To another colleague, Stephen Wilson, I am indebted for introducing me to many of the authors whose work is drawn on in the present study.

Subsequently I was researching on family structure in early modern Andalusia when the editor of the series, R. I. Moore, proposed the topic of this book. Without his faith, this more ambitious project would not have got off the ground. Matching his breadth of vision has been a challenge and a pleasure. To his careful editorship of the final typescript readers may attribute whatever clarity it may possess.

Finally, to my own nuclear family I am indebted for their forbearance during a time in which it must have seemed that I was more interested in lineage than in household.

Editor's Preface

Ignorance has many forms, and all of them are dangerous. In the nineteenth and twentieth centuries our chief effort has been to free ourselves from tradition and superstition in large questions, and from the error in small ones upon which they rest, by redefining the fields of knowledge and evolving in each the distinctive method appropriate for its cultivation. The achievement has been incalculable, but not without cost. As each new subject has developed a specialist vocabulary to permit rapid and precise reference to its own common and rapidly growing stock of ideas and discoveries, and come to require a greater depth of expertise from its specialists, scholars have been cut off by their own erudition not only from mankind at large, but from the findings of workers in other fields, and even in other parts of their own. Isolation diminishes not only the usefulness but the soundness of their labours when energies are exclusively devoted to eliminating the small blemishes so embarrassingly obvious to the fellow-professional on the next patch, instead of avoiding others that may loom much larger from, as it were, a more distant vantage point. Marc Bloch observed a contradiction in the attitudes of many historians: 'when it is a question of ascertaining whether or not some human act has really taken place, they cannot be too painstaking. If they proceed to the reasons for that act, they are content with the merest appearance, ordinarily founded upon one of those maxims of common-place psychology which are neither more nor less true than their opposites.' When the historian peeps across the fence he sees his neighbours, in literature, perhaps, or sociology, just as complacent in relying on historical platitudes which are naive, simplistic or obsolete.

New Perspectives on the Past represents not a reaction against specialization, which would be a romantic absurdity, but an attempt to come to terms with it. The authors, of course, are specialists, and their thought and conclusions rest on the foundation of distinguished professional research in different periods and fields. Here they will free themselves, as far as it is possible, from the restraints of subject, region and period within which they ordinarily and necessarily work, to discuss problems simply as problems, and not as 'history' or 'politics' or 'economics'. They will write for specialists, because we are all specialists now, and for laymen, because we are all laymen.

Anthropology's oldest and greatest gift to history is the realization that the family is the fundamental element in the constitution of human societies, that the ways in which it is conceived and regulated are infinitely variable, and that these variations govern much not only of private, but of social, political and cultural life. Yet all too often, and perhaps especially with the enormous growth of interest in local and domestic aspects of the family and sexual life, kinship studies as pioneered by anthropologists and family history as described by historians have been pursued with little reference to each other. James Casey's lively and lucid discussion brings them together. His account of the place of the family in the evolution of social thought puts family history in a broad intellectual and historiographical perspective which in turn provides a secure basis for his fresh and wide-ranging exploration of the emergence of the peculiar family structures that are universally agreed to lie at the heart of 'the European miracle', however defined. Many will enjoy even more his rich appreciation of difference in time and place, in which he provides a valuable corrective to much enthusiastic but facile discussion of recent years. This is one of those rare books which can both demonstrate the complexities of its subject and show how they can be made clear. The result is that deepening of understanding to which social history aspires.

R. I. Moore

Preface

The topic of the family is at once attractive and dangerous. Its very popularity has ensured that it is covered by a vast literature which is difficult for one person adequately to master. Then again, the subject is shared among different disciplines, being at the very core of one, social anthropology, and increasingly popular in another, history. It touches all of us in our daily lives in a way in which, arguably, political events do not. Because it is so much part of the fabric of everyday life, its features tend to be indistinct through too great familiarity. How does one begin to probe this amoeba-like structure?

There was a time when the enquiry could be organized along relatively simple lines. For the Victorian pioneers, McLennan, Morgan, Robertson Smith, the history of the family was part of that great march of civilization which had raised man from the level of brute beasts and given him a set of norms by which to live. The historical and anthropological data could be assembled within a theoretical framework as simple and cogent as that of Darwin for biological evolution. Since their day history and anthropology have pulled apart, asking more sophisticated questions of an increasingly diverse store of evidence. Historians have tended to limit the scope of their enquiry to those problems which in the West preoccupy us most today, the relationship between husband and wife or between both and their children, the emergence of the nuclear family and of domesticity. These are important questions in their own right, but arguably they tend to pre-empt the terms of the debate about the significance of the 'family' in the wider sense (kinsmen, godparents and the like) to the political and economic framework as a whole. Such enquiries become more significant the closer we approach to modern times, where the rise of domesticity is indeed a major historical issue. The further back in time we go, however, the relevance of the questions currently being asked seems marginal to our understanding of social relationships.

Here the social anthropologist, with his interest in kinship, may be of more help. But social anthropology has tended to become a discrete discipline, as we have said, since the days of the Victorians. Its practitioners have built up in this century an enormous corpus of field studies, based on enquiry into the identity of self-contained communities. The aim has been to understand the family, or any other aspect of the culture of a particular people, as part of a whole, a variable dependent on the economy, politics, religion of the area. This 'functionalist' approach, pioneered by Malinowski and Radcliffe-Brown at the beginning of this century, has given some outstanding insights. It has destroyed the old evolutionary certainties of the Victorian school, made it difficult to think in terms of the development of forms according to some general plan, and consequently cut most of the bridges with history.

Dissatisfaction on the part of both historians and anthropologists in recent years with the autonomy of their respective disciplines holds out new hope of co-operation. From the anthropological side Eric Wolf (1982) has reminded us of the difficulty of analysing communities as if they were truly self-contained, when we know that their structures have been moulded by centuries of contact, war and commerce with foreign powers. It was a point which the Victorian pioneers, with their solid grounding in the history of the ancient world, had perfectly grasped, but which really needed restating for a generation which has forgotten the primitive peoples of Greece, Rome and Judaea. The problem facing the historian is, in a sense, of the same order: that of making sense of a proliferation of detailed case studies. We know more than we ever did before about how men and women lived in the past, their ambitions and the concepts they had of their respective roles. We know about the kinds of household they lived in, and the way they organized their work and transmitted their wealth. A lot more remains to be done, but the quantitative material at our disposal, after a couple of decades of research, is quite impressive. Perhaps too impressive: the tunnels being sunk into the past are numerous, short and uncoordinated, with the consequent risk of fatigue, asphyxia or a cave-in. To change the metaphor, family historians give the distinct impression of having lost sight of the wood for the trees. It is time that we paused for breath and asked ourselves the question: What is it that we are trying to do?

The pages which follow have a double objective. They are written, firstly, on the assumption that social anthropologists and historians have partial aspects of the truth about social relationships, and that it is time to see whether the two can be brought to complement one another. Secondly, the book is an attempt to provide an interpretative framework within which studies of family structure in the past may make sense. It is not meant to be a résumé of knowledge about the family as such (though I hope it is that too). Rather, it aims to suggest why a proper understanding of what the 'family' was can help analysis of some major debates about the nature and development of the modern economy and the modern state. The emphases are, no doubt, personal to the author, for such a study cannot claim to be comprehensive or even objective. The questions I raise are shaped by two decades of thought on the development of early modern Spain, the failure of capitalism in that country despite its access to American silver, the failure of a modern state to develop despite the bureaucratic legalism of a great empire, the enduring strength of local community ties despite massive migration and centralization. But the guiding thread to the pages which follow is really the thought of three great Frenchmen: de Tocqueville, Le Play, Durkheim. Their concern with understanding the traumatic social changes through which their own society, that of nineteenth-century Europe, was passing has given them an enduring fascination for historians. Their desire to explore the contrast with the old world, then in its agony if not quite dead, led them by very different paths to a common preoccupation with defining 'individualism'. It is this search for the individual and his network of relationships to his fellow man, conceived of as a problem in its own right and not assumed as determined say, by class interest, that is the hallmark of their thought. I have adopted it, as best I could, as a way of understanding the significance of the family in the past. It forces the family historian to keep repeating to himself the questions: What am I trying to explain? How does my material link up with broader social developments? In that question of context resides the main possibility of dialogue between the more pragmatic historian and the more theoretical anthropologist.

1
The meaning of family

There is a tendency, in judging people of other periods or societies, to start from the values important in one's own time and to select significant facts in the light of these values. This approach blocks access to the special context of the people whom one is trying to understand. They are detached from the structure which they actually form with others, and placed heteronomously in contexts determined by contemporary values, to which they do not belong.

Norbert Elias, *The Court Society*

Much recent writing by historians on the family has aimed, in one form or another, at exploring the origins of a system which is most familiar to us in the West: the domestic hearth, round which are grouped a man and a woman, equal companions, dedicated to the education, in a broad sense, of their common offspring. The 'rise of the nuclear family' is beginning to take over the place vacated by the 'rise of liberty', the much decried Whig interpretation of history, as a way of making sense of the past. The problem with both concepts is not that they are necessarily wrong, but that they look at history through the wrong end of the telescope. The focus on the nuclear family, like that on parliaments, may give these bodies a spurious identity which they have come to assume only in more recent times. Because there were parliaments and households in the seventeenth century, we may be lulled into a false sense of security that they must therefore be much the same institutions, with much the same significance as they have nowadays. The danger there is that we forget to look for alternative ways of ordering constitutional and personal relationships – patronage, male sociability – which have not survived in the West. Our understanding of how older societies actually worked is thereby impoverished.

The pioneers in the exploration of the nuclear family were, and still are, exciting to read. Several decades ago, Philippe Ariès re-awakened historians' interest in the topic with a masterly book on childhood. His sensitive reflections on art, folklore and pedagogy from the later Middle Ages suggested the potential importance of seeing our own family arrangements, the domestic nuclear household, as part of a great historical change. We shall turn to explore his arguments in more detail in our last chapter, on domesticity. But it is interesting to note here a warning which he issued in the preface to the 1973 edition of his great work, *L'Enfant et la vie familiale:* 'Let us hope, though, that the history of the family does not get buried under an abundance of publications due to its popularity, as happened to its young predecessor, demographic history.' He was concerned, in his modest way, that too much specialization in the nuances of the themes he had raised, and too great a limitation to his own epoch, the early modern period, would cause people to lose sight of the object of the exercise, which was to understand ourselves in time. He urged the younger historians to go back in time: the earlier Middle Ages, he suspected, would be a more fruitful frontier. He would, no doubt, have been pained that he has been taken for – and criticized for being – the historian of 'attitudes', specifically the rise of affection within the household, when he was so concerned to get others to think in terms of the context which made that affection possible.

This has, of course, been one of the handicaps of family history: the tendency to treat the topic as a discrete field of enquiry. Two centuries ago Montesquieu demonstrated the value of looking at law as part of a total civilization, an expression of the way a society chose to organize itself, rather than as tablets of stone imposed by a lawgiver. Legal history, like religious history, continues to be influenced by this search for context. In the case of the family such fertile lines of enquiry are not so evident. It may be that the family has been regarded as an institution with visible boundaries, in a way in which religion or law are not, and that therefore its existence is unproblematical. If not an institution (i.e. a household), then the contours can seem so exasperatingly vague as to defy enquiry altogether. Of course, there is a substantial interest, especially among medieval historians, in the political significance of ties of kinship beyond the household. But the waters here tend to be murky. As J. C. Holt has recently pointed out, the fact that sixteen of the twenty-four barons chosen to enforce Magna Carta were somehow related to King John's great opponent, Earl Richard de Clare, does not of itself tell us very much. 'Relationships have been woven into an explanatory pattern, as if it were sufficient simply to say that men were kinsfolk, and that was that' (1982, pp. 193–4).

Alternatively, the fact that kin often quarrel (and who is not aware of the troubled relations of John or Richard III with their nephews?) produces maybe a shrug of the shoulders, a feeling that families then must have been much like their modern equivalents: a source of obligation for some, of resentment for others, of indifference for the majority.

Seeking firmer ground on which to build, historians have tended to reduce their focus to the household. Households can be measured; they figure in the historical record as identifiable units, whereas kin groupings have to be (mostly) inferred. At this level, family history links up with historical demography, and, at its best, can help our understanding of the economic development of traditional societies. The problem with this approach is that one may pre-empt any debate about what the significant categories for analysis of traditional societies should be. Anthropologists have cast doubt on whether households can actually be measured in the way in which historians often assume, given diverse arrangements for sleeping, eating or work-sharing, none of which need actually involve co-residence (cf. Jack Goody's contribution to Laslett and Wall, 1972, which seems to have found curiously little echo in the historical literature). The father of this kind of enquiry, Frédéric Le Play, was concerned with the relationship between household form and the economic and cultural constraints of any particular civilization within which it was moulded. We shall look at his ideas in detail a little later. But here we may note that his disciples have since tended to get bogged down in the minutiae of description of households as institutions in their own right. Le Play's attitude was rather that the household is a reflection of certain ways of organizing society and can be understood only in that context. The modern specialization of university research has ensured that we have switched the emphasis unconsciously, towards trying to understand a society through measuring the extent and form of something we rather arbitrarily label a 'household' or a 'family'. But it is precisely the definition of these terms that is the often unrecognized problem which may skew the results of the investigation.

It is the social anthropologist who has tried, more consistently, to see family relationships within their broader social context. Where histories of the family tend to pall for one reason or another – either because they are so specialized and ultimately marginal to our understanding of the society they aim to describe, or alternatively because they are so general, repetitive and anecdotal – the anthropologist's study has that theoretical framework which enables us to see the detail in a setting of general significance. The Victorian pioneers, McLennan, Morgan, Robertson Smith, are still of enduring importance because they asked the one question which matters above all: What is a family? Twenty marvellous years, from the publication of McLennan's (1970) *Primitive Marriage* in 1865 to Robertson Smith's (1903) *Kinship and Marriage in Early Arabia* in 1885, laid the foundations for a discipline. The idea which these three very different men held in common was that the primitive family was organized around the mother and her 'people', and only subsequently around the father. The idea is not much in favour today, though the arguments advanced are reasonably nuanced and rather compelling. But whether these thinkers were wrong or not on the substantive issue is of less significance than the fact that they raised the question of family organization as a problem – a problem over time and between cultures. They broke with that lazy view of the family as having developed vaguely out of associations of patriarchal heads of households and tribal chiefs into commonwealths and states which rendered the larger family groupings redundant, a view epitomized, perhaps, in H. S. Maine's epochal study, *Ancient Law* (1861). Under this schema, the family was not really a problem for analysis, merely a passive actor in a drama unfolding around it. McLennan, Robertson Smith and Morgan made us rethink our assumptions by underlining at least two points. One is that the concept of agnatic kinship is an artificial construct, which supposes a good deal of intelligence and abstract thinking: the natural relation of any creature is with its mother, that with its father and its father's people argues already for a higher degree of social organization. Secondly, the assumption that the conjugal family household is at the base of a pyramid which reaches up to the tribe and the state is to invert the true historical order: the emergence of the conjugal family is a problem for analysis in its own right, since it comes to supplant alternative ways of ordering human relationships where the mother or the father takes the child into her or his own group. Rearing, education, social solidarity: their concentration within the conjugal family entails a breakdown of older structures, therefore raising a historical problem.

These eminent Victorian thinkers were, of course, much influenced by discoveries in geology and biology at the time (Darwin had published *The Origin of Species* in 1859, though there is no evidence that it had a direct influence on their thought). It seemed reasonable to apply the same evolutionary dynamics to the understanding of family structures: the family was a system of conflicts, internal contradictions and adaptations rather than a chrysalis gradually shedding a cocoon of kin entanglements to reveal its true inner core. Where their method has come in for criticism is on the score of evidence. They tended to assume that human evolution was uniform, and that there were common stages of development, so that one could understand the past of one civilization by a direct transfer of evidence from another. The stimulus for McLennan's reflections on the history of marriage was the feigned reluctance on the part of brides to join their grooms, which he noted as a feature of wedding ceremonies among many peasantries persisting to his own day. He speculated that this was a relic of an older tradition of bride capture, of which echoes could be found in ancient literature. 'The symbolic forms that appear in a code or in popular customs,' he wrote, 'tell us as certainly of the early usages of a people as the rings in the transverse section of a tree tell of its age' (1970, p. 9). Whatever we may now think of his particular interpretation, his methodology is still quite interesting. He noted in connection with the development of marriage in ancient Rome that, if we confined ourselves solely to the written record, we would come away with a misleading impression of the direction and pace of historical change. We sometimes need to complement the paucity of the sources for a particular culture by analogy with better-documented ones elsewhere (p. 8).

Essentially his argument may be summarized as follows. In a primitive, hostile environment there would be considerable female infanticide and a consequent scarcity of women; brides would be shared and captured, and little knowledge could be had of physical paternity; children would trace descent through their mothers. At a certain stage men would try to regulate the competition for brides, and there would be a move first towards patriarchy (that is, control by a man over his wife and children) and then patriliny (that is, tracing descent through the father's line). Recognition of the potential clash between two principles of descent, or continuing attachment to the mother, would explain the rule in patrilineal tribes that one took one's bride from outside the circle of paternal relatives.

Morgan was less interested in matrilineal origins. His main achievement was to show how patrilineal descent came to be defined more precisely and exclusively as civilization developed. 'Instead of a natural and obvious conception, the *gens* was essentially abstruse; and, as such, a product of high intelligence ...' (pp. 388–9). His second contribution, further developed by Engels (1884), was to

explore the shift from tribal to household organization. They empha-
sized the importance of economic development and the accumulation
of capital. As settled agriculture spread and manufacture fostered exchange, households began to acquire patrimonies, which men wished
to transmit to their offspring. This led to efforts to monopolize the
sexual services of wives, with a view to establishing clear lines of
paternity. The patriarchal family was given an immense boost with
the introduction of iron-working, which made agriculture and warfare possible on a hitherto unknown scale and forced men to group
together for protection. Eventually the state rendered the tribe redundant, and left the conjugal family household as the basic focus of
human loyalties.

Modern scholars feel somewhat uneasy about the use of evidence
by these pioneers of family history. Perhaps what we really mean by
this criticism is that we get too little sense of context, too little sense
of family shaped by definable, observable constraints. The researches
of Morgan on the Iroquois, or of Robertson Smith on the Bedouin,
of course, are immensely detailed. But it is really, perhaps, with
Fustel de Coulanges's *La Cité antique* (1864) that we may feel that
family structures have been integrated in a significant way with a
well-researched historical environment. *La Cité antique*, like much
historiography of the nineteenth century, starts as a reaction against
its own civilization, a commitment which gives it, as with de Tocqueville and Marx, a universal relevance. Fustel warned his readers
that the revolutions in France since 1789 stemmed, in their sterile
repetitiveness, in part from a false reading of Greek and Roman ideas
of liberty. 'Our system of education, which causes us to live among
the Greeks and Romans from childhood,' he wrote, 'accustoms us to
compare them constantly to ourselves, to judge their history by our
own.' Nothing could be more mistaken. Greece and Rome needed to
be studied on their own terms, 'as if they were quite foreign to us,
with the same detachment and as unprejudiced a mind as we would
bring to the study of ancient India or Arabia' (p. 2).

It was this revolutionary approach which led Fustel to his discovery that, instead of 'citizens', Greece and Rome were in their
formative stages composed of 'clans'. The family was no mere private refuge, but a powerful corporation at the heart of public life.
This *gens* was patrilineal: Fustel had nothing to say about any matriarchy which may have existed in earlier times, since that was not
part of the historical record.

What he sacrificed in breadth of enquiry he gained in depth, linking the family more precisely with the religion and politics of the commonwealth. In a brilliant insight, akin to that of Robertson Smith on the totem cult of the ancient Arabian tribes, he suggested that a family was not necessarily defined by objective criteria like property or descent, but by a certain idea of itself. The cult of the ancestors gave the Roman lineage an identity just as sure, if less measurable, than common landholding might have done. Nothing has a more powerful grip on the soul, he wrote, than an idea: 'a man may tame the environment, but he is a prisoner of his own thought' (p. xvi). Fustel's definition of the family was so subtle that it became clear, perhaps for the first time, that the thing itself could not be grasped without a solid grounding in the culture of a particular people. It is a lesson that, as historians a century later, we are still sometimes slow to learn.

Fustel's memory is more honoured today among social anthropologists. But it has tended, paradoxically, to drive a wedge between them and the historians, as the emphasis came to be more on reconstructing cultures as a whole rather than, as McLennan, Morgan and Robertson Smith had tended to do, pursuing changes in the family over time. The father of modern social anthropology, Radcliffe-Brown, was impatient with what he called the 'speculative history' of the Victorians. He showed how elements of culture which these writers had interpreted as survivals of earlier forms – the 'bride capture' ceremonies beloved of McLennan, or the classifying of maternal or paternal uncles as 'mothers' or 'fathers' which Morgan had noted for many primitive peoples – could profitably be understood in terms of present need. In a superb article of 1924 entitled 'The Mother's Brother in South Africa' he argued that the importance of the maternal uncle in some tribes was related to particular patterns of property-holding and culture rather than to survivals of some supposed earlier stage of matriarchy (1952, pp. 15–31). Attitudes to the mother's brother will be found to vary as between cultures, and will provide an insight into how the society is organized: there will be a respectful distance in tribes where property passes in the matriline, and greater intimacy, even joking irreverence, where the father controls the property and the maternal uncle is an emotional substitute for one's father, a senior male in whom one can have unbounded trust. The significance of this way of exploring relationships will not be lost on the medieval historian, who has often pondered on the role which the mother's brother plays in the great epic poetry of feudalism. In both cases Radcliffe-Brown would say that one learns more by exploring the context of the society one is studying than by speculating on the origins of a particular custom.

This attempt to see the family in the wider context of a specific culture was facilitated around the time Radcliffe-Brown was writing, in the 1920s, by a burgeoning of field studies in the colonial territories of Africa and Polynesia. But as the family came to be seen more as a strand in local systems of social organization and less as a thing for study in its own right, the problem arose whether any general conclusions could be drawn. Radcliffe-Brown began to advocate what he called a 'comparative sociology' which would bring order to the proliferation of case studies. Cultures, he thought, might be classified according to certain broad principles or 'structures', such as whether they reckoned descent through the father's or the mother's side, and whether property passed at marriage from the groom's family to the bride's (bridewealth) or the reverse (dowry). It was then the task of the anthropologist to investigate how these structures were adapted to the routine needs of real human beings in specific contexts, the 'process' of everyday life. The way in which the structure fitted this process could be described as its 'function', a term pregnant with meaning for a generation of social anthropologists (see his collected articles, 1952).

Radcliffe-Brown's method might have been expected to appeal to the historian, whose task it might be to show how structure and process diverged over time and had to be reshaped. The author confessed to a personal attachment to history, but of the documented and not 'speculative' kind. He noted the change which had taken place in Europe from the agnatic *gens* or patrilineal clan, characteristic of ancient Rome, to the bilateral kindred or *Sib* introduced by the Germanic invaders. But he doubted whether historians could find full enough records to illuminate such change in most cases. Ultimately more light could be shed on the family or any other institution by studying its context rather than its origins. His approach had more in common than he may have realized with the developing school of French historiography at the time, centred on the foundation of the journal *Annales* in 1929, and its spokesmen Lucien Febvre and Marc Bloch. For they too were desperately concerned to break with an older form of linear history, and to explore the function of institutions, political, economic or cultural, within a total social context. But the triumphs of the *Annales* school were to be achieved in the marriage of history and geography, not history and anthropology.

The legacy of Radcliffe-Brown has been felt particularly in the multiplication of case studies of local communities studied as organic wholes. His hope that this might prove complementary to the elaboration of comparative structures of behaviour across communities has not, however, been fulfilled. As more and more local studies show the great variety of family forms, adapting to their particular environments, it has become more difficult to draw general conclusions. The problem is partly one of method. Institutions like bridewealth and dowry can be compared across cultures, but it may not always be helpful to do so. The anthropologist Pitt-Rivers (1971) has expressed the dilemma most forcefully in the introduction to his 1954 study of an Andalusian village: 'I went, therefore, into the field armed with the models of lineage systems and age groups, but devoid of any which turned out to be relevant to the social structure of Andalusia' (p. xv). It is the French, drawing on a richer sociological tradition, who have held most firmly to the concept of general laws or structures. Claude Lévi-Strauss, most notably, has drawn attention to the patterns which can be detected in the apparent randomness of marriage customs throughout the world. Peoples seem generally keen to work out a code for themselves regulating the pairing of male and female, and the kinds of barriers they erect can tell us a great deal about the organization of human society generally.

The problem of this kind of structuralist model is that of comparing like with like. Cousin marriage, for example, can take two forms: parallel (with the child of one's father's brother or one's mother's sister), or cross (with the child of one's father's sister or one's mother's brother). The anthropologist Jack Goody has noted that cousin marriages of the latter kind seem characteristic of both simpler societies, where there is little property to be handed on to descendants, and of more complex ones, where girls inherit property as well as boys and their matrimony becomes of strategic interest for the reuniting of inheritances (1976, p. 16). Clearly two different explanations are involved here, one concerned with property and another, in the simpler societies, with political alliances. They illustrate the difficulty for the comparative anthropologist in defining the variables he must use if any significant comparison is to be made among cultures. The problem has become more acute in the modern age of systematic, computer-assisted enquiries into world structures. As Goody warns, it is important not to lose sight of the data-base, the original field-work, the local variations, out of which the model is constructed. Ideally there needs to be a continual testing of broad theories about how kin marriages or dowry exchanges operate against a rounded case study, where one can see their function as modified by the local economic, religious or political context.

One of the exponents of the anti-structuralist approach, Pierre Bourdieu, warns us that rules of marriage and inheritance can be a kind of optical illusion in the eye of the beholder. Individual lives are adjusted flexibly to the needs of the local society. People who marry a father's brother's daughter are not obeying rules as such; rather, the prevalence of this form of marriage in their culture has to be studied as a series of responses to particular pressures. Certain expectations, it is true, are built up over time – notions of the right way to behave. But family structures are not self-contained institutions; rather, they are imperfect, ramshackle adaptations of the human psyche to the culture and ecology of a particular area. The interesting thing is not the 'structures', which do not really help us understand the complexity of a local society, but the way in which the norms of conduct evolve and can be adapted to individual needs. Bourdieu's divergence with Lévi-Strauss could be summarized, perhaps, by saying that to classify cultures in terms of marriage or inheritance rules is to impoverish one's understanding of how the family relates to its social context (1977).

This nuance is relevant to the analysis of tribal groups or clans, whose exact boundaries are notoriously difficult to define. The leading anthropologist in this field, Meyer Fortes, tended to see the clan as a structure greater than the mere sum of the individuals of which it might be composed at any one time. His field-work was done among African tribes, the matrilineal Ashanti and the patrilineal Tallensi. For these peoples the clan is the very framework of social life, conferring rights to citizenship and property. Fortes acknowledged that clan structures did not encapsulate the reality of individual ambition or the occasional waywardness of human behaviour. Among the Ashanti, where men were supposed to hand their property and status on to their sister's son by the rules of the tribal structure, they often favoured instead their own offspring. This informal 'web of kinship' could be at variance, then, with the structures of clanship. Nevertheless, Fortes argued, it still made sense to see Ashanti or Tallensi society in terms of tribal rules, even though these were 'dynamic' and not static (1970).

The historian of European society is likely to be more interested by the 'web of kinship', for, by training and by the nature of his evidence, he is more attuned to tracing individual behaviour than fitting it within a set of rules. The danger of such pragmatism is that it may overstress the significance of the individual in old-regime cultures and underestimate the importance of the family as a corporation. But the study of the European family as a problem surely begins as an attempt by nineteenth-century observers to make sense of their increasingly fragmented society. Where the old constraints of hierarchy were overthrown in religion and politics after 1789, sensitive men began to explore the nature of the ties which held a social order together in the first place. This is a common thread running through the work of the early French sociologists and historians, Fustel de Coulanges, Alexis de Tocqueville, Émile Durkheim, Frédéric Le Play.

These four thinkers have fashioned the framework which I, as a historian, have found most useful for family studies. Only one of them, Le Play, was directly concerned with the family as such. But their ideas on the nature of society give us that much-needed context within which the study of the family can alone make sense. Le Play has come to be as much cited in the historiography of the family as, say, Marx in that of class; but, as with Marx, he is perhaps more cited than read. He wrote a rather bad book, *L'Organisation de la famille* (1871), designed to recreate for his country those family institutions characteristic of 'frugal and fertile populations, with their dedication to hard work'. It has to be seen in the context of the defeat of France by Germany in the year of its publication, and Le Play should not be judged by this schematic essay, but by his mature work of several years before, *La Réforme sociale en France* (1864). Here is a book which, in its sensitive, probing analysis of social structure, has some claims to rank alongside de Tocqueville as a profound commentary on early liberal society.

Its impact in scientific circles was weakened, no doubt, by its strong moral tone. The most common view of Le Play is that he was a utopian or a reactionary, and therefore a poor guide to the reality of his own time. The stress he laid on abnegation and the sacrifice of individual sentiment by the members of a family for the good of the whole does not endear him to a modern readership. Le Play was not a psychologist but an engineer by training, with an acute insight into formal structures, and into the relationship of parts with the whole. Much of his observation of the family was made in the course of official visits to study the working of mines in various European countries. He was scarcely a reactionary in the conventional sense. He admired, for example, the growth of free trade, though he had some harsh comments about the degradation it inflicted on under-developed peoples: 'as big a scandal as free trade with children would be in our civilized societies' (vol. II, pp. 39–53). On the whole, though, the free exchange of goods was like the free exchange of ideas, the condition of human progress, to which he had a sincere commitment. It is too often forgotten that he was a supporter of the Enlightenment, and a stern critic of most pillars of the old regime – the church, the monarchy, the nobility, all of which he condemned for abuse of power. He regarded the Revolution of 1789 in somewhat the same light as de Tocqueville: an inevitable collapse of a political system which had concentrated too much, or not enough, power at the centre, undermining those intermediaries, like the family or the community, which had maintained social harmony before.

Le Play saw the great challenge facing his generation as that of coming to terms with the legacy of the twin revolutions, industrial and political. In spite of what he regarded as its undeniable benefits, the revolution of 1789 had failed to bring France stability. The further upheavals of 1830 and 1848 convinced him, like Fustel de Coulanges, 'that instead of incessantly altering our institutions as we had been doing with such futility since 1789, we needed to shake the soul of the nation into rethinking its beliefs and customs' (vol. I, p. 32). The problem might lie in the lack of a generally agreed social hierarchy, undermined by an unregulated competition for property. The Civil Code of 1804 had instituted a general equality of inheri-tance among siblings. Le Play was aware that this Revolutionary legislation could have had little effect on its own had it not been matched by the burgeoning of a market economy, which enabled young people to earn money at an earlier age than ever before and use it to supplement what would otherwise have been an uneconomic fraction of their parents' holding. Subdivision of the patrimony had become feasible for the first time without causing financial ruin. From these humble beginnings there developed a general moral climate of 'individualism', with competition between siblings gener-ating a more selfish and turbulent society than anything Europe had known before. Beggary and riches came to depend on the talent or luck of the individual; 'and so there arises a special group of men, unknown to earlier periods, for whom we have had to invent the word pauper' (vol. I, p. 169). Pauperism was not poverty, which had always existed. It was, rather, the utter destitution of the poor when the old props of family and community solidarity were no longer available to them. It was a problem aggravated by the lack of self-discipline of those to whom money and inheritance had come too early in life, encouraging feckless marriages and the transmission of pauperism to the next generation.

What was to be done? Le Play was against indiscriminate aid to the poor through a state bureaucracy. His experience of the state workshops set up during the revolution of 1848 convinced him that this would not solve the problem in the long run. Rather, he feared it would aggravate another undesirable trend which he perceived at the time, the growth of state power. The liberty of the individual would have to be safeguarded by fostering a proper sense of self-reliance in the citizen, and here the family must be the keystone of any structure. Le Play had no desire to revive the past. Referring to the patriarchal family of the Slavs, once characteristic of the medieval West too, he suggested that it was incompatible with political liberty and economic progress. It was, rather with the advocacy of a more streamlined, still living form, the 'stem family' that his name is chiefly associated in this respect. But what did he mean by the term? In principle, one child would inherit the paternal estate, and manage an enterprise substantially enough endowed to maintain the old couple for the rest of their days and set up his younger siblings in life. But such a schema does not do justice to the subtlety of Le Play's ideas. He was an engineer, a member of the middle class, worried by the degradation and political instability of the towns. He was not primarily concerned with the efficiency of the family farm, though he thought that that was a commendable objective too. Rather, it is the social or moral implications of family organization which intrigued Le Play.

The family for Le Play was not to be found in a set of walls or of fields, but in an attitude of mind, in a culture, or (as his contemporary Fustel might have said) in an idea. He drew his readers' attention to the preference of French businesses for recruiting their clerks outside France, in Germany and Switzerland, whose youth 'recommended themselves particularly by their strong religious belief, their inclination to obey and keep faith, and their assiduous commitment to work and save' (vol. I, pp. 216–18). The reason, he thought, had to do with the good upbringing provided by the stem families of the Germanic lands, which no amount of formal schooling could compensate for in the case of French youth. Germans learnt early in life the crucial virtues of patience, loyalty, team spirit, through working for the good of the stem family. And they could count on the continuing support of the head of their household. Le Play's em-

phasis on the moral significance of the family led him to look
approvingly at the English model. Here there was no peasantry, no
stem family in the strict sense. But what there was, he believed, was
something more fundamental: a climate of confidence between man
and wife and between parents and their children, which created the
reliable yet self-reliant citizenry needed by a liberal society. The
reason, he thought (and his ideas again echo de Tocqueville in
places), was that the Anglo-Saxon home was free of conflicts over
dowry and inheritance, since absolute property rights were invested
in the father for the good of the family as a whole (vol. II, pp.
67–79). It was a stem family in spirit if not in form.

The explanation is a little bit technical, and we shall leave its
elaboration for later chapters. Whether Le Play was right or wrong
seems ultimately of less significance than that he set up a challenging
agenda for family history, and directed attention to its subtle moral
dimension. This chapter has argued that the discovery of the family
as a problem begins with the economic and political upheavals of
the nineteenth century. The collapse of the old hierarchy induced a
range of talented thinkers in Western Europe to elaborate some idea
of how societies were held together in the first place: if not by the
force of the state, then by what? Men like Le Play stimulated a range
of empirical enquiries into household structures which are still quite
useful. But even more valuable was their theoretical standpoint: that
the family is best understood as a moral system rather than as an
institution in the narrow sense of the term. Very much in line with
French thinking since Montesquieu, they believed that moral values
do not flourish in a vacuum, but are subtly related to social structures. The family is a critical link between the two. To define the
family too narrowly at the outset, in terms of consanguinity or
household, may pre-empt the terms of the enquiry. It could be
argued, indeed, that 'definition' is what all family history is really
about, the last chapter of the book rather than the first. For it is in
defining it that we become aware of the significant features of the
society and culture we are studying. The niggling question may
remain whether this chameleon is worth studying on its own. In this
regard it is worth reminding ourselves from time to time, when
spirits flag, of the encouragement of thinkers like Durkheim and
Meyer Fortes to treat societies as something more than the sum of
their individual parts. The family does surely constitute such a
society, evolving to some extent with a rhythm of its own, which
responds to the dying echoes of past beliefs.

2
The role of the ancestors

> The ability to see ourselves as individuals is not something we are born with but which we have to learn. At bottom it is a requirement demanded of us by the society in which we live.
>
> Louis Dumont, *Homo hierarchicus: essai sur le système des castes*

Caste

Anthropologists distinguish between societies where status is 'achieved' and those where it is 'ascribed'. In the former, the individual can make his own way in the world, rising to the position where his talents will take him; in the second, he is tied down, Gulliver-like, by a myriad of petty (and sometimes insubstantial) strings, which we can call family, caste, community, custom ... In a modern society the individual generally stands in a simple relationship with those with whom he comes into contact: his relationship with his wife or his friends can usually be distinguished in kind from his professional dealings with colleagues, clients or employees. This is such an obvious point that its significance can escape us. Yet the conquest of individualism and professionalism, the separation of private and public space, has been one of the great, if silent, stories in the recent history of the West. Elsewhere, and in traditional Europe, something which we now label 'corruption' is more apparent. The individual finds himself drawn into a complex of interwoven ties: his marriage is part of his professional career, a conventional private life is a condition of the confidence which others will accord him in the public sphere, 'what' he is professionally is liable to be of less account than 'who' he is as a person. The reconstruction of this lost world can still best be achieved, I think, by studying the writings of those Europeans who lived through the transition, and particularly those of the French sociological school: Durkheim, de Tocqueville and others. Though not directly concerned with the family, everything they have to say provides the basic framework within which one can see the relevance of its study.

The English anthropologist Radcliffe-Brown once told his readers that 'the status of an individual . . . may be defined as the totality of all his rights and duties as recognised in the social usages (laws and customs) of the society to which he belongs' (1952, p. 37). This seems fairly straightforward, until we pause to reflect upon it. The characteristic of a modern Western society, one might argue, is to limit the formal specification of 'rights and duties', except in the most general terms, for fear of discriminating against specific sections of the population. Instead of inherited 'social usages' we prefer the simpler morality of the market place. That is, the exchange of professional services becomes the basic means of establishing a hierarchy of respect and responsibility; indeed, the very word hierarchy becomes redundant in a modern society, because it suggests too much form and permanence. We are left, at most, with clusters and networks. Durkheim's major work, *The Division of Labour in Society* (1893), underlined – in contradistinction to the way in which capitalist society is supposed to work – the importance of alternative ways of allocating status.

For Durkheim, the specialization of tasks and the exchange of services resulting from it were not mere steps in economic or technological history. Work is dictated in large measure – and increasingly so beyond the level of minimal biological satisfaction – by culture rather than by need as such. In traditional society, before the division or specialization of labour, the individual is very small indeed. He finds himself tied to a rank, caste or occupation which is, in great measure, hereditary in his family. Given that specialist skills are so few, this causes no great problem: soldiers need bravery rather than a knowledge of mathematics, scholars hand on the tradition of a few sacred rituals from father to son. The distinction of ranks, paradoxically, is always greater in such societies than in the more diversified modern West. There are elaborate differences in clothes, comportment, access to resources, even physique (leisure and food being concentrated overwhelmingly at the top echelons of society). The great challenge for such societies is to fashion a workable hierarchy to regulate human competition. Since careers require such minimal skills, they have to be allocated on some basis other than mere talent. In fact, they are generally filled by agreed custom or law: that is, certain kinds of people are assigned to specific tasks on a 'moral' rather than economic basis. A 'caste' system will thus develop, of which the best known example is that of India. Since there is a danger in such highly stratified societies that the various layers will draw apart (given the minimal exchange of services needed), co-operation has to be specified in other, non-economic ways. The sense of community has to affirm itself essentially through the proclamation of common values. Objectionable conduct has to be ritually spelled out. The law codes of early peoples, as Durkheim pointed out, are extremely detailed by our standards, picking out and condemning a range of particular actions. Above all, religion provides a sense of harmony and cohesion for the group. Durkheim used the word 'mechanical' to refer to the solidarity of such communities, as contrasted with the 'organic' character of their modern counterparts, held together by the continuous exchange of professional services.

Durkheim was not directly concerned with family, but his whole treatise can be read in one sense as about nothing else. He made the basic point that a 'family' was not a chance biological grouping, but a rule-based corporation which might exclude certain consanguines altogether – for example, the maternal uncle in ancient Rome. It has to be seen as one part of the hierarchical ordering of pre-industrial communities. A more specific illustration of Durkheim's largely theoretical discussion is to be found in the contrast drawn by Alexis de Tocqueville (1963) between Europe and America, in his classic work of 1835–40, *De la démocratie en Amérique*. The democratic society which de Tocqueville set out to describe was essentially that individualistic and professionalized world so familiar to us but so different from the Old World of the 1830s. A tradition of political decentralization, Protestant sectarianism and the open frontier (permitting the easy circulation of wealth) had fostered, in combination, that most novel phenomenon, individualism. 'Individualism is a recent word invented to define a new concept: our forefathers knew only egoism' (p. 269). Individualism was distinguished from egoism by professionalism, by something very akin to what Max Weber would later call the 'spirit of capitalism'. Unlike egoism, it was a fascinating new definition of the relations between the individual and the community. De Tocqueville noted that in America the division of labour, the relentless pursuit of work and the accumulation of wealth had replaced every other kind of hierarchy. Without guilds, without an aristocracy, without priests as such, the Americans were thrown back on the exchange of specialized skills, and ultimately on money, as the regulator of their relationships. Like Durkheim, de Tocqueville suggested that such a development was not solely an economic but also a cultural phenomenon.

By contrast, and despite 1789, France had retained many of the basic features of what de Tocqueville called an 'aristocratic' society, a term very close in meaning to Durkheim's 'mechanical solidarity'. That is, it was a society where the individual found his niche as a member of a group – family, parish, even perhaps guild (though these were nominally abolished in France) – which assigned him rights and obligations. 'In aristocratic societies, families stay for centuries in the same social group, and often in the same place ... A man will almost always know and reverence his ancestors; he can have some idea of his great-grand children, and feel affection for them. He is happy to undertake commitments to both ...' (p. 270). The ties of an aristocratic people were personalized, localized and quasi-sacral. Its virtues were religious: self-sacrifice, abnegation, heroism; whereas those of a 'democratic' society were more utilitarian: the doing of one's duty. In France, lineage and patrons enveloped the individual; in America he stood alone within an anonymous collectivity, releasing a tremendous force for economic progress and political centralization. De Tocqueville was aware of some of the dangers here: as money became the regulator of social relations, the accumulation of wealth would create much greater social divisions than in the past, while the state would arrogate exceptional power to itself as the other intermediary bodies faded away.

I have dwelt at length on Durkheim and de Tocqueville because they seem to me to be two of the clearest exponents of the difference between a modern society, where status is 'achieved' by the individual, and traditional cultures, where it is 'ascribed' to him by virtue of the group. Reversing the usual order of progress, Durkheim suggested that 'collective life is not born from individual life, but it is, on the contrary, the second which is born from the first' (1964, p. 279). The words constitute a challenging agenda for the historian of family life under the old regime. The problem facing students of pre-industrial Europe is that of understanding the factors making for economic and political cohesion, when the component parts of the society were so little differentiated and non-complementary in the Durkheimian sense. The conventional wisdom holds that Europe before 1789 was an 'estates' society, with individuals located in corporations – lineages, guilds, chartered fraternities – which regulated their political and social life. The hierarchy could be seen as one of honour rather than wealth, with social distinctions being fixed in law (privilege or charter), rather than, as today, through the demand for one's services in the market place. As de Tocqueville noted, the old hierarchy had to justify itself in terms of moral worth or 'virtue', playing on the ambivalence of the term 'honour' as at once exalted rank and the justification of that rank.

When the usurping king of Castile, Henry of Trastámara, granted the lordship of Santisteban near the frontier with Moorish Granada to his supporter Men Rodríguez de Benavides (1371), he did it 'that you and the men of your lineage may be worth more, and may be honoured and have the wherewithal to serve us the more, and that this may be for a memory to others who come to know and hear of it ...' (Argote, 1957, p. 500). The memory in question was the loyal defence of the king's cause at the decisive battle of Montiel and the subsequent defence of Jaén against the Moor. Such memory was necessary as a stimulus to loyalty and political obedience in the states of Europe at least down to the civil wars of the seventeenth century, perhaps down to the clear legitimation of power in modern polities, where government is held to be by the will of the governed, and is buttressed by a near-monopoly of physical force. Heroic actions by the nobility of the old regime were symbolized in myth, and frequently in ballads, as examples of the generosity or courage which a pre-industrial polity requires of its leaders. The sixteenth-century Valencian chronicler, Martín de Viciana, stressed that honour was the 'reward of virtue'. The plastering up of coats of arms above tombs, doors and beds was no mere vanity, but a way of 'telling and recalling who the now dead owner once was, for people who see the arms fall to talking about the man and how he obtained them' (1972, vol. II, f. 21v).

Virtue, honour and 'honours', in the sense of titles and lands, were three pillars on which old regimes rested. Inevitably the dominance of 'nobility', again, in a two fold sense, is one of their characteristic features, and an area in which family history and politics meet. It is interesting to note how the concept continued to be defended by the flourishing school of Spanish genealogists into the age of liberalism. One of the best of their number, Francisco Piferrer, writing in 1857, came up with a rather Tocquevillian justification, opposing those who attacked nobility for its association with political abuses: 'As if there were no nobility before feudalism and entail! ... The cornerstone of nobility is religion, honour, talent and valour' (1857, vol. I, p. 3). Essentially the stimulus to virtue – or citizenship – in these older societies was regarded as a collective phenomenon. One did what one did because one was sprung of an honourable line or a reputable people. Duby has remarked upon the

significance of early 'nationalism' in the thirteenth-century life of
William Marshal, with its distinctions between French and English,
which may surprise those of us accustomed to seeing the early
Plantagenet nobility as steeped in both cultures. A little before, the
early twelfth-century epic, *The Song of Roland* (which I surmise was
composed shortly after the taking of Zaragoza from the Moor in
1118, given the prominence of that city in the text) is very clear
about the special characteristics of Poitevins, Normans or Bavarians.
It reckons that these can be expected to fight best if grouped on the
battlefield with their fellow 'nationals'. The 'natio' had not yet
acquired the hard territorial edge which it would later have; but as a
kind of tribalism it instilled some of the virtues of citizenship and
public responsibility A seventeenth-century Granadan chronicler
summed it up: 'a noble city ennobles its citizens', and lays them
under a special obligation 'to love and honour her with a more
sterling love' (Bermúdez de Pedraza, 1981, p. 147).

This emphasis on community sense is fundamental to our understanding of inherited status. Anthropologists working on Mediterranean peasant societies at the present day have tended to see status as
a function of 'political' considerations (in the broad sense). It is not
that wealth is not important to social stratification: it very clearly is.
But money needs to be channelled into socially acceptable ways. The
wealthy must, as it were, 'purchase' consideration by the prominent
public role which they adopt, involving the 'protection' of the less
fortunate. In fifteenth-century Florence, as in eighteenth-century
Frankfurt, historians have made us aware of a rather similar phenomenon: that the hierarchy was formulated in terms of political
responsibility rather than of mere wealth. The seventeenth-century
French theorist, Charles Loyseau, summed up the situation by
saying that the orders or estates in a particular society were marks
of 'dignity, with access to authority' (Mousnier, 1967, p. 18).
Not only the occupation of official posts is involved here. Before
about 1650, claim to power came from a high public profile, and
signally by participating in ritual celebration. Wealthy merchants'
sons in Andalusia demonstrated their patrician status by lancing
bulls, or trying to stay on a horse in some great masquerade before
the assembled populace, on the occasion of recurring public festivities. To be a noble or a patrician before about 1650 meant demonstrating qualities of courage and magnanimity, in a great theatre of
virtue. What is exemplified here is a concept of hierarchy more like
that of the caste system of India than one cares to think. A calling

was both a function and a moral quality. Warriors were brave, plebeians were not; being a warrior (or a priest or a merchant) was not only an occupation but a showing forth of traits of character which fitted one for the occupation in the first place. Only by stressing 'virtue', it was believed, could a properly integrated polity be constructed at all.

Hereditary moral traits were important not only in the political but also in the economic sphere. Not only did one frequently have to be admitted to citizenship of a particular town in order to practise as a master craftsman there – especially, of course, in the city states of Germany – but certain categories of people were excluded. Traditionally these were 'children of constables, wardens, gravediggers, night watchmen, jailers, cleaners of streets and waterways, shepherds', whom the great Imperial edict of 1731 ordered to be admitted, as well as the illegitimate, whom we shall consider in a later chapter. Spain was facing similar problems round this time, with the desire of statesmen to open the guilds more widely in the interests of economic progress. One of the writers on the subject, Antonio Pérez y López, argued against throwing them fully open to mere talent. The reason was that they had too vital a role to play in 'education for citizenship', which could be defined as a combination of pride in work and political self-discipline (1781). In order to understand the position of these defenders of the old order, like Pérez in Spain, or Justus Möser in Germany whom we shall come across in a later chapter, one has to appreciate the nature of manufacture in a pre-industrial economy: high-cost, labour intensive, exquisitely detailed in even the most ordinary articles like locks or buckles. The elaborate guild regulations in defence of quality and workmanship made sense only if they could be addressed to 'honourable' craftsmen, whose corporate pride would ensure that they would be carried out.

Since the eighteenth century, since Mandeville's *Fable of the Bees* (1714), significantly subtitled *Private Vices, Publick Benefits*, or Adam Smith's *Wealth of Nations* (1776), the West has increasingly adopted an alternative view of social structure. This stresses the moral neutrality of private virtue in the public sphere, as economics replaces politics as the force which is seen to hold society together. The new science emphasizes that the exchange of professional services, according to the law of supply and demand, will reward the competent and draw the idle perforce into rendering what they can to the community. As Benjamin Franklin, spokesman of that early

America which de Tocqueville found so novel, expressed it in his *Autobiography* of 1771–84, it might be 'that vicious actions are not hurtful because they are forbidden, but forbidden because they are hurtful, the nature of man alone considered; that it was therefore everyone's interest to be virtuous who wished to be happy even in this world' (1948, p. 82). Such a utilitarian ethic spelled the end of caste, or indeed of a society of orders.

The concept of caste will tend to lead to a fascination with genealogy. Where a people lacks the organic unity of a modern society, men like to 'situate' an individual before doing business with him. It is possible that genealogical memory has been most highly developed in those vast, ill-tamed frontier regions of Europe – Spain (and North Africa), Russia – with their unusual degree of geographic mobility, military or pastoral. From the vantage point of 1639, one eighty-year-old priest in Granada recalled how his elders would gossip about the origins of those who had come to settle in the newly conquered city: 'in those times ... there was talk about everyone's background, for the disturbances and upheavals in this kingdom were still recent, and there were so many Moors ...' (testimony in a lawsuit, in the Chancery Archive of Granada, 301/115/8). I wonder if a similar state of affairs did not underlie the vigorous *mestnichestvo* system of allocating office by clan in Russia at the same time. All cultures need some way of regulating their economic and political life. Where both are unstructured, as occurs typically in frontier conditions, then caste may be particularly important.

Clan

If we may suggest, then, that the family plays a fundamental role in the classification of individuals in traditional, small-scale societies, we need to tackle the question: What kind of family? Anthropologists have noted the wide variety of such possible groupings. Meyer Fortes, whose field-work was done among two tribes of Ghana, the matrilineal Ashanti and the patrilineal Tallensi, has given us one of the clearest definitions of what we might look for. In the first place, one should not be over-sanguine about the objective reality of the clan. Genealogies can be manipulated in these oral cultures, at least beyond the fourth generation, in order to validate the occupation of a particular territory by a particular set of people. Segmentation will take place, possibly every seven or eight generations, by which the original clan, having outgrown its resources, will invent a new 'sub-lineage' for itself, classically through the marriage of one of its members to a propertied outsider. These segments of the original clan may be rivals rather than friends. Though the clan will continue to have a formal, 'jural' structure, the living reality of human relationships will tend to go beyond its boundaries. Thus, though the Ashanti trace descent in the mother's line, a man must have an acknowledged father in order to enjoy full matrilineal status; though inheritance passes from a man to his sister's son, the man will also try in practice to endow his own children; finally, though a person will enjoy full citizenship rights only in the territory of his mother's tribe, he may actually live and work in his father's tribal area (Fortes, 1970, p. 110). As one can see, the clan is important in providing a formal structure but has no monopoly on human relations, any more than a house is the same thing as the people living there.

This view of the tribe as 'process' recalls the fundamental research of Evans-Pritchard in the 1930s among the Nuer of the Sudan. This pastoral people, about 200,000 strong, was composed of a number of tribes, each containing from 10,000 to 20,000 members. Rather than a real descent group, the tribe seemed to be fundamentally a community in occupation of a particular territory. It was made up of a number of 'clans', the most powerful of which would give its name to the tribe and the territory. The clan had a certain cohesion in that its members could trace descent from a common ancestor in the male line. But the genealogies beyond the fourth or fifth generation seemed somewhat fictitious. What intrigued Evans-Pritchard was that there was only a fixed number of clans, all beginning about ten or twelve generations back, though the Nuer had probably been in the area for a longer period of time than that. Weaker families and outsiders seemed to have been absorbed through manipulation of the oral memory into the stronger groups. The Nuer were less interested in the exact steps of the genealogy than in situating their neighbours as kinsmen, and for this it was enough to 'remember' the name of their ancestor who had branched from the main stem.

Nevertheless, the clan does provide a language for defining social solidarity here and throughout Africa generally. More problematic is its role in areas of settled agriculture. In the Swat Valley, in north-west Pakistan, focus of another outstanding study of a clan society, the formal structures disintegrate almost entirely. This area, described for us by Fredrik Barth, was more developed economically than the tribal lands of Ghana, with greater use of arable and landlord–tenant contract. Ownership of land was validated by reference to the clan, to descent from the grandsons of an eponymous ancestor, Yusuf, who had conquered the territory in the sixteenth century. Genealogies could be foreshortened, but were not manipulated to admit outsiders; so the clan here does seem to have some objective reality. Perhaps because of that, it has become too rigid to accommodate personal ambitions. Since all sons shared equally in land, the clan has grown enormously, and access to property has caused much rivalry and competition. The descendants of Yusuf, the Yusufzai, are certainly a corporate group as far as status is concerned; but the clan for them appears to have little other importance.

If we define a clan as a unilineal descent group – that is, a group of people who can trace a common ancestry through either their father or their mother to a founding forefather – then we may conclude, with Fortes, that such bodies are more significant in zones of intermediate economic development, dominantly the pastoral territories of Africa. Where there is an absence of herds or of kingships, as among the Aborigines (and perhaps fairly generally in Polynesia), one will find more flexible, smaller-scale hunting bands rather than clans. Equally, where an economy reaches a superior stage of settlement, as in Swat, rivalry over property may rupture the clan. With these principles in mind, let us turn to examine the formative stages of European society.

There is considerable obscurity, and some controversy, about whether the early Germans had much awareness of the unilineal descent group at all. The most careful recent study of the family institutions of this people, by Alexander C. Murray (1983), suggests that the classical literature (Caesar, Tacitus), on which we must depend for a view of Germanic society before the Invasions gives little evidence of such groupings. The equally meticulous analysis by P. D. King of the earliest extant Barbarian law code, that of the Visigoths of 681, can speak of the virtual absence of the kindred as a significant social force (1972, p. 222). Admittedly the Visigoths were among the most Romanized of the Germanic peoples, and may have lost whatever early tribalism they possessed. Also, law codes are not necessarily good places to find evidence on the role of the ancestors. They are concerned, rather, with protection of the individual, with the *Sippe* or Sib, rather than directly with descent.

Sib and lineage are not mutually exclusive, and should not be confused. The Barbarian codes are concerned with the feud, and with the men on whom a man can count to help him, either by swearing to his innocence (oath-helping), or by contributing to the blood-money to the victim's kin (the *Wergeld*) 'to buy off the point of the spear'. Among the Franks this Sib may have extended to descendants of the first cousins of one's four grandparents. This bilateral kindred – that is, a grouping which is formed out of relatives on both one's father's and one's mother's side – has a very different structure from that of the clans with which we have been concerned so far. Thus, at each generation a man will have a different set of obligations from those of his father, for his set of grandparents will be different. Among tribal peoples, by contrast, there is less need to spell out in codes of law the kinsmen to whom one owes solidarity in the feud. Like the segments of a worm, the various bits of the tribe will coalesce as and when needed – brother with brother against cousin, first cousins against second, up to the solidarity of all those who claim descent from a common ancestor against an outsider. Perhaps one can understand the Sib better if one takes into account the exceptional mobility of the Germanic peoples. Whatever unilineal descent groups may or may not have existed among them before, they must have given way before the formation of warbands under charismatic leaders at the time of the Invasions. It is interesting to compare them with that other mobile, plundering people, the Mongols. There too one notes an inevitable tendency for clans to fragment under pressure of constant migrations and warfare, with more random assemblages of bits of tribes coming together to constitute effective fighting groups (Cuisenier, 1976, pp. 214–18). Admittedly the Mongols did keep to the concept of unilineal descent groups as far as possible. Is there any evidence that the Germans even tried to do the same?

'The most striking feature of the history of the dominant families in the first feudal age', Marc Bloch tells us, in a memorable phrase, 'is the shortness of their pedigrees' (1965, vol. III, p. 284). To the father of the study of the medieval nobility it seemed that genealogy was relatively unimportant to status in European society before about AD 1000. This was a rough-and-tumble world, where a broad sword and sharp wits were enough to bring a man to the highest positions. Though the picture is still very plausible, it clearly is not the whole truth. Our best informant on the early Barbarians, the sixth-century chronicler Gregory of Tours, was in no doubt that the Franks had both a nobility and able warleaders, and tried to combine the two where possible in the course of their wanderings. They 'set up in each country district and each city long-haired kings chosen from the foremost and most noble family of their race' (1974, p. 125). The myth which the Frankish kings began to put about rather later, in the seventh century, about their descent from the fabled Merovech, suggests they were also operating with some concept of 'clan'. It is, of course, the exasperating vagueness of the genealogies which we find surprising. It is not enough just to blame the remoteness of the time and the lack of records. Peoples with little or no written culture can do better: the Tallensi of Ghana have no trouble describing their descent over eight generations (though they tend to invent names after three), the Yusufzai of Swat can go back nine to the conquest of the sixteenth century, and back at least another three to their founder Yusuf. If the German genealogies are vaguer, is it because they served a much less useful purpose?

The question can possibly not be answered directly for the Dark Ages, given the paucity of sources. But by analogy with better-documented periods one may shed some light on the issue. The first point, I think, is that the obscurity of the descent line among the nobility of Europe does not mean that it was unimportant. Much could be learned here from studying the numerous petty gentry of frontier Europe – Russia, Poland, Spain – down to the seventeenth century, where family structures and social conditions were quite fluid. The sixteenth-century Basque chronicler, Esteban de Garibay (born 1533), gives us a vivid insight into the way in which genealogies were handed on in a mobile, basically oral culture. His mother, he tells us, 'was very close to her kinsfolk, and her head was full of the doings of her forefathers and those of her husband, many of which ... I heard from her lips' (1854, pp. 247–8). But when it came to actually reconstructing a formal genealogy for this petty nobility, as Garibay tried to do in 1584, it proved very difficult, since he had moved away from his village, the old men had died, archives had been lost. Complaint about loss of papers and the confusion of genealogies is the great, universal cry from men who began to try drawing them up in the sixteenth century in Spain. As the doyen of the school, Luis de Salazar y Castro, commented in the later seventeenth century on the problem of tracing the medieval ancestry of the Castilian nobility, even as late as the thirteenth century, 'apart from a few lineages ... none of the Castilians had a surname, and all were happy with patronymics' (1959, p. 257).

The vagueness of genealogies tells us perhaps something about the openness of family structures. As the great Andalusian chronicler of

THE ROLE OF THE ANCESTORS

the sixteenth century, Gonzalo Argote, observed, 'it is a very common thing in the most noble lineages for the name to be used by those who do not belong to it, as we see slaves nowadays take that of their masters . . .' (1957, p. 9). Constantly at this period there was a tendency for the stewards of noble households to be assimilated to the kin of their employer. This phenomenon of the assimilation of clients into the clan is found even in societies which clearly do have unilineal descent groups: for example, in the Rome of Fustel de Coulanges, or the Swat of Fredrik Barth. It is also visible in fourteenth-century Ireland, if Froissart is to be believed. His account of the Englishman Henry Crystede, captured by a Gaelic tribesman, married to the man's daughter and incorporated as a son of the house, recalls the importance of the mother's family even in this patrilineal, clan society (1978, p. 413; cf. Herlihy, 1985, pp. 34–43). This same passionate love of a grandfather for the heirs of his daughter comes through in the fascinating chronicles of the fifteenth-century Basque clans told by Lope García de Salazar. The two bastard sons of one Martín Ruys kill the son of another Lope García de Salazar for seducing their half-sister; but the child of the guilty pair is spared at the pleading of old Martín Ruys, who raises him as his heir and even gives him the name of his paternal grandfather, so that yet another Lope García de Salazar takes the stage! (1884, fo. 23 v). The Salazar name clearly means something, but membership of the clan is very fluid, not least because inherited property from the mother's side is so important. May it not have been the same among the early Germanic peoples?

Descent lines are perhaps not as rigid in such societies as in our own day, precisely because the clan was too important to be left to random biological production of a male heir. Useful men had to be annexed if they could not be acquired in any other way. But, one might object, does the existence of descent reckoning in both the male and female line not rule out clans (properly reckoned as groups of men claiming descent from one ancestor, not two) altogether in Germanic Europe? Clearly much depends here on the interpretation of the evidence about descent through females. Historians have pointed to the enormous importance of the maternal uncle in the French epics of the High Middle Ages, so beautifully symbolized by the bond between Roland and Charlemagne. They have observed the way noble families at that period (the twelfth century) would trace their descent from an important woman, whom some wandering knight had married in the distant past. It is hard to know what

exactly to make of all this, but it does not of itself suggest that the
mother's side was more important among the Germans than among
patrilineal peoples. Since clans will tend to go on expanding indefinitely from a common ancestor, there will come a time, after
perhaps seven or eight generations, when they must 'segment': that
is, a branch will hive off and establish a certain autonomy. The
genealogies of their descendants will be unconsciously refashioned
to take account of the split. As in the example of the Salazars cited
above, one branch will want to explain its settlement in Ruys territory: marriage with a Ruys heiress will be the obvious, and typical,
legitimating myth to be invoked. As regards the warmth of affection
for the maternal uncle, Radcliffe-Brown pointed out many years ago
how this could be combined with a strict emphasis on the patriline.
Roland does not expect to inherit from Charlemagne, hence his love
is disinterested and intense; meanwhile, considerations of property
sour or efface the relations of Roland with his stepfather Ganelon, or
even those of Charlemagne with the second-rate Louis, his son, who
creeps in towards the end of the poem as a consolation prize for
Roland's widow!

Pride in the father's name, the 'clan', may not have been as
important in medieval Europe as it was in African societies; but the
evidence is not as unambiguous on this point as it sometimes seems.
Nor is the absence of clear-cut lines of descent among the nobility
of the Dark Ages – and among their counterparts in the outlying
frontier areas of Europe, like Spain, down to quite modern times.
We started this discussion by suggesting that primitive societies need
caste as a way of fixing economic and political obligations, and that
family is one channel for allocating places in the hierarchy. One can
take the point a stage further, and argue that, where caste is important, family structures will tend to be fairly open in order to
accommodate individual mobility within the system. A few words
may be said, in order to make the point clearer, about the knight.

The European knight long remained in an ambiguous position, at
once part of a quasi-sacred order by his function, yet increasingly
'useless' because of a growing insistence that he should be well-born.
Marc Bloch called attention to the new emphasis on family background for membership of the warrior class from the twelfth century. In Spain one can still hear echoes of the debate into the
sixteenth century: is knighthood a function or a dignity – indeed,
does it make sense to distinguish the two? The Valencian chronicler
Viciana records the ritual formula for the arming of a knight: 'that

he may be favoured and rewarded thereby, and his lineage ennobled, in return for the good and loyal service which he has done and can be expected to do, for his person is worthy of the honour of knighthood ...' (1972, vol. II, pp. 38–40). Viciana's discussion highlights the ambiguity inherent in the expression 'worthy of honour'. He had in mind nobility, but a nobility perhaps less fixed juridically than we are accustomed to, for it will be 'all the greater the older the lineage'. Now there is clearly just enough vagueness here about genealogy still to allow the knight to function as a soldier and not a mere ornament. De Tocqueville said something similar about the French nobility. In the fourteenth century they were still an order of the realm, with a recognizable political function; but by 1789 they had become a social group, stripped of their function by a professional army and bureaucracy, and increasingly exclusive.

Part of the explanation was that genealogy had become an exact science during the interval. Viciana was proud of the fact that he was one of the first genealogists not to be in the pay of a noble family, but to be doing objective research (though he did have a patron, the duke of Gandía). His Andalusian contemporary, Argote, equally prided himself on the twenty years of research he had done in the archives, armed with a royal warrant, to clear away some of the myths surrounding the origin of noble families. But it is really the seventeenth century which sees the new rigour in genealogy flourish, the age of Salazar y Castro in Spain, of d'Hozier in France. D'Hozier's method can be seen at work in a case referred to him by Nicolas Fouquet, the famous finance minister of the young Louis XIV. Fouquet, great-grandson of a merchant of Angers, tried to link the latter with an extinct gentry family of the same name, which had disappeared about 1545. D'Hozier warned that his titles were not very good: 'it is easy to see that these documents have been got up for the purpose, both from their style, which is not in the old fashion, and from the parchment on which they are written' (Dessert, 1987, p. 21). The Fouquets never quite lived down the gossip, though they eventually did establish themselves as a noble dynasty.

Thanks to the generalization of parish registers from the mid-sixteenth century, it was becoming difficult (though not impossible) to forge ancestry. But there was something more than a mere technical development at work here. As the nobility ceased to be an order with a political function it could afford to become more exclusive. This was the point which de Tocqueville made in *L'Ancien Régime et la Révolution* (1967, originally 1856). He noted that this loss of a sense of function affected other ranks within society: the bourgeoisie, too, had a specific political role in the fourteenth century but none in the eighteenth. Rather, a new elite was struggling to define itself, in terms of both wealth and birth. The concept of aristocracy in the eighteenth century narrowed, attaching itself less to family name, and more to descent from a known house, in possession of a fixed (and preferably large) patrimony. This narrowing posed some of the political problems for the old regime in France which de Tocqueville analysed so acutely. But it also raises a question about how the transmission of property became the framework within which a family defines itself. To that we must now turn.

Lineage

The importance of a fixed patrimony for the maintenance of nobility was highlighted by Chateaubriand, whose *Mémoires d'outre-tombe* give such a vivid insight into the world of the provincial nobility of France on the eve of the great Revolution. The Chateaubriands were proud of a long ancestry stretching back to AD 1000; but their family had to struggle for recognition because it was so poor. The patrimony had continued to be divided up among several married children at each generation (though there was a main heir). As with the Chateaubriands, so with the Breton nobility as a whole. 'In the old noble families we see a number of younger sons. We can follow them for two or three generations, then they disappear, gone back little by little to the plough, or absorbed by the labouring population, and no one knows what has become of them' (1982, vol. I, pp. 21–2).

Chateaubriand's description would be familiar enough to the medievalist, concerned with what he sees as the emergence of a clearly defined nobility from about 1000. The vague 'clans' of the Dark Ages seem to be giving way to narrow groups which define themselves by their ownership of a piece of land handed down from father to son. In common with the French medievalist Georges Duby, I prefer to call such groups 'lineages', distinguishing them from clans, though there is some controversy over the use of these terms (see glossary). Duby has given us the richest insight into the nature of the feudal family, on the basis of the archives of the great abbey of Cluny, which record donations of property from the nobility of southern Burgundy. Landholding round Cluny in the early part of the eleventh century resembles a patchwork quilt, of a kind which would not be unfamiliar to the Yusufzai or other patrilineal clans. Land is held in small parcels by males, who seem, by and large, to have been settled round Cluny for several generations past. A limited number of old Carolingian families, perhaps six, with huge patrimonies in a depopulated territory, had apparently gone on splitting up their estates among their sons, so that by 1050 the number of old landholding families had risen to twenty-four, augmented by ten new ones (which had possibly married in?). As among the Yusufzai, the separate families tended to go their own way. Then in the course of the eleventh century this process of splitting or segmentation slows down. It becomes more difficult, for example, to alienate land to the monastery of Cluny without the consent of the males of the kinship group; joint holding of lands by brothers becomes more common, a first step towards practical (if not yet legal) primogeniture; younger brothers are encouraged now to join an increasingly aristocratic and crusade-orientated monastery (Cluny, or its Cistercian offspring), or to stay celibate as landless knights in this new, crusading age; finally, daughters and their husbands will be preferred as heirs to the patrimony, rather than letting it be broken up among a range of male cousins. Duby sees the precondition here for the growth of a wealthier and more clearly defined nobility in the High Middle Ages, now organized around hereditary family estates. An interesting development is the rise of the surname, taken from the name of the estate or castle, which comes to replace a more flexible system of patronymics (Duby, 1976, pp. 16–40).

Bonnassie, working on Catalonia, sees a similar development there in the eleventh century: a rise of unigeniture, a greater solidarity among cousins as a defence against the anarchy of this violent age of early feudalism, when kings ceased to be able to guarantee public order (1976, vol. I, pp. 281–2; vol. II, pp. 547–9). But this drawing together of the lineage, round a fixed patrimony and a surname, is less evident in the frontier regions of Europe, where perhaps greater opportunities for plunder ensured the maintenance of an older system. Thus in Germany the patriline seems very slow to take shape among the nobility. And indeed into the early modern period, subdivision or joint holding of estates by siblings kept the Prussian aristocracy small and rather poor. The great lawbook of King Alfonso the Wise of Castile, of the mid-thirteenth century, still envisages division of the patrimony as the most satisfactory solution, to avoid the 'very great disagreements which arise among men ... for each one feels happy with his own share when he gets it, and looks after it better, and makes greater use of it' (Las Siete Partidas, 6/14/1).

It is doubtful, in fact, whether there is any clear relationship between nobility and control of a fixed patrimony. Down to the nineteenth century the Russian elite, like the Yusufzai of Swat, seem to have combined a remarkable genealogical memory with considerable geographic mobility. The Aksakovs, for example, known to us from the famous autobiography of one of their number, Sergei, allow a vivid insight into this world in the early nineteenth century. This family had, indeed, been remarkably fortunate in having only one son at each generation in the eighteenth century. Yet there were daughters to be provided for. When they married, 'their portions took the shape of a certain number of serfs, and a certain amount of land. Though their shares were not large, yet, as the land had never been properly surveyed, at this time [that is, in the days of Sergei's grandfather, Stepan] four intruders asserted their right to share in the management of it' (1917, p. 1). Frustrated by quarrels with his in-laws, Stepan moved out across the Volga into the colonial territories of the Bashkir tribes under Catherine the Great to make a new home for himself. Or again, the more famous Alexander Herzen has left us an equally vivid portrait of the splitting of the joint patrimony of his father and uncles. Keeping the grandfather's estate together had not been a great success. The eldest of the three siblings 'was not even on speaking terms with his two juniors. In spite of this, they all took a share in the management of the family property, which really meant that they combined to ruin it' (1980, p. 14). By analogy with the Russian example, but *mutatis mutandis*, one senses that the little noble families round Cluny, with their fractured holdings before 1000, were all perfectly aware of who they were, though they did not write down their genealogies. Their ability to keep their domains together after 1000, whether as joint holdings or as single inheritances, must have represented a quite dramatic cultural revolution.

It seems clear that land ownership set up a centrifugal tendency within the clan. Unlike the more simple, pastoral societies of Africa, Europe and Asia were powerfully influenced from an early date by the economic and political constraints of settled agriculture. What one finds, therefore, is a constant tendency towards segmentation within the clan at perhaps every third generation, as the sons of brothers fail to agree on how to run the joint estate. The Basque clans of the fifteenth century, memorably described by one of their number, Lope García de Salazar, were perpetually engaged in this process. The genealogies are like a tangled skein, until the moment when a lucky man breaks from the pack, makes his fortune and carves out a 'lineage' for himself, based on a fixed surname, which is derived from the tower or village he has planted. This process was still going on in the sixteenth century, and is interestingly described for us by the Valencian chronicler Viciana: 'if today someone should, by his courage or fortune, establish a home for the lineage [*solar conocido*], those who succeed him will call themselves after the home, where he first settled ... Some such houses were established in Aragon around 812, others around 1100, others in Valencia around 1240, and those who go off to the Indies nowadays do the same' (1972, vol. II, p. 38). What was tending to happen, in the days of Salazar and Viciana, was a settling down of known lineages as the patrimony came to be protected by entail.

We can see the complex process of segmentation within the clan accompanied by increasing stability of lineages in control of particular fiefs by looking at one of those families studied by Viciana, the Buyl. They claimed descent from a semi-legendary Pyrenean warlord, García Aznares, who had captured the castle of Buyl from the Moors and become its warden in the mid-twelfth century on behalf of the crown. The family began to adopt a hereditary surname, derived from the castle, to replace the old patronymics or nicknames like García or Aznares. By 1364 the castle was formally transferred to one Don Pedro Buyl by the crown, and Don Pedro entailed the estate on the head of his eldest son, as was becoming increasingly common at this time throughout Spain. But the opportunities of the Reconquest had drawn members of the family south to Valencia, where they carved out new lordships for themselves. By the mid-sixteenth century there were at least three separate branches of the Buyls, each with its own fief, and not a little confusion as to which was the senior line. The dispute centred round control of the main burial chapel in the Dominican convent of Valencia, and it was fought before the royal courts. It concerned also the control of the old castle of Buyl itself, and resulted in the raising of a private army by one of the claimants under Philip II – surely one of the last such *coups de main* in the increasingly ordered polity of that Prudent King (Viciana, 1972, vol. II, pp. 87–90; Escolano, 1878, vol. II, p. 135).

What is interesting in the case of the Buyls is the development of the concept of a 'senior line'. The clan chief, or *pariente mayor*, becomes a quite significant feature of late medieval and early modern Spain – at the precise time, one feels, when the clan itself was breaking down into propertied lineages. The recent biography by J. H. Elliott of *The Count-Duke of Olivares* (1986) reminds us how the rivalry of that great statesman with his cousin the duke of Medina Sidonia for headship of the House of Guzmán nearly provoked a rebellion in Andalusia in 1641. In societies where clans are very important for status or defence, the concept of such hereditary headship would be hard to maintain. One has to have moved towards some kind of system of a single heir taking over the old tower or main property of the house from his father – and that was a fairly slow development in Europe, especially on the Russian or Spanish frontiers. Clearly the early modern period does see a well-nigh universal drive in western Europe towards keeping the noble patrimony together by some kind of 'strict settlement', or even (in Spain and Italy) perpetual entail on the head of the eldest son at each generation. The celibate Doge of Venice, Leonardo Donà, echoed a typical attitude when he entailed his fortune in 1609, 'to maintain the well-being and good-standing of our family, by providing in this way against the thoughtlessness or frivolousness' of later generations (Davis, 1975, pp. 78–83). Was this attitude on the part of the elite, perhaps, a response to the greater fluidity of wealth in an increasingly mercantile age? Or to the settling down of western Europe, as frontiers closed and wars of plunder became less feasible? In any case it would seem that property had become more important than sturdy sons.

Keeping a noble patrimony together, however, required more effort than might appear at first sight. In France, as in England, by the seventeenth century, entails were not perpetual; rather, a father would specify the arrangements for the succession of his grandchildren at the marriage of his heir – a 'strict settlement', then, subject to modification every other generation or so. The eldest son of a noble family in France before the Revolution could take at most two-thirds of the estate; if there were more than two children, in the custom of Paris, or four elsewhere, then his share fell to a half. Chateaubriand has described for us the sometimes disastrous consequences of this process. Even in the Mediterranean, where entails tended to be perpetual, younger sons seem often to have shared the patrimony through the sixteenth century, according to studies of the nobilities of Piedmont, Sicily and Venice. Increasingly in the seventeenth century, it is true, these cadets seem to have been restricted to life pensions from their elder brothers. But this might work to the detriment of the latter, as reformers pointed out in the Spain of the Enlightenment, noting the reluctance of noble fathers to invest in repairs to their entails, since the improvements would have to go to

just one son (Castellano, 1984, pp. 311–12). The money was diverted
instead to the education and placement of the younger sons, who
'gain honour and fortune, and protect the silly heir and rule him,
and so deserve to be called his masters' (Pineda, 1963–4, vol. IV, p.
77). We are here moving into the realm of the 'stem' family, as Le
Play might have defined it: that is, the moral unity of the siblings,
with one of their number inheriting the patrimony, but educating
the others for important positions in life. He argued that this kind of
family was perfectly adapted to the requirements of a modern economic and political system. Unlike the clan, it was suited to a centralized government; unlike the Aksakov and Herzen households, with
their multiple families in charge of a common patrimony, it was
geared to an efficient, market economy.

It is one of Le Play's disciples, Charles de Ribbe, who has given us
the best case study of how the aristocratic 'stem' family worked, and
how it fitted in with the flexible requirements of a more settled,
post-medieval society. This came with his publication in 1879 of the
memoirs of a sixteenth-century Provençal lady, Jeanne de Laurens.
Jeanne, born in 1563, wrote the story of her parents and ten siblings,
her father being a doctor from Savoy and her mother the daughter of
a petty noble called Castellan. The memoir is designed to point out a
moral: that, by dint of hard work and the solidarity of siblings, each
can be found a place in society and the whole family will prosper.
The strategy depended on exploiting educational opportunities, and
being able to place the graduates in government or church employment. The widowed mother served as a focus of obedience throughout her life, while the siblings consulted each other's interests. At
the next generation, as is only to be expected in this kind of stem
family, ties of kinship will weaken: Jeanne is much less interested in
and knowledgeable about the fate of her nephews and nieces. The
stem family is not a clan, not necessarily even a household, but
rather a culture which emphasizes solidarity among the siblings. In
the case of the Laurens it was a way of providing for large numbers
of children in a world with some, but not too many, professional
openings.

The evolution of this kind of family strategy in Europe depended
upon the growth of a celibate, bureaucratic church. The relationship
of Christianity to the structure of the European family is a complex
one, and has recently been the subject of a stimulating monograph
by the anthropologist Jack Goody (1983). He has traced a long-term
conflict over property and inheritance between two powerful corpora-

tions, the lineage and the clergy, which the latter eventually won, with major consequences for the structure of marriage in particular, a topic which we shall examine in more detail in chapter 4 below. Goody is probably right to draw attention to a latent conflict between christianity, at least in its early stages, and the family. The words of Jesus himself come to mind: 'For I am come to set a man at variance against his father, and the daughter against her mother, and the daughter-in-law against her mother-in-law. And a man's foes shall be they of his household' (Matthew x, 35–6). The continuing tension between earthly and spiritual brotherhood is highlighted in the writings of St Teresa of Avila. Praising the determination of one aristocratic acquaintance to see all her children enter the religious life though it meant the end of the dynasty, she commented that such parents 'love their offspring truly, for they would sooner have them lay up wealth and patrimony in that fortunate realm which has no end' (1951, pp. 60–1).

But there was an alternative principle at work in the history of the church as that body became a powerful landowning corporation. R. W. Southern, in some memorable pages, once described the inheritance strategies of the counts of Barcelona around 1000, whereby the kaleidoscopic subdivision of the patrimony among all the sons 'was to some extent compensated by the mingling of secular and ecclesiastical offices, and the concentration of both in the hands of the ruling family' (1987, p. 117). David Herlihy has speculated that this accumulation of bishoprics and abbeys in unworthy hands became less feasible as a result of the great reform movement of Pope Gregory VII (1073–85) and his successors, and that this may explain why aristocratic fathers were beginning to try at about this time to keep the inheritance undivided (1985, pp. 86–7). But the editor of this series, R. I. Moore, has suggested in a note to me that the Gregorian reform itself could be seen, at least in part, as a reaction to the exclusion of younger sons from their fathers' estates. These cadets of the nobility, increasingly vowed to celibacy, needed to secure their own careers through a monopoly of ecclesiastical benefices. The greater professionalism of the post-Gregorian church can thus be seen as an adaptation to changing family strategies rather than a complete rejection of them.

The latter interpretation does seem to fit better with the continuing interaction of church and family among the aristocracy, even after the Counter-Reformation and down to the end of the old regime. The career of the great poet of the Golden Age of Spanish letters,

Luis de Góngora (1561–1627), is testimony to that. The Góngoras were a gentry family of Córdoba, roughly equivalent in status to the Laurens. They depended on advancement in learning and office rather than on an inherited patrimony. In order to pay for young Luis's studies at the famous university of Salamanca, his maternal uncle, Francisco de Góngora, prebendary of Córdoba cathedral, resigned a couple of local benefices which he held on the young man in 1577. In 1585 the prebend itself was handed over, though Luis was not ordained a priest until 1617, at which point he actually resigned the prebend in his turn, in favour of his sister Francisca's child. Meanwhile uncle Francisco had provided, out of the prebend, the dowry with which Francisca had married back in 1579 (Artigas, 1925, pp. 28, 52, 55).

The Góngora family strategy depended on the existence of an economic and political system which generated considerable wealth outside the control of the family as such. Eventually that process of wealth creation would go so far that the solidarity even of the stem family, restricted, that is, to siblings and nephews, would be as redundant as the solidarity of the wider clan. By shedding his obligations to collaterals, now no longer needed as fighting men, the eighteenth-century noble was abandoning not only a family but a political function; by concentrating on the cultivation of his entailed estate, he was also becoming something of an economic problem. Fiscally exempt, holding down inefficiently exploited *latifundia* whose political *raison d'être* had largely disappeared, he seemed for the first time to be enjoying meaningless privileges. Chateaubriand summarizes some of the contradictions inherent in the eighteenth-century nobility, with its uneasy compromise between individualism and caste. His father had been forced to trade in the West Indies in order to reconstitute a fief in Brittany; he himself failed to get the naval commission for which his education had partly prepared him, but settled instead for a lieutenancy in the Regiment of Navarre, obtained for him through the patronage of his brother at court. From being a mark of political function, nobility had become by the last century of the old regime merely a channel for political favour. In an increasingly centralized regime, this created problems. One thinks again of the point made by de Tocqueville: that the French nobility by 1789 had virtually lost its political function, and this was reflected in the ease with which the juridical category of noble could be purchased or usurped; but thereby its social exclusiveness became all the more intolerable.

In order to understand what de Tocqueville was getting at, one has to have some concept of how the self-definition of family had evolved in France over the previous century or so. One aspect of this 'exclusiveness' will be dealt with more fully in our last chapter under the heading of domesticity. I would like to limit myself here to a more general illustration of the decline of lineage towards the end of the old regime, the decline of the cult of the ancestors in the religious sphere. Chantries, or endowments of masses for the souls of the dead, had proliferated in later medieval Europe. Abolished in protestant countries, they received a new lease of life in Catholic Europe after the Council of Trent (1545–63). But by 1700 some very interesting changes were becoming apparent. Michel Vovelle for Provence (1973, pp. 114–22) and Francois Lebrun for Anjou (1975, p. 361) have noted a concern by the ecclesiastical authorities that the clergy were being saddled with more masses for the dead than either their numbers or the endowments warranted. With a stagnation or fall in the numbers of clergy in Catholic Europe during the eighteenth century, the situation could only grow worse. In fact, Vovelle's classic thesis on the cult of the dead notes a decline in provision for masses, particularly among the middle classes in the latter half of the eighteenth century. Though Spain is not so well studied, a similar trend seems to have set in there too, reflected in new statements in last wills and testaments that the testator is not leaving many masses for his soul because he has taken care to have them said in his own lifetime. This trend is what we would expect in those Spanish circles exposed to Jansenist spirituality. But, as in France, may it not have led to a significant rupture with a centuries-old cult of the ancestors, reflecting and encouraging a declining role for the lineage?

Let us try to summarize some of the conclusions of this chapter. My argument has been that the lineage is less an institution in its own right, with clear boundaries which can be traced, as it were, by drawing a genealogical tree, than a kind of molten glass or metal which takes its form from the mould into which it is poured. Civic responsibility in a pre-industrial society reposes to a large extent – in the absence of a mass exchange of services or of 'rational' domination by a centralized government – on a concept of caste, which means simply purity or honour. A pride in ancestors, and a reverence for them, were ways in which that purity was maintained. The breakdown of this way of envisaging social relationships has been a major feature of modern European history, traditionally explained in terms of economic development, which fostered the concept of contract in place of inherited obligation, and in terms of the growth of the state, which submitted its citizens to an egalitarian respect for the rule of reason. But one part of that development seems to have been a narrowing of the notion of caste as such – and here the family historian might bring some light to bear.

It is perhaps ironic that the fully-fledged concept of the Three Orders of the realm – those who pray, these who fight, these who work – came in the eleventh century, according to Duby, that is, around the time when a clearer definition of genealogy would begin to create problems of recruitment of talented outsiders into the ranks of the nobility. The process was, indeed, a very gradual one, and lines of descent seem to have been still satisfactorily vague in the sixteenth century in many parts of Europe. But as they became more clearly defined, by being attached, in particular, to a patrimony which passed to a single or main heir, it became inevitable that civic responsibility would have to be secured in some other way – that the talent required for government would have to be sought outside the caste system. This is surely one of the features of the promotion of the 'vile bourgeoisie', for which the Absolute Monarchies were criticized in the seventeenth century.

The attempt of the monarchies to compromise with their critics, and buy off challenges to their authority, was an intriguing feature of the last stages of the old regime. In the eighteenth century a system of Orders or castes could be said to have reached its apogee: never had the nobility received such enthusiastic endorsement of its special right to lead the people in war and government, never had the guilds been more solidly entrenched in the monopoly of manufactures. It was the great merit of de Tocqueville to have shown how artificial and unstable this compromise between caste and centralism really was. Nobility, he tells us in effect, had lost its political significance, since government was based on bureaucratic control from the centre, rather than on honour and the memory of the ancestors. The nobility, however, had become virtually the only arm of government, for the latter ensured that its servants became noble if they were not already so. But the compromise did not work well, de Tocqueville tells us, because the new nobles were not fully accepted on the social level. In a beautiful, apparent paradox, nobility in 1789 was at once more open and more closed than ever before.

It is on the latter aspect that the historian of the family may hope to shed some light. He can show that genealogies had, indeed, become clearer over the early modern period. He can point out the relationship of this to a changing definition of property – no longer a source of patronage for the clan, but a capital asset to be exploited for the income it could yield, and to be husbanded for one's children alone. The retreat of the great families of Western Europe into their own households from the later seventeenth century, and the disbandment of their retainers, symbolized a shift from a society held together by personal ties to one based on wealth and the indirect power which comes from money. That other bastion of the political order, the guilds, posed problems of a similar kind. The whole rationale of the old regime was that the ties which held a society together were 'moral'; but those ties – of good lordship, family piety – were clearly now subordinated to the impersonal rule of bureaucracy and the market. The sense of disorientation and resentment at the change comes across quite well in the Chateaubriand memoirs. The historian of the family cannot 'explain' the French Revolution; but his research can help deepen our awareness of the frame of reference within which the protagonists operated, and the nature of the new bourgeois society from which the ancestors had been banished.

3
The politics of family

Now that the advance of civilization has made us more aware of the
natural and legal rights of all men, which royal authority is sufficiently
powerful to enforce, we no longer readily appreciate the significance
and importance of protecting life and property. In the Middle Ages it
was enjoyed only at great cost. No one could live peacefully without a
godfather.
> Juan Sempere y Guarinos, *Historia de los vínculos y mayorazgos*

The quotation which heads this chapter, from the procurator fiscal of
the chancery court of Granada, reminds us of the key role once
played by the solidarity of the group in securing life and limb. It is
more than a question of mere physical protection. Politics in the
small-scale societies of the old regime included a wide variety of
personal relationships which in our modern world are generally
regarded as part of the private sphere. Politics was crucial for the
allocation of status, which today is left to the more informal mechanism of the market, the exchange of professional services and the
build-up of wealth thereby. Defence of status in the old regime,
therefore, occupied proportionately more time and resources, from
the private warfare of the Middle Ages to the duels and litigation so
characteristic of the early modern period. In this world, whether the
Florence of the Medici or the villages of the present-day Mediterranean described by anthropologists, wealth has to be translated,
through gifts and patronage, into control over men if it is to purchase respect. Direct competition for prestige in the public arena,
rather than the anonymous exercise of power through control of
property, characterizes a traditional society. The hierarchy is determined, as it were, by political contest rather than by economic laws.

In such communities the lines of personal obligation tend to the
multiple and complex. Because the services he can render are so
irregular and often inherited from his father, a tradesman or servant
will often fall into a general relation of dependence with his customer
or master. He will become a client, perhaps a friend, the quarrels of

his superiors his quarrels. Since his relations with the market are too irregular for there to be a standard price for what he has to sell, he will fix his demands by non-capitalist criteria, by what he knows of the other party to the contract – whether he is a friend to be favoured, a potential enemy to be placated, a fool to be cheated. Private lives are, of course, matters of gossip in such small-scale societies and powerfully affect an individual's standing in the eyes of his contemporaries. After all, the capital with which the trader works, or the land which the peasant ploughs, will as likely have come to him from his father, his uncle or his wife as from his own skill at his job. Anthropologists of the Mediterranean have found, unsurprisingly, that a good relationship with one's womenfolk – daughter, sister or wife – is crucial to one's functioning as a full member of the community, as a man of respect, to be treated seriously in contracts. Sexual honour is (if we may twist La Rochefoucauld's famous phrase) the homage which public life pays to the family in traditional communities, where the two cannot be easily separated. The great Castilian lawbook of the mid-thirteenth century, the *Siete Partidas*, reserved no fewer than twenty-three paragraphs to the question of honour (as against sixteen, for example, to homicide). It listed the ways in which a man could be dishonoured, by wounding, robbing, spitting, satire, or following a woman around too closely. Some of these actions would, of course, attract a penalty anyway for assault; but there was a separate legal suit for the dishonour attached.

We shall be looking in more detail at the reasons for this in a later chapter, when we come to consider the role of women in traditional societies. I mention it here in order to suggest the great potential for violence in such closed communities. As Barth notes for the Swat Pathans, honour is an important ingredient in the prestige which enables a chief to attract followers. It must be defended by the humiliation of any who seek to undermine it. One murder may thus have to be avenged by that of two or more persons from the other side, perhaps together with destruction of their property. In societies with long memories, such hatreds will become hereditary, ready to be reactivated on the slightest provocation (1965, pp. 81–6). In the absence of a strong central authority, there is a great need for the support of friends if an individual is to survive at all. In Swat, such friends are not necessarily kinsmen; in less developed societies they often are. Evans-Pritchard has given us the classic description of one such society, that of the pastoral Nuer of the Sudan. 'Fear of incurring a blood-feud is, in fact, the most important legal sanction within a tribe, and the main guarantee of an individual's life and property' (1969, p. 150). The feud depends, in the ideal type, upon a segmentary family structure: that is, brothers may quarrel between themselves and no one will intervene, but they will stand shoulder to shoulder if one of them is attacked by a cousin, and again they will postpone disputes with cousins and rally to their defence should these be attacked by any outsider. In this way a rambling, pyramidal structure of mutual defence gives a whole people, up to a certain point of genealogical awareness, a sense of belonging to a rule-based, though leaderless, polity. Where the sense of obligation to the clan ends, there ends the 'feud', and there begins random, unstructured warfare with strangers.

Evans-Pritchard has given the classic definition of the feud as a 'rule-based' structure. Those who abide by its rules are members of something akin to a state. Internal disputes are not evidence of the weakness of the clan (and here, perhaps, the historian could take note); rather, they may bring into operation that mechanism for settlement which reinforces a sense of common solidarity. Some of the most interesting work on the feud has been done for North Africa. Here the predominant pastoralism of the Nuer or other sub-Saharan tribes begins to give way to a more settled agriculture in what was, after all, part of the old Roman empire. Nevertheless, population is more scattered and towns are much fewer than on the northern shore of the Mediterranean. Settlement seems to be frequently in hamlets, populated by men of one blood. The authority of the state in these areas was never very great under the native Muslim rulers. Over against the *makhzen*, the territory under the effective control of the sultan, stood the *siba*, the land of 'dissidence', where peace was maintained by the feud. Transhumance and the conflicts to which it gave rise into our own times remind us of a world, like that of Spain three centuries ago, where pastoralism is slowly giving way to more settled cultivation. Public order depends on the solidarity of the agnatic kin (that is, the relations of a man through his father) with the victim of an assault. Gellner has given us a classic account of one such system among the Berbers of the Atlas Mountains. After a murder the culprit and his ten closest kin will flee to safety. Negotiation for reconciliation may lead to the payment of blood-money by the culprit and his associates, half to the victim's sons and half to his ten closest agnates. Alternatively the accused may seek to establish his innocence by the 'co-juring' of his paternal

kinsmen, whose number will be fixed in accordance with the seriousness of the charge. The oaths must be sworn on holy ground to avoid
the risk of blasphemy, for a false swearing may be expected to attract
divine wrath. If this fear deters enough kin from swearing, then the
man is presumed 'guilty', and the co-juring kinsmen who do turn up
will be fined (Gellner, 1969, pp. 106–14 and 125–6).

The Berber system may recall some aspects of trials in medieval
Europe. One thinks of *The Song of Roland* and of the thirty kinsmen
of the false Ganelon who 'pledge him by faith and trust' after he was
accused of betraying the hero (lines 3846–7); or of the deceitful
Yseut, accused of adultery in *The Romance of Tristan*, who is allowed
to clear her name with an ambivalent oath on holy relics (pp.
140–2). In both cases a modern readership has some difficulty in
understanding what is going on, since the participants are all fully
aware of Ganelon's treachery and Yseut's fault. Clearly, as among
the Berbers, the oaths are not meant to establish innocence but
'oath-worthiness' – that is, the good-standing of the accused with his
own friends and supporters. If these are prepared to stand by him or
her, it may be in everyone's interest to seek some face-saving formula of reconciliation. As Roland's companions put it, faced with the
need to fight Ganelon's champion and kinsman Pinabel, 'Roland is
dead – he'll never more be seen – / One can't restore him for money
or for fee./ Fight Pinabel? Who'd be so rash? Not me!' (lines
3802–4). In societies where the public peace is so fragile, it seems
best not to insist on the letter of one's rights against wrong-doers
who have too powerful backers. Persistent troublemakers will be
disciplined ultimately by their own group: either murdered or refused further help with oaths.

There are limits, though, to the effectiveness of the feud as a way
of keeping the peace in more settled societies: after all, Ganelon was
ultimately answerable to some kind of 'public' authority. In practice,
it may be difficult to raise wider groupings of kin than the men of
one household to pursue a grievance. Among the transhumant
shepherds of the Epirus region of Greece, a man's obligation of
actively pursuing the quarrels of his brothers ceases once a son is
born to him: his first duty is not to jeopardize the lives of his own
household (Campbell, 1964, pp. 70–1). Communities will have some
kind of mediator in feuds, not bound by blood ties to the lineages. In
medieval Europe this was typically the ecclesiastics. Among the
Berbers of the Atlas, as among the Pathans of Swat, it is a class of
holy men, the 'saints' in Gellner's phrase, who exude a spiritual

authority because of their descent from the prophet Mohammed or because of the asceticism of their private lives. Such men can arrange for apologies to be made in time from the weak to the strong, without loss of face, or they can avoid unnecessary bloodshed by appealing for magnanimity from those perhaps not too sure of their own strength if matters came to fighting. In the less exclusively kin-based society of Swat, it is sometimes difficult to determine in advance the strength of the other side. Some use has to be made of 'public opinion', through meetings of local assemblies, which may serve as a kind of jury not unlike that which we have encountered in the trial of Ganelon. At one of these meetings a culprit may be denounced by the aggrieved party in order to test the water, as it were. If the man's friends do not rally openly in his support, he will find himself under the ban of the assembly, branded as a trouble-maker, and liable to summary chastisement at the hands of his opponent, who will run no risk of incurring a feud thereby.

Though the 'family' provides a basic framework within which the individual can find shelter in stateless or near-stateless societies, it is obviously misleading to make it the exclusive focus of attention, at least in any part of Eurasia. Robert Montagne, pioneer of the sociol-ogy of the Maghreb, defined the solidarities of the Berbers at the time of the French occupation of Morocco more in terms of settle-ment than of kinship (though the two tended to overlap). The kin-based hamlets formed a township, with a mosque and a political council comprising the able-bodied males, the *jama'a* (the *aljama* of Muslim Spain four centuries earlier). These *aljamas* (to use the Spanish derivation) were grouped in cantons, or petty republics, one to each valley in the Atlas, comprising 200–400 families in occupa-tion of forty to fifty square kilometres of territory, under a council of notables. When a canton had a dispute with its neighbour, it sought an alliance with the next 'republic' but one. This association or *Leff* could be extended over a whole region, to the friends of friends. The military obligations thus contracted could give an able cantonal leader an opportunity of exerting headship over a considerable population, as he intervened to pacify the quarrels of his friends and lead them against their enemies. Such warlords, or *caïds*, will begin building fortresses and collecting their own permanent bodyguards. The old family/township-based feuding republic will give way to a petty principality, only to recover its force as the *caïd*'s sons fall out over their father's inheritance (Montagne, 1973, pp. 62–4).

Barth has given us a rather similar picture of the ebb and flow of political leadership in Swat. Here, where the kindreds are often split internally by feuds over land, alliances between powerful men are built up on a voluntary basis. The treaties oblige the parties to settle their disputes amicably, and to support each other in all circumstances against outsiders. They build up into extensive blocs, which split the territory of Swat and its 400,000 people into two factions. Membership of these factions is hereditary, though a man can renounce his allegiance if he feels it to be in his interest to do so and a suitable pretext presents itself. Lords or *khans* tend to develop, as military leaders or patrons of their weaker brethren. The construction of a state, though, is ultimately frustrated (until modern times, at least) by the subdivision of a *khan*'s patrimony among his sons at his death, and by a constant tendency for emergent strong men to lose friends, who rally in fright to the opposing faction (Barth, 1965, chapter 9).

The analyses of Montagne and Barth remind us that in the more settled societies of Eurasia there is much room for manipulation of the feud in order to build up structures of authority which may ultimately be inimical to it. Historians of Europe are not too familiar with such a model. We are inclined to see the growth of states as hampered by the existence of too strong a consciousness of clan. The concept of ebb and flow is less easy for us to grasp. Yet that most exciting of medieval historians, Ibn Khaldūn, has left us a memorable analysis of how this mechanism works. This fourteenth-century Arab writer seems to have been very much influenced by the Greeks as well as by observation of his own civilization. His interest was in the city as well as in the tribe, as one might expect from someone living on the southern flank of the Byzantine empire. He cited with approval an old dictum: 'Men persist only with the help of property. The only way to property is through cultivation. The only way to cultivation is through justice' – which for him meant government (1967, pp. 40–1). He looked with admiration to the strong states of the Umayyads or Abassids. For Ibn Khaldūn politics was the very basis of civilized life; natural man was but a brute. One senses in him something of that old tension between the *polis* and the kin which one can find in the Greeks as early as Homer. Defining the barbarism of the Cyclops, Homer declared: 'They have no assemblies to debate in, they have no ancestral ordinances; they live in arching caves on the tops of high hills, and the head of each family heeds no other, but makes his own ordinances for wife and children' (Book IX, lines 112–15).

Ibn Khaldūn's well-known model is that of a successive ebb and flow of civilizations, as cities are invaded and conquered by tribes, which in turn settle down as ruling urban dynasties. The strength of the tribe came from its cohesiveness, based on the loyalty of its members to one another. Such loyalty could come from awareness of common descent; but biological kinship alone did not ensure its presence, for (as Ibn Khaldūn pointed out) most clans existed only at a latent level, with a marked tendency towards segmentation into smaller interest groups. Pride in genealogy was known in the cities, but had no political significance. 'The consequences of common descent, though natural, still are something imaginary,' he writes. 'The real thing to bring about the feeling of close contact is social intercourse, friendly association, long familiarity and the companionship that results from growing up together, having the same wet nurse and sharing the other circumstances of death and life' (1967, p. 148). His analysis at this point might recall some pages of Fustel de Coulanges describing the Roman *gens*, a grouping based around a household, but including clients and adopted outsiders as well as biological kin. Indeed, when Ibn Khaldūn is talking about the rise of dynasties like the Umayyads or Abassids, I think he may have had in mind something closer to an extended household and its clients than to a sub-Saharan tribe. But the biological kindred clearly is important to him, as constituting the nucleus of a successful dynasty. There is mention at one stage of its self-awareness extending perhaps to four generations (pp. 97–107). Where such consciousness is missing, as typically in urbanized societies like Muslim Spain, then true dynasties will fail to evolve, and each city will fall prey to a petty local warlord, as happened to Spain under the Taifa kings.

This tremendously important group feeling (*asabiya*) of the clan, then, is the very condition for the construction of a proper state. Such solidarities are to be found only in the countryside, especially in the desert, where they play a vital role in protecting a man against his enemies. City dwellers, by contrast, will rely on their walls and their hired militia, and, because they are greedy for gain, will marry rich women and forget their kindred. Of course, this is precisely the trap which lies in wait for all successful dynasties which have imposed their will on cities: they too will come to rely on their walls and paid soldiers, which are no match for the hungry new clans already forming in the desert.

Ibn Khaldūn's analysis bears a striking resemblance to Robert Montagne's account of how Moroccan warlords operated six centuries later, if we substitute 'petty court' or 'walled fortress' for city. Montagne noted that the instability of these North African states stood in contrast to the pattern in Europe. He observed that the power of the warlords, unlike that of medieval barons, lacked vital supports at the top and bottom of the social hierarchy. The Berbers acknowledged no dependence on a feudal superior, and they did not structure their gifts to dependants in the form of 'fees' conditional on continued service (1973, pp. 68–9). The rule of a *caïd*'s family might last a couple of generations, but then it would disintegrate through the division of the patrimony among several heirs, allied with pressure from opposing forces: the sultan seeking to extend his authority, the erstwhile friends and clients of the *caïd* rallying for a while to the sultan in order to make life difficult for an unbearable superior. After a certain point, political authority in North Africa seemed to become dysfunctional as it ceased to correspond to the real needs of the local people. 'It is generally felt in most regions that when the sultan is in control of the area, law and order is maintained but justice is not upheld' (p. 75). This is the perpetual dilemma which gnaws at the foundations of power in a tribal society, stimulating rebellion and the return of the feud.

The contrast with Europe, highlighted by Montagne, is intriguing. Here a centralized authority seems to have met fewer difficulties in countering the influence of the feud and in maintaining its own permanence. The words of the Spanish essayist, Luis Zapata (1532?–1600?), observing the demise of self-help among the barons in his own day, come to mind: 'principalities have been joined one to the other, fanning a glow into a mighty blaze, with which no grandee can compete' (1859, pp. 231–4). This ability of European rulers to concentrate power so effectively poses questions for the historian of the family. It may have its roots in antiquity. Plato, father of Western political philosophy, was less interested in the family than in the commonwealth. Writing in the fourth century BC, he looked back to a then vanished age of patriarchal rule, for which his main source seems to have been Homer and the passage from *The Odyssey* which we quoted above. Such structures were still to be found, he noted, where population was scattered and lived by herding. 'The next step is to come together in large numbers, which will increase the size of the communities, and turn to agriculture.' The city would then form out of a coalition of family heads, who would delegate their chiefs as magistrates, thus making 'the patriarchal groups into an aristocracy, or possibly a monarchy' (1960, pp. 59–60). This concept of how political society forms has been enormously influential in European thought, and perhaps we tend to take it too much for granted. Yet, though Rome was strong enough to dispense with the family feud, the Greek cities seem to have had to incorporate some aspects of it within their system of peace-keeping. There was the *anchisteia*, the mourning and vengeance circle, which included second cousins on both the maternal and paternal sides, and the neighbourhood grouping or *phratry*, responsible for exacting blood-money or vengeance, though only after the city magistrates had passed sentence (Roussel, 1976, pp. 143–4). The family, then, continued to have a certain political importance even within the framework of the city or state.

The blood-feud as such came into its own with the fall of Graeco-Roman civilization in the West. The law codes of the Germanic invaders are not as forthcoming on the subject as we would like, and there is always the problem of knowing how far they really corresponded to practice. The Salian Laws of the earlier sixth century (which have, unfortunately, come down to us only in incomplete manuscripts from a couple of centuries later) seem to have the fullest specifications regarding the feud. A man could apparently count on the support of both maternal and paternal kin in a quarrel, out to the desendants of his grandparents' first cousins (Murray, 1983, p. 143). These would be called upon to swear oaths to his innocence if he were accused of a crime, and they would help pay any blood-money or *Wergeld* to the kin of the victim. As among the Berbers, if the oath-helpers did not come forward in the numbers required, then the accused was found guilty. One half of the *Wergeld* went to the sons of the victim, the rest being shared among his kin.

As Wallace-Hadrill pointed out some years ago, the sixth-century chronicle of Gregory of Tours gives us an insight into how this code actually worked. Clearly the kindred was not free to avenge its own grievances without interference. Always there seem to be intermediaries, royal orders not to pursue in particular cases, and reconciliations, as well, of course, as the uncontrollable, unpredictable fits of anger of individuals which play havoc with the rules (1962, pp. 121–47). The classic study of the feud among the Germanic peoples (or 'Teutonic races', as one could still call them in 1913) is that by Bertha Phillpotts. One gets the impression from her work that the feud was often less structured than it might appear in the laws. The rise of strong monarchies in England after 1066, and on the continent during the thirteenth century, substituted alternative forms of

peace-keeping. The 'forswearings' in Flanders, by which the kin
could renounce solidarity with a troublemaker, date from this time
(Phillpotts, 1913, p. 179). In Castile one notes how much more room
is left for the kin in the *fuero*, or local law code, of Sepúlveda,
incorporating customs from as far back as the tenth century though
drawn up in its present form in the thirteenth, than in the *fuero* of
Cuenca, introduced after that town's conquest from the Moors in the
late twelfth century. In Cuenca the kin have virtually disappeared
from criminal jurisprudence, whereas in Sepúlveda one finds them
(out to the 'fourth degree', or descendants of a great-great-
grandfather) helping an accused swear to his innocence, or pursuing
a man who has seduced the daughter or wife of one of their number
(Dillard, 1976, pp. 71–94).

Nevertheless, the feud, though regulated by the courts, continued
to play a major part in criminal jurisprudence in some parts of
Europe into more modern times. Though the *Wergeld* was formally
abolished in Denmark in 1537, the kin of the culprit would still
readily buy his freedom from the victim's family, encouraged by the
pardons available from the crown, into the seventeenth century
(Phillpotts, 1913, pp. 82–98). The situation was not greatly different
in Spain. Alonso de Villadiego, *corregidor* (district judge) under
Philip III (1598–1621), noted that some crimes interested chiefly
the kin and might be pardoned if these were reconciled. The judge
would have to act only 'to satisfy the commonwealth' in cases of
robbery, or murder 'with malice aforethought' (1766, p. 80). The
notarial registers are full of reconciliations in other cases between the
culprit and the victim's immediate family, though these become
much less frequent from the end of the seventeenth century. The
widow and the children tended alone to figure as recipients of
compensation. But the wider grouping of 'friends' would play a key
role in the trial itself, where verdicts often depended less on the
material evidence to the crime than on the common fame of the
accused. This was, indeed, true of litigation in the civil sphere as
well, which was often a prelude to, or substitute for, a bitter feud.

We, who live in a policed society, where our lives and property are
so clearly identified, measured and documented in such a variety of
registers, find it easy to forget how recently this world has come into
being. The general registration of births, marriages and deaths, like
the generalized identification of property for fiscal purposes is essentially an achievement of the later seventeenth and eighteenth centuries. Before that, the practice of the civil courts in Spain (and, I

would presume, elsewhere) was to permit the constant re-opening of civil suits as fresh pieces of evidence appeared a generation or more after the previous judgement. New members of the family would come to light; fresh doubts would be cast on the authenticity of manuscript copies of documents whose original it was too costly to bring from some inaccessible mountain village; women (who owned so much property but were judicial minors) had the privilege of reneging on contracts unless their fathers or husbands could establish that they did freely consent to them. Stirling has noted in his *Turkish Village* how difficult it is to establish the validity of the sale of land in a traditional community, where parties are not expected to insist on the letter of the contract but to act as friends (an echo, perhaps, of *The Merchant of Venice?*) (1965, p. 263). In early modern Spain legal documents were signed in order to comply with official requirements, or sometimes (as in marriage contracts specifying the amount of the dowry), in order to 'look good'. But the parties, as we learn afterwards from other sources, had tacit agreements ('between friends') which cancelled the letter of the agreement. Subsequent court cases would turn not on the material signatures to the contract, but on the 'common fame' of the parties and what each had really intended. Here, built into a modern-looking civil law system, was a very traditional jurisprudence, which it is sometimes hard to distinguish from old-fashioned compurgation or oath-helping.

It is this impreciseness of adjudication in the old regime which helps explain the notorious 'corruption' associated with the law. It is not that judges were particularly venal, nor that litigants did not believe in fairness; it was rather that fairness could rarely be found in an application of the law of contract. Since this was so generally known to be so, a 'strict' verdict could only be construed as an unfriendly act. This was, of course, even more true in the realm of criminal jurisprudence. In his advice to a friend who was taking up a judgeship in Córdoba in the early seventeenth century, the Murcian chronicler Cascales wrote that he must above all administer justice discreetly, so that it did not cause resentment among a man's kinsfolk. If a troublemaker had to be punished – and where possible, leading figures should not be punished, only detained at pleasure until the dust settled – then 'let your worship make his peace with the man's kin ... and make amends to them by doing them kindnesses when the occasion arises' (Ochoa, 1856–70, vol. II, pp. 529–31).

The fact is that the judge in early modern Europe was in a problematical situation when any action he took against an individual might plunge a whole family into disgrace. As the fifteenth-century Florentine writer and architect Alberti noted, a man had a special bond with his kinsmen, 'for every honor that you gain brings them honor also, and part of the dishonor attached to any disgrace of yours falls on them' (1969, p. 201). Since the feud was technically illegal in early modern Europe, we perhaps forget what a great role it played indirectly underneath the official calm of the courtroom. Since the law codes themselves, unlike in the early medieval period, are no help here, we have to be more than usually attentive to the unfolding of particular individual dramas. One which I have found quite illustrative – and since it is in print, may not be too abstruse – concerns the fate of a petty nobleman from Toledo, by the name of Diego Duque, who murdered his betrothed and a rival for her affections in 1607, when he was only eighteen. His guardian and 'step-brothers', with whom he had been reared, helped him escape. The law caught up with him only in 1611, in the person of a judge who took a personal dislike to him, decided to enforce the warrant for his arrest and duly packed him back to Toledo to stand trial. On his arrival, the widow of the murdered man (who apparently had been innocent of more than a mild indiscretion in respect of Duque's betrothed) had the four-year old mourning drapes taken down from her house and invited her kinsfolk to celebrate. The investigation by the *corregidor* turned into a personal confrontation with the accused and his family, who intervened with the prime minister of the day, the duke of Lerma, and obtained a stay of execution. The issue was resolved in time-honoured fashion by the escape of Duque from gaol (1613), and his disappearance from the wasps' nest in Toledo for good (Duque, 1860, pp. 54–9). The case of Duque illustrates, I think, how careful the governments of early modern Europe had to be of fuelling kin resentments by too high-handed a defence of public order.

Villadiego, the *corregidor* of Philip III's reign, whom we have come across before, warned his fellow judges: 'there is no city, town or village which is not divided into bands or factions, even between friends and kin ...' (1766, p. 162). His analysis is instructive, but at the same time perplexing. He seems to be saying that the kindred will as often be found to be divided within itself as acting collectively on behalf of each of its members. What is true of the Spanish towns seems equally the case in the Italian city states. Shifting alignments of individuals within the factions which dominated communal politics have caught the eye of Renaissance historians. How could solidarity with the kin have any significance, when a prominent Florentine like Filippo Strozzi the Younger could have ties of marriage and friendship with the Medici around 1500, while his brothers were obviously Republican in sentiment? (Goldthwaite, 1968, pp. 85–107).

Clearly, it would be unrealistic ever to expect the same degree of cohesion from a bilateral European kindred as from a unilineal descent group. The Germanic *Sippe* had functioned as a defensive grouping for its members in the feud, but its membership was not as stable as that of a clan, broadening in one direction and contracting in another as each new generation shed obligations to distant cousins on the father's side and took up new ones towards its mother's people. One of the most interesting insights into the tensions caused in Europe by these 'rights of the woman' comes, appropriately enough, in that great epic of the German people, *The Nibelungenlied*, which was composed around 1200. Written probably on the Austrian frontier, it reflects an unsettled world of plunder and of conflict with the heathen, not too different (one may assume) from the fifth-century wars against the Hungarians, which are its starting point. It is a world in which – unlike aristocratic France at this time – women have strong political personalities. This can make for instability, because they have claims on the patrimony of their father (the notion that the Germans did not have dowry – that is, a right to some portion of the wealth of their family of origin – finds no support in the poem); yet, having married out, their loyalty to their siblings is undermined by that to their husbands. This is the unfolding drama of the poem, the feud over status and treasure which leads Kriemhild to avenge the death of her spouse Siegfried against her brother Gunther. Though most clearly expressed in *The Nibelungenlied*, the same tension underlay most aristocratic family relations in Europe. It stemmed, I think, from the inheritance rights of women, which we shall discuss more fully in a later chapter. Perhaps I may just cite one real example, from Spanish history, of the trouble it could cause. The third son of the newly elected king of Aragon, Ferdinand of Antequera, married in 1422 his cousin, sister of John II of Castile. She supported him, in ways which recall Kriemhild, in his demand for the marquisate of Villena as part of her dowry, helping to spark off a border war between Castile and Aragon in 1425 (Viciana, 1972, vol. II, p. 70).

Loyalty to the mother's side, because of expectation of inheritance, actually makes it very difficult to see clear-cut lineages in action in any European feud. That does not mean that kin solidarity was not very important, but simply that the threads of allegiance are very tangled. A man could look in many directions for support in quarrels, but he would generally start out by addressing himself to his kinsfolk. Some of these would be unavailable, because on the other side anyway. Again, as with the influence of the kin in the courtroom, it is only through studying actual feuds that one can see how the kaleidoscopic changes of party actually did constitute a coherent family strategy. We shall take the published memoirs of one gentleman of Seville, Alonso Enríquez, which cover the years 1518 to 1543. He describes an interesting confrontation with an old enemy of his house, the commander Garci Tello, which erupted into violence after a period of slumber, in the way of all feuds, because of a few, ill-chosen words (which struck the bystanders, including the marquis of Ayamonte, who had connections with both sides, as of little importance at the time). Alonso subsequently ambushed and wounded Garci Tello, with the support of his brothers and the brother of his wife. The important question now was whether the violence could be stopped from spreading, for both sides were well connected – Tello was a client of Ayamonte, Alonso of the future first duke of Alcalá. 'Although our kinship was slight, for he is of the Enríquez of Castile, and I am of those of Portugal', he tells us with regard to Alcalá, 'we are all of one house, though the exact relationship is unclear. But obligations [deuda, as against deudo, kinship] were great on both sides, such was his love for me and my desire to serve him' (Enríquez 1886, p. 69). Since Ayamonte was a kinsman of Alcalá as well, he tried to patch up a reconciliation. But this rambling Enríquez connection could never function as a proper clan, because Alcalá looked to his mother's side, the Ribera, for the bulk of his inheritance, and Ayamonte to his own wife, a Zúñiga, through whom hoped to succeed to the duchy of Béjar and the headship of a new connection. In fact, bitterness between Alonso Enríquez and Ayamonte continued to rumble on for a few years as a result of the Tello wounding. What one notices here, I think, is a vague uneasiness among kinsmen at finding themselves on opposite sides, with an inevitable tendency to drift apart into the separate obligations imposed by their wives and mothers.

The problem in medieval Europe had been that the Sippe, even if technically allowed to exact retribution for an injury done to one of its number, was not sufficiently cohesive territorially to make this feasible. Given the exogamy of early feudal society, which we shall be looking at later, a man would very likely be living quite far away from his mother's people, on whom he was supposed to count for half his strength. Again, *The Nibelungenlied* gives as good an insight as any into the forces at work here – I mean, the sheer dispersal of aristocratic women in the earlier Middle Ages away from their families of origin. The situation is far different from that which Gellner describes for the Atlas Mountains, where the obligations to one's agnatic kinsfolk coincide with those to one's neighbours, since fewer than 10 per cent of the males in a particular village will be immigrants (1969, p. 63).

More generally, though, historians have tended to blame the weakness of the feud in Europe on the sheer confusion which is likely to arise (as in the Enríquez memoir) when obligations are owed equally to two different camps, mother's as well as father's kin. Perhaps because of this, one notes in Europe a precocious rise of a sense of territoriality as a substitute for kinship: that one's prime obligation was to neighbours rather than family. Some such concept seems to me to underlie the medieval commune. All civilizations, in a sense, have had towns; but Europe may have been unique in the autonomy and cohesiveness which hers came to enjoy in the eleventh and twelfth centuries. The communal movement of that period was as much about protection of the person as about fiscal privilege. It aimed to establish a 'brotherhood' among neighbours, which would ensure that disputes were resolved peacefully and that loyalty to the city would take precedence over the older ties of family – a quite revolutionary development. The statutes of the Guild of Our Lady, which grouped the conquerors of Andújar in 1245 shortly after the conquest of that Andalusian town from the Moor, specified: 'that among all the brothers of this our guild there should be love and full concord, with each looking out for the honour of the other, and for the good of this town of Andújar' (Argote, 1957, pp. 237–8). More radically, the gentlemen of nearby Baeza swore in 1442 'ever to stand by and defend the magistracy of Baeza and one another, and to be friends of their friends and foes of their foes ... and also not to be in the dependency of any persons ... from outside this city' (pp. 713–14).

Historians of medieval and Renaissance Italy have been concerned in recent years to emphasize the continuing importance of the kindred within the commune. The towers which still dominate the skyline of San Gimignano are a mute testimony to the bloody factional feuds which tore the early communes apart, though the towers were often built by the men of more than one clan. Did the punitive legislation of the Later Middle Ages against magnates and their followings drive a stake through the heart of kin solidarity? F. W. Kent's seminal study of *Household and Lineage in Renaissance Florence* (1977) makes a good case for thinking otherwise, or at least for redefining the terms of the debate. True, the Florentine great families tended to live in nuclear households by the fourteenth and fifteenth centuries; but they still congregated in particular districts – almost all the twenty-three Rucellai households in the Red Lion quarter in 1427, for example. Though siblings would split up the father's estate after death, networks of patronage continued to link the rich and poor of the clan. Though bilateral inheritance may tend to confuse loyalties, one's name came from one's father, and that created a potential badge of identity. After all, the sixteenth-century Florentine goldsmith, Benvenuto Cellini, who has left us a well-known autobiography, has both the typical Renaissance pride in personal achievement, and a traditional sense of pride in all those who bear the Cellini name, even though he cannot trace the exact connection (1956, p. 17). The significance of this in republican Florence, where voting for office took place in district assemblies like that of the Red Lion, was that a family name could easily become the nucleus of a political party, especially since one's namesake was also one's neighbour.

My own impression, from a reading of the situation in late medieval Spanish towns, is that one should not define these communal clans too narrowly. It is not until the fifteenth or sixteenth centuries, as I have suggested in the previous chapter, that the genealogies of the patricians in Spain can be accurately documented. Before that we have such a kaleidoscopic pattern of subdivision of patrimonies, proliferation of collateral branches through the marriages of cadets, integration of illegitimates into the line as full sons through formal adoption or insinuation, that it is difficult to mark off the frontiers between one descent group and the next. Clan names are certainly used, and become very important as party labels – Villavicencio and Dávila in Jerez, or Altamirano, Añasco and Bejarano in Trujillo. But these clans are perhaps best seen as analogous to the *alberghi* of Genoa: associations of different families for protection.

The useful study of the *albergo* by Jacques Heers (1977) reminds us how important such associations were. The commune in Genoa seems to have been weaker than in Florence, as is suggested by the urban landscape itself – the absence of a city hall and square as dominant as that constructed by the Florentines in the mid-fourteenth century, the parcelling out of city space into clearly defensive quarters. The sixty-four *alberghi* of the late fourteenth century, reduced through amalgamations to twenty-eight by 1528, were constituted by treaties among families who agreed to settle disputes peaceably and support one another against outsiders. One, that of the Giustiniani, arose out of an agreement among merchants specializing in the alum and mastic trade; but the majority kept trade separate from politics, concentrating on the needs of defence. The *alberghi* drew much of their strength from association with particular neighbourhoods, where a grouping would have its own retail outlets, church, fortresses of the wealthy and necessary complement of artisans. Since elections for communal office went by neighbourhood, as in Florence, it was important to belong to an association if one had any hopes of a political career.

The study of Heers throws light indirectly on the situation in Castile as well. Down to the reign of Isabella (1474–1504), the Castilian towns seem to have constituted so many autonomous republics, in spite of the nominal overlordship of the monarchy. As such, they were torn apart by the faction fighting so familiar to scholars of Renaissance Italy. These factions or *bandos* often acquired a near-hereditary lien on a certain proportion of the communal offices, though the intervention of the monarchy in appointments from the fourteenth century, and particularly under Isabella, helped to break their stranglehold. Quarrels for office gave kinship, as in Florence, an enduring political significance. Towers were built to serve as places of refuge. Most were knocked down in the reign of Isabella, but one, that of the Carvajal lineage, still survives in Cáceres. In the intervals between elections, clan feeling was kept alive by tournaments, of which the best known are the five annual jousts organized by the Dávila and Villavicencio in Jerez. Unlike the individual combats of north European knights, these were family affairs – mass charges by two factions across the public square, hurling toy javelins at each other from light ponies, and all clad in party colours (red and white for Villavicencio, purple and yellow for Dávila) (Moreno de Guerra 1929, pp. 64–6). These *bandos* were not family groupings in the strict sense, though they were built around a family name. Their framework was that of a unilineal descent group, because such cohesion was necessary for power; but recruitment was open to the illegitimate, to descendants through women, and probably to mere clients.

What is intriguing about the Castilian situation is the way in which faction fighting became worse as the power of the monarchy grew from the fourteenth century onwards. Historians have tended to see this as an inevitable response to the weakness of the Trastámara dynasty after its usurpation of the crown in 1369, allied with personal failings on the part of individual kings. I think the evidence could be read the other way: that the crown's servants were intervening ever more in the regulation of competition for municipal office during this period and provoking the disintegration of the old party solidarities. In classic feuding societies real violence tends to be rare, as the opponents measure each other's strength and seek a compromise. Where a third party, such as a king, seeks to impose a solution, the feud risks becoming a 'vendetta', that is, an unstructured series of blows and counterblows, often indirect and secret, utilizing special access to the forces of law and order themselves. Secrecy and treachery render compromise impossible. The essayist Luis Zapata noted precisely this effect in the once lawless territories of the Crown of Aragon, then coming under the strong government of Philip II (1556–98). Forbidden the traditional resort to duels, the aggrieved parties took to the hills, 'and if they cannot take vengeance on the man who injured them, they kill his cousin, his son, his wife, his dog or his horse' (1859, p. 469). This kind of vendetta or banditry will arise in a transitional phase, where the feud as such is outlawed or restricted by the action of superiors, but where the latter do not yet have a coercive monopoly of force.

There is a further, related point which helps us explain the proliferating factional violence of the later Middle Ages – and not just in Spain or Italy. This is the growing integration of local units into a much vaster, region- or nation-wide system of alliances, a kind of *leff* collision, to use Montagne's model. The municipal feuds in late medieval Castile fed on national disputes, in particular a long series of wars among the princes of the usurping house of Trastámara after 1369. During the later conflict between Isabella and the Portuguese-backed pretender to the throne, the duke of Medina Sidonia and the marquis of Cádiz took opposing sides in deference to the old feud of their respective families, fighting their battles through their clients in the municipal councils of Seville and Jerez. Time and again the politics of faction within the Castilian communes tied up with the wider struggle of the great magnates at court. In one sense these blocs of alliances remind us of the *leff* in Morocco, or its equivalent in the Swat of the Pathans. But the intriguing thing about these power struggles of the later Middle Ages in Spain and other parts of

Europe is the way in which they led towards the creation of more stable, more centralized political authority after 1500: the absolute monarchies. Now this story goes far beyond the confines of aristocratic family strategy. There is a history of military technology, political philosophy and economic development involved here as well. But I would like to raise one matter of debate which seems appropriate in the present context. That is, that it is difficult to write the history of the European state, in this crucial period of its formation around 1500, in terms of gunpowder, the tearing down of baronial castles, or the implantation of royal judges. The old lineages did not die out in the civil wars of the fifteenth century, though we are accustomed to that model for England after the Wars of the Roses. In Spain, at least, they flourished under absolutism as never before – after all, many of them, like the Mendozas, had helped to place Isabella on the throne in the first place. Their influence at court and in the provinces continued for at least another century. Unlike Swat or Morocco, strong 'factions' did not seem to find it necessary to check the progress of their superiors; in the rise of the European state, rather, what we have to explain is the dovetailing of faction, and its nucleus the lineage, with the advent of monarchical absolutism.

One fascinating case study is that of the Mendoza family, one of the greatest and best-studied of the Castilian lineages, supporters of Isabella, whom they helped put on the throne, hereditary governors in one branch of her recently won Moorish kingdom of Granada (after 1492), and, finally but not least, patrons of humanism in Spain (an interesting example, incidentally, of how a lineage can acquire or cultivate a distinctive ethos – like the house of Cavendish in England, patrons of the Reformation, of the Whigs and eventually of science, or the house of Howard, with its traditional allegiance to Catholicism). In 1568 the Mendozas faced the greatest test of their identity as a significant intellectual and political force. In that year the bureaucratic monarchy of Philip II sought to enforce cultural uniformity on the Moorish people who lived under the Mendoza governorship. The programme included measures against the Arabic dress and language, as well as a more indirect campaign against the vendettas of this mountain people and their customary forms of land tenure. The rebellion which broke out in Granada at Christmas 1568, and which led to a bitter, two-year guerrilla war, is a turning-point in Spainsh history in more ways than one. But it interests us here because of the testimony left by a cadet of the Mendozas, Diego Hurtado de Mendoza, who happened to find himself detained in the family 'fief' during much of 1569 for having brawled in the king's palace. He put his enforced leisure to good use, like many another detainee since, by writing about his environment, a *Historia de la Guerra de Granda*, which is not only a classic of Spanish literature but an interesting family document, since one of the protagonists was the local governor, nephew of the author. The manuscript was written for public consumption, though not published immediately. We are fortunate, therefore, in having a more intimate, running commentary on the author's attitudes in the form of the letters he wrote from Granada to the first minister of the crown, Cardinal Espinosa.

Both documents reveal the battle which the governor was fighting, not just against the Moors, but against other Andalusian nobles who were hereditary enemies of his house, and against the machinations of the central bureaucracy in Madrid. Significantly Diego did not show himself to be a wholehearted supporter of his nephew's cause. His attitude is perhaps understandable. He had quarrelled with the governor's father, his elder brother, over the division of the family estates, and had had to make his own way at court. He depended more on the good will of men like Espinosa than on the head of his own lineage, and was concerned not to compromise his own reputation with government officials. So the great rebellion of 1568 which finally undermined Mendoza power in Granada, failed to provoke a concerted response by that family, though the governor and his uncle actually shared many of the same political attitudes. The problem was that the ties of patronage led away from the lineage strictly defined towards the network of friends (González Palencia, 1941–3, vol. II, pp. 366–80).

This pattern of patronage beyond the clan goes very far back in European history. It seems to have impeded that feeling of solidarity within the blood group which Ibn Khaldūn regarded as so vital to political success in the civilizations of North Africa. The Germanic tribes were, after all, heirs to a Roman world already quite urbanized and traversed by major trade routes. The rise of the Vikings from the eighth century depended not only on the existence of things to plunder, but also on controlling trade; as in the eighteenth century, trade and piracy seemed indistinguishable. What strikes the reader time and again in *The Nibelungenlied*, is the enormous contribution which wealth made to status. Birth alone is not enough; poverty degrades and dishonours – hence the concern throughout this heroic poem with crassly material things like dowry. Wealth, of course, is needed for the lord or lady to show the 'generosity' to inferiors which is the way to respect and power. For the ties of dependence are not those of blood; rather they are built up through gifts, hospitality, marriage. These sacred bonds of gratitude are very far from creating the exclusive loyalties of a unilineal descent group. Rüdiger's excruciating dilemma, caught between the conflicting claims of different benefactors, the feuding Kriemhild and her brothers, is one of the highlights of the epic.

On another frontier, that of medieval Spain, and around the same time (1140), the great epic of the Cid tells how this warrior built up his following through both kinship and patronage. His 115 original companions on the expedition against the Moor grow with the Cid's success and the desire for plunder. These later followers are integrated into the patronage network of their lord through marriage to the ladies of his household. Shortly after this time, that famous lawbook of mid-thirteenth century Castile, the *Siete Partidas* (as much a disquisition on human relationships by the philosopher king, Alfonso the Wise, as a code of laws) summed up the practice described in *The Poem of the Cid*. Though 'kinship by lineage' (*parentesco de linage*) was a great thing 'which binds men in great love, for they are like one by blood and nature', nevertheless lordship and fostering could create yet stronger ties. Rearing a person (*crianza*) 'is one of the greatest benefits a man can bestow on another', and the recipient must treat his benefactor 'just as if he were his father' (4/20/3). The author reserves some of his most eloquent passages for the delights of lordship, especially the 'long usage of loyal love' which will grow between a man and the lord of the area where he was born, for their roots are sunk deep in the local homeland (4/24/2).

This emphasis on nurture at the expense of blood, and a strong sense of physical as against genealogical space, are significant characteristics of European compared with other world civilizations. Pirenne, in his classic thesis on the continuity of the classical world (1939), contrasted the way in which the Germanic invaders were absorbed culturally by the peoples of the northern shore of the Mediterranean with the disappearance of the Romano-Christian civilization of North Africa under the Islamic invasions of the seventh and eighth centuries. Though he was inclined to stress the religious dynamism of Islam, one may wonder whether part of the explanation may not lie in contrasting family structures. The Arab tribe, as Ibn Khaldūn explained, had a great capacity for absorbing outsiders. By contrast, the Germanic invaders seem to have arrived in more loosely-jointed war-bands, whose leaders settled down quickly as exploiters of land, alongside the existing Roman population, with whom they intermarried, eventually shedding their own identity. There are some pages of interest on this in Engels (1968, pp. 561–2).

It may have been easier in Europe than in Africa to accumulate the capital from which to dispense the gifts on which a lord would rely in order to create a personal following and thereby dispense with the help of his consanguines. Is the explanation, as we suggested earlier, that there was more opportunity in urbanized, post-Roman Europe for chiefs to build up the capital required for gifts? But, of course, the *caïds* and the *khans* were not without resources of their own. If we ask why their authority showed a cyclical tendency to wax and wane, whereas that of the European lords grew into states, perhaps we should return to the question of dynastic succession. The tradit-tion of the Muslim world is egalitarian – the sharing of all the sons in the patrimony and authority of the father. As Montagne has pointed out, this makes for great instability in the nascent polities of North Africa. So long as social space is marked out by lines of blood, it is difficult to see what else can be done. The rather different European tradition is curiously epitomized in the description of father–son relationships by the poet of *The Song of Roland*. Though nominally referring to a Muslim emir, Baligant, the portrait actually fits better the poet's own Christian tradition. Baligant, in order to get his son to fight valiantly, can think of no greater honour than to enfeoff him, to make him a vassal (lines 3206–11 and 3375–7). Turning to his other knights, Baligant makes the significant cry: 'Long years I've kept and fed you, lords of mine./See how my son in search of Carlon rides,/ And with his arms so many lords defies;/ A better vassal I could not wish to find.' Now this emphasis on nurture at the expense of nature is in the purest European, but not Muslim tradition. There are many instances of this same contrast – that the vassal whom one has reared or maintained in the household is worth more than a descendant by blood – in the literature of Christian Spain.

The point is, I think, that the automatic claim of sons on the patrimony of their father was quickly sacrificed to an alternative principle of dependence on the house. From 987, if I interpret rightly Andrew Lewis's useful account (1981) of Capetian family strategy, the younger sons of French kings were endowed to marry, and they went on to establish many collateral lines, which was necessary enough to the survival of the dynasty in that age of high mortality. However, their patrimonies tended to be small. Even when they were large, as classically for the offspring of a very successful king like Philip Augustus, who had conquered many new lands for his house, the cadets were obliged to do homage for their endowments to their elder brother in Paris. The chaotically mismanaged strategy of Philip's contemporary, the English King Henry II Plantagenent, for the division of his realms among his four sons, caused more political turmoil, but seems broadly to conform to the Capetian model. By the fourteenth century the 'Princes of the Blood' in France seem to have acquired a greater sense of their collective identity. It is a process analogous to that described by Duby (1976) for the Mâconnais nobility at the beginning of the High Middle Ages: the keeping together of the patrimony, the emergence of a sense of family cohesion round the head of the lineage. Of course, it will not do to exaggerate the speed of the process. The enormous fief handed over to his favourite younger son Philip by the characteristically inept John the Good of France (1350–64) laid the foundations of an autonomous power in Burgundy which was to shake the French throne for a century. And even Louis XIV was preoccupied in his memoirs with the threat to kingship posed by younger sons of the house. But by this time restriction on the marriages and endowments of princes was so great that the political historian can afford to pass over the family quarrels of the ruling house as a rather secondary topic.

If a restrictive inheritance strategy enabled the patrimony of European princes to grow, one still has to explore how this wealth was translated into political authority. One of the features of Swat society, which Barth has identified, is the automatic check to strong leadership which will come into play at a certain point in its development, through the regrouping of rivals. Equally, Montagne was impressed with the social isolation of ruling families in the Atlas, always menaced by a coalition of superiors and inferiors. Though there are elements of this kind of blocking technique throughout European history as well, it is perhaps relevant to contrast the very strong ties of European vassalage with the weaker ones of North Africa. The social isolation of the ruling dynasties there is surely in part attributable to a policy of marriage within the clan. This is too simple a statement and we shall have to introduce further complications in our analysis of marriage in a later chapter. But it may be allowed for the moment that the marriage strategy of the Arabs has traditionally been directed towards consolidating that sense of tribe, whose co-ordinates mark out their social space. By contrast, European princes have operated, like the Cid, with a more down-to-earth model of the household and its followers, who are tied to their lord by adoption as sons-in-law. It has been calculated that about half the great families of Charlemagne's empire had the blood of the ruling dynasty in their venis, either through fathers or mothers (Gerd Tellenbach, in Reuter, 1978, pp. 207–9). The very 'ordinariness' of this situation is well brought out in *The Song of Roland*, where the two protagonists, Roland and Ganelon, are both members of Charlemagne's family. No matter how bad Ganelon's relations with Roland, one feels he will not easily betray his brother-in-law, the emperor – 'I deny treason against the state' (line 3760). Here, surely, is that missing link in the power structures of the Berbers on which Montagne commented: the emotional bond between inferiors and the prince equivalent to the tie of family. And let us remember how enduring this concept of the barons as part of the ruler's family, as well as of his household, was in Europe. It is intriguing, for example, to see how many of the great families of early modern Spain were sprung, often quite recently, from the line of kings – the Borjas, for example, illegitimate sons of Pope Alexander VI on their father's side, but of María Enríquez, first cousin of Ferdinand the Catholic on their mother's, while María's brother Pedro was grandfather of the first duke of Alcalá, whom we have come across before.

Marc Bloch summed up this situation with his usual acumen: 'the tie of kinship was one of the essential elements of feudal society', though he went on: 'its relative weakness explains why there was feudalism at all' (1965, vol. I, p. 142). We have got thus far without using that controversial term, feudalism. The topic will be with us again in a later chapter, on inheritance. But we may note here that it is not perhaps useful to treat the political organisms of the medieval and early modern worlds as if they were 'institutions' in a nineteenth- or twentieth-century sense. There has been such a clear delimitation between private and public space since 1789 that it is sometimes hard for us to capture what politics was about in a world where the two spheres overlapped. Perhaps the concept of the family and the household is one way of refocusing our thoughts.

The dilemma of the modern state is, in the words of the Berbers, that 'where there is much order, there is little justice' – the classic conflict between concepts of self and the community. Some form of mediation had to be available for the latter to triumph in the end, as it did in Europe. A readily accessible insight into the transition is provided by that marvellous pair of Scottish writers, Scott and Stevenson, who captured so vividly the lineaments of the conflict between law and family. We may just consider here *The Heart of Midlothian* (1818), set in the mid-eighteenth century and based on a true story of presumed infanticide. The law on infanticide was harsh: if the baby could not be found, the mother was presumed guilty of its death unless she could prove her innocence – an interesting clash of two concepts, the need to uphold 'order' against the 'justice' of allowing an unmarried mother (and her kin) to hide their shame. The heroine of the tale, Jeanie Deans, anxious to rescue her innocent sister from execution, turns to the great Whig courtier, the duke of Argyle, better known to his Scottish vassals as the 'great Campbell' or 'MacCallummore'. Argyle's role in the affair is curious: as a protestant Hanoverian, he is part of a culture which prizes law and the state, but as a Campbell, he is bound in with the patronage network of a clan society (albeit, in this case, extending to Edinburgh and the Lowlands). Jeanie has several claims on the great man's attention, going back to the persecution of the Covenanters under the Stuarts, when her father had stood by Argyle's father, and her friends the Butlers had saved the old duke's life. Though neither Jeanie nor the young duke knew each other, the old memory still lingered, kept alive in ballads peddled by 'Peter the Packman', in tales told by parents to their children, in a treasured scrap of paper from the old duke conjuring 'my friends, kinsmen and whoever will do aught for me, either in the Highlands or Lowlands, to protect and assist the said Benjamin Butler, and his friends or family, on their lawful occasions ...' (1952, p. 320). It is nice to be able to note that, even if for the wrong reason, Argyle did obtain a pardon from the king for Jeanie's sister.

At a certain stage this old system of patronage, so essential to the creation of the modern state, came to be seen as redundant or corrupt. This is evident, I think, in the outcry against *lettres de cachet* in France in 1789. These secret warrants from the king were mostly used in that twilight zone where private and public space overlapped – for example, to have errant sons detained, at the suit of their fathers, in order to prevent the disgrace which they might cause to their families by a *mésalliance*. They had been a perfectly serviceable and popular instrument of rule for centuries. That they now came to be called into question as an infringement of the due process of law is a fascinating example of that desire to delimit clearly the public and the private, which is the hallmark of nineteenth-century liberalism. The *lettres de cachet* belonged to a small-scale society where the ruler could act indiscriminately as a 'father', where his household was the state (as witness Louis XIV at table, importuned by courtiers, or holding council next door to his bedroom – in Saint-Simon's memoirs it is not the king who 'is the state', it is his family in the broad sense). By 1789 France and Europe were outgrowing the limits of such patrimonial government. We may leave the last word on the transition to de Tocqueville, describing the new world of America, where the family had lost its political functions: 'we may say that in America a man never obeys another man, but only justice or the law' (1963, chapter 5).

4

The arranged marriage

> The Ancient fathers, for their part, were concerned that the ties of kinship itself should not be loosened as generation succeeded generation ... And so for them it was a matter of religion to restore the bond of kinship by means of the marriage tie before kinship became too remote ... Yet no one doubts that the modern prohibition of marriage between cousins is an advance in civilized standards.
>
> St Augustine, *The City of God*

It has been the merit of Claude Lévi-Strauss's classic study, *The Elementary Structures of Kinship* (1969, first published in 1949), to direct attention away from the ancestors and towards wives as a keystone of social structure. Throughout much of Asia and Polynesia in particular, he argued, the individual defined himself in relation to categories of people that he must, could or could not marry. These were the 'elementary structures of kinship', to be contrasted with the more complex societies of Europe and much of Africa, where the individual was attached to a clan at birth and the choice of his marriage partner was therefore less crucial. It is, indeed, through rules for the exchange of women that more primitive societies seem to acquire cohesion, and perhaps become aware of the possibilities of social organization. As Robin Fox, most Lévi-Straussian of English anthropologists, puts it, 'No Australian Aborigine sat down and worked out a blueprint for the complicated systems of kinships and marriage for which he is justly famous; but his ability to conceptualize and classify was as much a factor in this successful development [sc. of mankind] as the claws of the tiger or the neck of the giraffe were in the survival and success of these species' (1967, p. 31). The frequent rule here that a man would marry his mother's brother's daughter, and give his own sister in return to the girl's brother, created some primitive social groupings.

Among peoples already organized into clans by descent, the basic rule of marriage is that of exogamy – that is, that one should marry outside the group. Among the Chinese, for example, marriage with relatives on one's father's side was forbidden, though there was no objection to relatives, even close ones, on the mother's side. The point seems to be that the patrilineal clan in China constituted a sufficiently defined and important group in its own right, united in the ritual worship of the ancestor, not to require strengthening by matrimony. Rather, the fear was that a union of cousins would create more limited and exclusive solidarities which would prejudice the health of the whole. Incest of this kind would be, in the revealing Chinese phrase, 'a confusion of relationships', a confusion of loyalties.

Endogamy, by contrast – that is, marriage within the group – is likely to become more prevalent in societies where daughters inherit property as well as sons. Jack Goody (1976) has drawn attention to this as a distinguishing feature of Eurasian civilization. Black Africa, though enjoying some settled agriculture, had never got beyond cultivation with the hoe; the failure to utilize the plough limited the amount of land that could be exploited by one household, and its ability to accumulate resources. In these predominantly pastoral societies wealth continued to be reckoned in terms of manpower, with the fundamental social unit being the clan rather than the household. Here exogamy remained the basic rule of marriage. The Mediterranean, India and China, by contrast, had more developed economies, where control of property became very important for the family and concern for its transmission to the next generation a dominant concern. By the normal laws of demography, one out of five couples would have only daughters to succeed to their estate, and the temptation to make these into heiresses, at the expense of uncles or cousins, has been very great in Eurasia. Interestingly, China continued to exclude daughters from inheritance, preferring the clan. Might the explanation be the solemn, jural significance of the latter, united by a religious bond, the cult of the ancestors? By contrast, in Eurasia the clan was virtually destroyed as a religious unit at the beginning of our era by the rise of those two egalitarian brotherhoods of 'true believers', Christianity and Islam with their levelling, universalist claims. This has made it easier for the Muslims to adapt the residual strength of clan feeling to the pressing demands of a developed economy, allowing daughters to inherit, but preferring them to keep their inheritance within the clan by marrying their father's brother's son. This is not a rule but a preference, a 'noble' or 'proper' thing to do, even though the reality of family strategy often rules it out in practice. What has intrigued Goody is that Europe has not followed suit. While allowing daughters to inherit, it has tended to stress exogamy – that is, marriage outside the group – as the norm, thereby letting property pass into the hands of strangers. One explanation, Goody suggests, might be found in the cultural norms imposed on Europe by that unusually powerful and celibate corporation, the Christian Church, a rival with the family for men's inheritance. Certainly, much of medieval history is dominated by the legislation of that body on marriage, and, in particular, by the setting out of an unusually extensive list of kinsmen whom one could not wed.

These 'prohibited degrees of kinship' evolved slowly and rather obscurely. The authority sometimes invoked was an obscure and difficult passage in Leviticus, which seems basically concerned with household incest in a patriarchal society where men had several wives and lived alongside their married brothers. It is probably not until St Augustine, in the fourth century AD, that we get a fully elaborated doctrine of the desirability of not marrying close kin because this limits social ties to the clan and impedes the development of wider social intercourse. In *The City of God* he advocated exogamy not only because 'the ties of kinship are thereby multiplied, in that one person cannot stand in a double relationship', but also in terms of a 'certain mysterious and inherent sense of decency', which inhibits carnal lust among men and women whose paths cross daily. In other words, he is drawing partly on a concern with household incest, to be found in Leviticus, but also on a wide tradition, whose roots seem to me to be more secular than religious. For him, the affection or *caritas* which came about through marriage was one of the foundations of that civilized society, the world of Greece and Rome, to whose passing he was an early witness. The nearest parallel to his thought is that of Plato, for whom too, as we suggested in the last chapter, there was a basic incompatibility between the exclusiveness of the clan and the construction of the well-ordered 'city'.

The early Christian communities legislated little on marriage. In the mixed confessional world of late antiquity they left that to the Emperor. After the fall of Rome, bishops in the West came to assume greater responsibilities in this regard, though it is really only with the Carolingians in the ninth century that ecclesiastical or canon law and a network of Church courts begin to take shape (Gaudemet, 1987, p. 111). One has to remember in this context the tendency of medieval law to grow organically through custom and consensus rather than through legislation in our sense. In the early Middle

Ages, when each diocese had its separate customs, it was the responsibility of the canon lawyer to interpret 'discordant canons'. The
authority of his work came from its perceived wisdom, buttressed by
its supposed conformity with tradition, though the latter was malle-
able in an age which had to rely on oral memory. The marriage law
of the Jews of medieval Cairo seems to have evolved in some such
way, as a series of opinions put forth by recognized scholars like
Maimonides (Goitein, 1978, pp. 213–14 and 344–6). It may be more
helpful, therefore, to see the law of Christian matrimony as a series
of adaptations to the local environment, rather than as a ready-made
formula handed down by a corporate clerical leadership. In any case,
as Goody has noted, the Church did eventually spell out an impressive range of prohibited partners. No marriage was to be contracted
within seven degrees of kinship on either one's father's or one's
mother's side – that is, with cousins descended from a common
ancestor seven generations back. The seven degrees corresponded to
an old Roman formula, which specified this as the outer ring of the
kindred for the purposes of intestate inheritance. But ancient Rome
had forbidden matrimony only within four degrees, and defined
these more restrictively, by a different way of reckoning, as extending out to first cousins alone (see the excellent tables and discussion
in Goody, 1983, pp. 136–9). Was the Church, then, setting up new
barriers to marriage in its own interest, and going against an older
tradition?

More likely, the slow evolution of the canons on this matter
corresponded to the norms of matrimony among the Barbarians who
overran the Roman empire. *The Nibelungenlied*, though written
down in its definitive form only around 1200, has strident if de-
formed echoes of an early time when women were prizes to be taken
from strangers and foes. When the hero, Siegfried, announces his
intention of wooing Kriemhild, who lives in a far-off land and whom
he has never met, he discounts the warnings of his father that the
girl's family may refuse to surrender her. 'How should that trouble
us?' he retorts. 'Whatever I fail to get from them by friendly re-
quests I shall take by my own valour' (1965, p. 24). Winning a bride
was symbolic, in the poetry and practice of early medieval Europe,
of a sense of adventure and braving of the unknown familiar to the
warriors of a frontier society, and echoed in the concern of the
Carolingian lawmakers with abduction, a crime which they reserved
for the royal courts. The counterpart of this was the cosmopolitan-
ism of early medieval woman, taken away at marriage from her

homeland and brought to live among a strange people. R. W. Southern has some illuminating pages on the process, in his discussion of how an Anglo-Saxon masterpiece, the eleventh-century Gospels of Countess Judith, came to find its way to a monastery of southern Germany:

> It had been made, probably at Winchester, for a Flemish lady, Judith, the sister of the count of Flanders, who came to England about 1051 as the wife of one of the sons of Earl Godwin. Her husband Tostig, Earl of Northumbria, was killed at the battle of Stamford Bridge in 1066, and she returned to her native land. In 1072 she married Duke Welf of Bavaria and took with her to southern Germany manuscripts and relics which she had collected in England. (1987, pp. 76–7)

The Germanic peoples married outwards unlike their Arab counterparts, who tended to use the marriage tie as a way of consolidating friendships within the clan. The development of the feudal system of protection in Europe, as a substitute for the clan, really depended on this outgoing marriage policy. It created communities more extensive, and eventually more cohesive, than those of Islam. On the European frontier with the Moor, King Alfonso the Wise of Castile (1252–84) speculated on the social and political significance of exogamy in his great law code, the *Siete Partidas*. In a primitive order, he thought, men would live in exclusive groupings within which they would find their brides. The price of constructing an ordered polity was the abandonment of this system, for otherwise 'men would live apart from one another, each in his own clan, which would turn into a vengeance group (*bando*)' (4/6/introduction). Yet exogamy did impose great sacrifices on a father, which the Emperor Charlemagne for one had not been prepared to accept. It meant sending one's daughter among a strange people, with imperfect guarantees of her security or status. Speaking of Charlemagne's daughters, his biographer Einhard tells us: 'These girls were extraordinarily beautiful and greatly loved by their father ... As a result of this, he kept them with him in his household until the very day of his death, instead of giving them in marriage to his own men or to foreigners, maintaining that he could not live without them' (1969, p. 75). Meanwhile, he 'shut his eyes' to the illicit liaisons they formed with lovers, finding their illegitimate offspring places in the Church. The ambiguous status of matrimony at the time was apparent in the instability of Charlemagne's own unions, the first of which ended in divorce, and several of which were with concubines. It is one of the marks of a tribal society to be less concerned about the status and permanence of the marriage, and more interested in the production of sturdy sons who can be incorporated into the father's clan. In Charlemagne's day there was a distinction between marriage and concubinage, with the offspring of the latter not being allowed to inherit property or office; but it was not yet as clear a line of division as it was later to become. It is, indeed, the issue of property which led to the more careful 'arranging' of marriage in Europe.

One of the main ways of distinguishing marriage from concubinage in Charlemagne's day was by the public endowment of the bride by her husband. Typically this would take the form of the *Morgengabe*, the 'gift on the morrow' following the nuptial night. It is possible that this was an evolution from an older practice alluded to by Tacitus in the first century AD, whereby the Germans would also pay a sum to the bride's family. Both kinds of prestation are sometimes lumped together, rather confusingly, under the term 'bridewealth'. Typically bridewealth is associated with exogamous, tribal societies, where outsiders come to take the women of the tribe away as brides and compensate it for the loss by generous gifts of cattle or the like. In early medieval Europe – as, indeed, among the Arabs after the conversion to Islam in the seventh century – this tradition disappeared, leaving the 'indirect dowry' paid by the husband to his bride, and to no one else. The significance of this arrangement is still a matter of some debate. It is, perhaps, helpful to see it as a guarantee of the stability of a new conjugal family, by which the man publicly assumes responsibility for the woman's welfare, and particularly for her widowhood. Under the system of exogamy practised by the Germans, of course, the woman would not be able easily to fall back on her own tribe in difficulty; nor would she be incorporated into her husband's clan, as she would have been in Africa; there was pressure, therefore, for some property arrangement which would guarantee her autonomy in widowhood. This the 'indirect dowry' assured. The laws of the Visigoths in seventh-century Spain treated the formation of the household as fundamentally the man's responsibility. When one of the partners died, any acquisitions made during the marriage were split equally with the survivor. English medieval law, which remained immune from later Roman influence, is an even more striking illustration of old Germanic practice. Here too the establishment of the household is fundamentally the responsibility of the husband; property arrangements are conceived of basically in terms of the dower – that is, the portion of his property which the husband must set aside in order to guarantee the security of his widow. English law is exclusively focused on the household, ignoring the claims of the lineage, which (as we shall see in a moment) crept back into continental law in the form of the dowry.

However, there is a danger when discussing marriage prestations of forgetting that, in small-scale, pre-industrial communities, they are often about status rather than property as such. In the *Turkish Village* studied by Paul Stirling (1965), the bridewealth is not only a transfer of funds, it is a symbol of honour for the giver, that he should have been able to afford so much. It is one part of a generous disbursement on nuptial festivities, lasting several days, which will enhance the status of the bridegroom within his community (pp. 185–9). The endowment, as well as constituting a public mark of the permanence of the union, is a sensitive indicator of the standing of the respective families of origin, and of the value attached to alliance with them.

Something of the same sort can be seen in early medieval society. Marriage, though fundamentally exogamous, was not anarchic. We are reminded of Einhard's words on the options open to Charlemagne of giving his daughters 'to his own men or to foreigners'. In fact, it seems that quite often in early feudal society it was the former option which was chosen. One of the best studies here is that by Ruiz Domenec (1979) on eleventh- and twelfth-century Catalonia. He finds a tendency among the Catalan nobility to marry their daughters down to 'their men'. Such marriages consolidated relations of dependence in a feudal environment. A man's lord was often his father-in-law, and his son would be reared at the latter's court. Hence, those strong ties with the mother's brother, which we find reflected in the medieval epics like *The Song of Roland*. Often, according to Ruiz Domenec, the young man would go on to marry his mother's brother's daughter. One would not expect to find dowry handed over with the bride; rather the husband would be expected to endow his wife, for she is of higher social status. This system, of the downward flow of brides, is an interesting way of maintaining hierarchy in the absence of alternative forms of stratification based on wealth. Societies like early feudal Catalonia belong to a recognizable category of world cultures, characterized by division between 'bride-givers' and 'bride-takers' (Mair, 1972, p. 88). The giving of women is a symbol of generosity, part of a culture of patronage, which places inferiors in one's debt. The system depends, of course, on a certain intimacy between inferiors and superiors, characterized by household fostering and an absence of any great disparity of wealth or culture between master and follower. It helps us make sense of certain features of early feudal society, not least the role of women in constituting networks of power.

One of the arguments which brought Hugh Capet to the French throne in 987 instead of the Carolingian pretender Charles of Lorraine, was that the latter's wife was not of high enough status to foster a line of kings (Bouchard, 1981, pp. 268–87). The role of the queen seems to have been undergoing an expansion round the same time, as she came to be crowned and anointed like her husband, and to be included in poems and prayers in honour of the royal couple (Wemple, 1981, pp. 97–8). She had to have a character which would command respect in her husband's vassals. Advising Giselher, youngest of the co-kings of Burgundy, to proceed with his marriage to the mere daughter of a frontier commander, his cousin noted that she was 'of such high lineage' that he and his companions 'would gladly serve her were she to go crowned to Burgundy' (*The Nibelungenlied*, 1965, p. 209). At the time when this was written, however, the role of women was undergoing a change. The spread of the practice whereby the father of the bride endowed his daughter (dowry), which replaced endowment by the husband (bridewealth or indirect dowry), was a significant feature of the twelfth century. It has been linked to a certain loss of judicial autonomy by women during the feudal period, and a revival of *patria potestas*, by which the bride, carrying property of her father to the groom, passed directly from the authority of one male to the other and reverted to the tutelage of her family of origin during her widowhood. Matrimony had ceased to be an exchange of women, but was coming to be a pledge of co-operation between two male lineages. Giselher, for example, endows his bride with castles and lands, following the norm of bridewealth among the early Germanic peoples. But the bride's father also contributes silver and gold and, significantly, goes on to promise his son-in-law that he will be his 'sincere and devoted friend always'.

It is possible to overstress the apparent shift at this time from bridewealth to dowry, and thereby miss its real significance (cf. Hughes, 1978). It is worth always bearing in mind the general point made by Goody that where human societies reach a certain level of economic development and accumulation of capital, inheritance by the daughters of the household – unless the clan structure is exceptionally strong, as in China – is very likely to be a facet of their culture. One can see this among some of the early Barbarians, heirs, in a sense, to the urbanized culture of Rome. Among the Visigoths, though they were somewhat exceptional, daughters inherited equally with sons. Interestingly, their portions might be transferred to them well before the death of their parents, at their own marriage, in order to enhance their status. When the Visigothic princess Galswinth brings her portion to her husband Chilperic, this is a demonstration of her high standing, and a way of distinguishing her from the king's concubines. Her property gives her a certain influence in her new household, emboldening her to demand the dismissal of her rivals, though the move fails and she is eventually murdered for being a nuisance (Gregory of Tours, 1974, pp. 222–3). *The Nibelungenlied* turns on the question of dowry, the difficulties and bitterness which the inheritance of sisters engenders being the main theme of the poem. It is not the men in the epic who demand big dowries at marriage – indeed, both husbands of the heroine Kriemhild are inclined to forgo it, for the significant reasons that they want neither to quarrel with, nor to be too indebted to, their in-laws. Rather, it is Kriemhild who pursues her inheritance rights relentlessly, as a safe-guard of her own status and power. *The Nibelungenlied*, like other medieval epics, is a palimpsest of different layers of culture. Its treatment of the question of dowry seems to reflect two traditions in conflict: an older Germanic one of female inheritance from the father, which can be traced back to the Visigoths, designed to enhance the autonomy and status of the bride among a strange people; and a newer, feudal concept of co-operation between a man and his son-in-law.

As Barbarian Europe began to settle down, and plunder give way to cultivation after 1000, one can detect the spread of dowry as the chief form of matrimonial prestation. The charters of the abbey of Cluny, examined by Duby for the eleventh century, indicate a fall in the value of the endowments which grooms were passing to their brides from about half to about a third of their property (1981, pp. 100–15). This is interestingly close to the figure at which the medieval English dower was customarily set – that is, of the posses-sions of the household, a third would be set aside for the mainten-ance of the widow. In any case, in southern Burgundy during the eleventh century the chief transfer of property at marriage was coming to be that from the bride's father, and not from the husband to his wife. Duby interprets the shift as an attempt to restrict the latter rather than as a recognition of female inheritance. This was the period, if we may recall the discussion in chapter 2 above, during which the noble family was seeking to consolidate its patrimony, transmitting it to just one son and encouraging the others to stay celibate as monks or knights. Women also, suggests Duby, began to feel the pinch. Their dowry was restricted to property from their mother's side, marginal, therefore, to the main patrimony reserved for their eldest brother. The latter, the only one of the males of his family to marry, was reluctant to divest himself of any substantial part of his inheritance as bridewealth for his own wife. Indeed, the need to do so was probably reduced at this time, since fewer males than females were coming on the marriage market. Dowry could be seen – and was seen by early modern writers increasingly (cf. Mello, 1923, pp. 154–5) – as a necessary financial inducement if a girl was to find a husband of her own social standing.

The exact significance of the rise of dowry, however, is still somewhat obscure and even controversial. The notion that it may reflect a baiting of the hook by which a woman of good family might attract the increasingly scarce suitors from her own class, is a modern (or early modern) interpretation, which does not do justice to earlier tendencies of women to marry down into the ranks of their father's vassals. It is not an explanation to be ruled out, and we shall return to it; but, in its bare form, it leaves too many assumptions unquestioned. The other question, whether the dowry was a way of restricting female inheritance, again poses many problems, since, during the Renaissance period particularly, it spiralled upwards throughout continental Europe, provoking widespread complaint that it was mortgaging, literally and metaphorically, the future of the family estate. Girls might be excluded from the patrimony, but that patrimony could be eaten up by the debts required to assemble their dowry. The distinguished Spanish jurist, Francisco de Cárdenas, explored a century ago the transition in his country from the bridewealth of the Visigoths to the dowry system found in the thirteenth-century royal law codes. The practical change was possibly not very great, for the dowry could be seen as an advance instalment of a daughter's inheritance rights to her parents' estate, guaranteed from the days of the Visigoths. But the shift in timing of the payment was interesting, from the death of the parents to the marriage of their daughter, and it appeared to be part of the general return at the time to the principles of Roman law (1884, vol. II, pp. 5–62). It is probably true that, in order to understand the dowry, we have to return to its roots in certain structures of ancient Mediterranean civilization.

Under the early Roman Republic, in the days of the patrilineal clans so lovingly described by Fustel, women were excluded from inheritance, as they were typically in tribal societies, and married strangers into whose clan they were incorporated. In the later Republic and early Empire, endowment of the bride by her father seems to have led to, or accompanied, her emancipation from the absolute power of her husband; in particular, she acquired rights of controlling her property, which reverted to her, and not to her husband's people, at the dissolution of the marriage. One seems to witness here the typical emancipation of the conjugal family from the clan, once a certain level of urbanization is reached, and transmission of property becomes more important than solidarity with consanguines. It is the nature of a household to be a joint enterprise between a man and a woman, and societies which privilege the household at the expense of the clan are likely to require some affirmation of its ability to survive economically on its own. This is where 'indirect dowry' or 'dower' becomes significant, since it is at once a guarantee for the widow and a public affirmation of the husband's wealth, standing and general ability to run his new enterprise. One would do well here to recall Stirling's (1965) words about the significance of bridewealth as display rather than actual property transfer in the *Turkish Village*. In any case, during the later Empire, the Romans began to develop the practice of indirect dowry, or *donatio propter nuptias*, an endowment of the bride by her husband, which anticipated the later practice of the Barbarians. Unlike the Barbarians, however, the urbanized Romans still held firmly to the transfer of property as well from a father to his daughter. The Code of Justinian (emperor between 527 and 565) summed up their basic principles at the waning of that great civilization by specifying that a household should be formed out of the confluence of the dowry and the *donatio*, which should be equal in amount (cf. Herlihy, 1985, pp. 8–16). It is scarcely too much to say that the code captured perfectly the spirit of the Mediterranean family, and has remained extremely influential throughout the region, albeit in modified form, down to the present day.

A vivid insight into the working of the Mediterranean family, at a time when the Barbarians were practising exogamy and bridewealth, is given by the voluminous correspondence of Jewish traders living in Cairo between the tenth and thirteenth centuries – a community which stood at the crossroads, in more ways than one, of Rome and Islam (Goitein, 1978). One notes the confluence in matrimonial arrangements of inheritance by daughters and endowment of the bride by the groom. The dowry seems often to have been larger than the assets at the disposal of the husband, so care was taken to secure its return to the bride's family if the couple, for example, had no children. Married women retained the familiar Mediterranean control over their own property, their authority being required for the sale of any part of the dowry by their husband. Inevitably in the circumstances, they tended to interact closely during the marriage with their father and brothers, bringing their husbands to live close by the latter, and sending their children to learn a trade with them. It is the kind of situation which is very familiar to students of the early modern Spanish city, and which, I suspect, was the practice Justinian must have had in mind when framing his code.

The revival of Roman law, including provision for dowry, was a significant feature of the history of the West in the thirteenth century. Reflected in the development of more rationalized national codes like the famous *Siete Partidas*, it has been seen as one facet of the growth of stronger, more centralized states at the time. It seems to have accompanied that strengthening of the male patrimony traced by Duby for southern Burgundy, and to have led to a loss of the old financial and juridical autonomy of women. But we perhaps assume too readily that the influence of Roman law led in only one direction: towards the enhancement of *patria potestas*, and of a male-dominated, patriarchal society. It would be truer to say that the new rules of marriage, and the operation of the dowry system, led to an increase of the rights of the lineage – in particular, of the bride's father and brothers – at the expense of the authority of the head of the household. Dowry was less a once-for-all settlement with a daughter by her parents than a symbol of their ongoing interest in her fate, less an exclusion of her from the inheritance than a major financial commitment to her happiness. Le Play and de Tocqueville would note the divisiveness which the dowry system introduced into the household, undermining the authority of the husband. They contrasted it unfavourably with the English system, which had held fast to the old Germanic principle of bridewealth or dower, and which invested absolute rights of property, during the marriage itself, with the head of the household. The difference in forms of endowment – dower as compared with dowry – might seem trivial enough, but over the centuries it had fostered a quite novel family culture. Whereas in the Anglo-Saxon world the 'home' was autonomous, in countries under the influence of Roman law its authority was flawed by the overriding claims of the lineage. One has to remember that, in a pre-capitalist society, it often took years to assemble a dowry. Instead of being a simple payment from the bride's father to the groom, the enterprise might need the support of kin and friends, all of whom retained a certain interest in how their investment would fare.

Rights of female inheritance, as Goody noted, may lead to some form of endogamy, or marriage within the group. Typically the Arabs resolve the potential conflict between lineage and household by marrying a girl to her father's brother's son. This kind of marriage is actually rare in practice for a whole host of reasons. One is that daughters often do not receive the share of the inheritance to which they are entitled by the Koran. However, their exclusion depends upon an arrangement with their husbands, an agreement that they will get satisfaction in some other way, through the ongoing co-operation and patronage of their in-laws (cf. Cuisenier, 1975, p. 428). The practical effect of the law of Islam is much the same as that of the Code of Justinian: it unites both shores of the Mediterranean in a common reverence for in-laws, and a common weakening of the autonomy of the household in the interests of the lineage.

Among the Europeans one can detect a similar trend, as in Islam, towards some form of endogamy, with the rise of dowry after 1000. A father wants increasingly to entrust his daughter to known people rather than to strangers. He wants to be able to trace the descent of the property which he has settled on his daughter to her offspring, his own grandchildren. He becomes more concerned, therefore, with the stability and permanence of the union, and more ambivalent about the easy repudiation of wives and serial polygamy which had characterized his Barbarian ancestors. A symbol of his changing aspirations was the great corpus of matrimonial legislation enacted by the Fourth Lateran Council in 1215, the very embodiment, in many ways, of the concept of marriage in the West which has lasted down to our own day. We shall be looking in more detail in the next chapter at the measures taken to enhance monogamy and distinguish marriage from concubinage. What concerns us here is the pruning back of the prohibited degrees of kinship, within which marriage could not be contracted, from seven to four – that is, to the descendants of a common ancestor four generations back (great-great-grandfather). The implications of the measure seem clear enough. It removed a device which, as Duby has noted, was used by princes in the early Middle Ages to repudiate wives who had become incon-

venient – the 'inventing' of distant degrees of consanguinity with
one's partner, so distant as not to have been perceptible at the time
the marriage was originally contracted. In this way the clarification
of the rules of incest at the Lateran Council may have contributed to
the stability of feudal marriage. May they also have marginally
facilitated endogamy?

Marriage within the kin group certainly seems to have become a
more notable feature of later medieval society, as the pressure to
keep property within the lineage grew. An example concerns the
succession to the lordship of La Guardia, near Jaén in southern
Spain. The fief had changed hands several times in the fourteenth
century through rebellion, confiscation and failure of heirs. A certain
Ruy González Mexía succeeded through marriage to the daughter
of the previous incumbent. At his death the lordship was contested
between his heiress and his brother's son, a characteristic conflict
between households, as represented by daughters, and the lineage.
The dispute was settled in a characteristic way too, by the marriage
of the two first cousins in 1396, 'to settle the lawsuit' (Argote, 1957,
pp. 496–8). But this kind of marriage, so honourable on the southern shore of the Mediterranean among the Arabs as a way of strengthening the patrilineal clan, was never valued in the same light by
Europeans. It might be necessary from time to time, in order to
prevent property leaving the lineage; but it was rarely a mark of
honour. That great letter-writer at the court of Charles V, Doña
Estefania Requeséns, registered her surprise in 1535 that a certain
noble lady was going to wed her uncle (a matrilineal one, admittedly): 'it seems a strange thing to everybody, given that there is no
need to keep property together ...' (March, 1941, vol. II, pp.
229–32).

Rather than being a way of strengthening the lineage, marriage
with relatives seems to have spread in Europe after 1000 as part of
the normal process of the settling down of a society. Ties of neighbourhood and of property provided the context within which cousin
marriage would occasionally occur. As a Spanish bishop put it in
1782, explaining the prevalence of marriage between consanguines in
his diocese, 'The women of one village will have been trained in a
single kind of work or craft from the time they were children ... so
that outsiders will not fit in well to the village' (Llorente, 1809, p. 2).
Consanguineous marriages were probably increasingly common in
the later medieval and early modern period, in Spain as in Europe
generally, especially among the aristocracy and the peasantry. In

both cases they seem to reflect the pressures of a tightly-knit local community rather than of a lineage. Most of the dispensations from the prohibited degrees accorded by the ecclesiastical authorities in Spain seem to have concerned the third and fourth degrees – that is, second and third cousins. They are routine, rather dull documents on the whole. The children of siblings might occasionally seek to reunite a property through their marriage (though rarely); at the level of second and third cousins this strategy is generally no longer feasible anyway, since the inheritance will have been too much dispersed in the interval.

The spread of consanguineous marriages was, it would seem, one part of a wider trend from 1000 towards keeping the bride and her property within the 'community'; but whereas for Islam this community was (notionally, at least) defined in terms of blood, for the Europeans it was fundamentally a territorial, a neighbourhood concept. In the age of wooden stockades and mobile warbands, such as had characterized early medieval Europe, loyalty to the tribe – Bavarians, Franks, Normans – had echoes of the tribal loyalty of Islam. The building in stone after 1000, and the technological sophistication which went with it, created a network of castles in Europe which had no real equivalent on the southern shore of the Mediterranean. These fortresses required an extensive mobilization of resources of a more continuous kind than anything a tribal group could provide. They became in the eleventh century the focus of early bureaucracy and taxation, and the basis of the 'peace' within which a territorial concept of family made sense. Europe was passing from a stage of armed companions, still typical of Islam, to one of hierarchy and command, of castle-owners and their retainers; from an egalitarian brotherhood of warriors to a society stratified in terms of command of material resources. The tremendous pressures on family structure to which this gave rise can, perhaps, be illustrated by one, fairly well-known example, that of the great warrior of medieval Castile, the Cid, whose half-mythical career was commemorated in song, and written down perhaps as early as 1140, within only half a century of his death.

The Poem of the Cid turns to a large extent round a marriage which sours. We noted in an earlier chapter how this hero had built up his following by marrying off the ladies of his household to his trusty captains, a downward movement of brides fairly typical of early feudal society, where no dowry was given, and where the main emphasis was on acquiring followers. However, the Cid pursued an alternative strategy, somewhat against his better judgement, of marrying his own two daughters, who were also his heirs, upwards into the high aristocracy, giving them to the Infantes of Carrión. The motive of the Infantes was simple: crass greed, duly sated by a munificent dowry of 3000 silver marks, which the Cid had plundered from the Moors. 'Let it be noised abroad in Galicia, Castile and León,' announces the proud father, 'that I am endowing my sons-in-law richly.' So far, so good. The rub came when he went on to tell the high-born Infantes: 'You are my sons, for I give you my daughters.' The problem with this remark, familiar enough in any dowry society, was that it inverted the hierarchy of early feudal Europe, by placing wealth above honour. The inevitable tragedy followed: the restlessness of the Infantes at their dependence on their upstart father-in-law, and their eventual repudiation of their wives as a means of deliberately dishonouring him.

The Poem of the Cid raises many fascinating questions. One of them is the difficulty of repudiating spouses in a dowry society – on which the Council of the Lateran was to have quite a lot to say in 1215. Another problem is the nature of the *mésalliance* or 'disparagement' (to use the old English word, whose Latin equivalent makes an early appearance in Magna Carta, also in 1215), to which the Castilian barons thought themselves subject. One of the features of early feudal society, we have suggested, is that women marry down: they are gifts bestowed by a superior, consolidating ties of patronage with dependants. There is no evident dishonour in the system, because the inferior will be close to his patron, educated in his household, possibly related to him on his mother's side. The arrangement works best in a society where wealth is still reckoned in terms of followers, and where there is no great disparity of culture and resources between these and their master. However the system will clearly not work well where pursuit of material resources, in the form of dowry, comes to dominate marriage strategy. One of the interesting features of later medieval history is the uneasy coexistence of the two systems: a failing effort to maintain a feudal hierarchy by giving out one's womenfolk as brides to one's followers; and a more realistic pursuit of big dowries, against which moralists and statesmen railed in vain. There is an echo of this in the marriages of the Alba family in the sixteenth century. Leonora, daughter of the second duke of Alba, married (probably slightly 'downwards') the first count of Alba de Liste. Leonora's son, Enrique, then married back up, in true feudal fashion, his mother's brother's daughter,

María, of the house of Alba, without a dowry. By contrast, when the Alba heir Fernando married an Alba de Liste girl in 1529 he exacted a big dowry – a rupture with feudal tradition, involving 'upward' movement of the bride, who carried with her a large property transfer. The whole Alba–Alba de Liste connection involved a complex interchange of partners best illustrated diagramatically, on the basis of the material supplied in William S. Maltby's biography of the great duke of Alba (1983, p. 17).

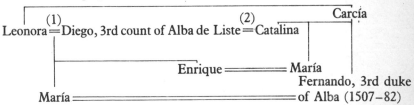

Fadrique, 2nd duke of Alba

The concentration of exchange within such a narrow circuit – so that the great duke of Alba, Fernando, was at once the son-in-law and brother-in-law of his 'uncle', the count of Alba de Liste – was somewhat exceptional. It argues for a system of child marriages, and sometimes a matching of girls to much older men, which we shall have to look at more closely in our next chapter, on sexual roles.

More generally, the Alba marriages suggest a continuing attempt by the Renaissance aristocracy to combine a hierarchy of honour with one of wealth, a dilemma which had first faced the Cid. It is during this period that statesmen in Spain and Italy lament the exorbitant increase in dowries, on which they blamed a perceived retreat from marriage, a stagnation or fall of population, and a creeping moral corruption. One anonymous writer, in a paper probably submitted to the great Olivares, who had made it his life's work to arrest the decline of the Spanish empire, laid considerable emphasis on the problem. For him, the enormous quantity of property being invested in dowry was not only making it difficult for honourable families to marry off their daughters, but undermining the foundations of an ordered, patriarchal society, since wives were now the property-owners, which made them 'so emancipated and scandalous in their conduct, spending with abandon ...' (González Palencia, 1932, p. 239). Olivares incorporated part of the advice into his law of 1623, which refurbished earlier legislation of 1573 setting an upward limit on dowries according to the income of the girl's father.

What was happening was probably a new way of structuring social relations in the age of nascent capitalism. The open households and bands of retainers, consolidated by the giving out of women as brides, were becoming things of the past. The power of the great families had now to be buttressed by more tangible, material resources, and that imposed a rethinking of marriage strategies. Countries with a more highly developed bourgeoisie than Spain generated a more extensive practice of 'disparagement' – the stooping by members of the aristocracy to pick up daughters of rich merchants and financiers, '*pour redorer le blason*', or '*pour fumer ses terres*' (to 'refurbish the coat of arms' or 'dung one's land'). Early modern historians are so familiar with this practice that we sometimes take it too much for granted. But one Spanish writer on marriage, towards the end of the old regime, looked on it with horror as undermining the whole hierarchy of feudalism. It was through membership of an order or caste, with its corporate tradition of honour, that a man learned the responsibilities of citizenship in the broad sense. If nobles pursued mere wealth, through marriage with commoners, then 'families in time would be indistinguishable', and the whole social hierarchy subverted (Amorós, 1777, pp. 179–85).

The words encourage us to set the study of marriage within a broad social context. We began this chapter by suggesting that the Christian prohibitions on incest during the early Middle Ages are related not only to the preoccupations of theologians but also to the actual practice of a mobile, plundering society. The reduction of the degrees of kinship within which marriage was forbidden, from seven to four, by the Lateran Council in 1215 seems to reflect an adjustment by the clergy to the needs of a more stable, feudal society, where the exploitation of land was becoming more important than the solidarity of tribal groupings.

The rise of dowry in this period as the typical form of endowment at marriage and the accompanying reduction of the dower have been seen as a loss of status for women, an infringement of their financial and juridical autonomy in a state increasingly organized along principles of male dominance, monarchical authority and Roman law. There is, no doubt, something to be said for this interpretation. But it seems to undervalue the importance of dowry as a recognition of female rights of inheritance. As de Tocqueville and Le Play were later to argue, dowry systems undermine the authority of the husband in his own home to the benefit of that of his financial patron, his father-in-law. 'You are my sons, for I have given you my daugh-

ters': the words of the Cid reflect a growing revolution in the structure of the European family, centred on co-operation between in-
laws. The rise of dowry marked a potential break with older forms of
hierarchy, placing the pursuit of wealth above that of honour, a
dangerous inversion which the Cid's epic biographer was among the
first to describe. The pursuit of heiresses must find its way one day
into the story of the rise of capitalism and the breakdown of the caste
system in Europe, for it is surely at the level of the family that the
cultural attitudes which underlay the economic transformation of
Europe are to be found.

Finally, where daughters inherit, control of their marriage becomes
very important. One might summarize the situation by saying that
in tribal society a woman is simply given a list of those whom she may
not marry (the rule of exogamy), whereas in the economically developed societies of Eurasia, her marriage is arranged for her by her
parents. This will lead to some form of endogamy: either marriage
within the clan, as typically among the Arabs, or marriage within the
neighbourhood, as typically among the Europeans. Advising his
fellow Florentines on the subject, the fifteenth century humanist
Alberti wrote:

> When by the urging and counsel of their elders and of the whole
> family young men have arrived at the point of marriage, their mothers
> and other female relatives and friends, who have known the virgins of
> the neighbourhood from earliest childhood and know the way their
> upbringing has formed them, should select all the well-born and
> well-brought-up girls and present that list to the new groom-to-be.
> (1969, p. 115)

This advice foreshadows the practice which the anthropologist J.
Davis found in the little town of Pisticci in southern Italy in the early
1960s, where brides brought their husbands to live in the neighbourhoods where they had been born (1973, pp. 67–8). In both cases the
system seems to be related to a concern with the bride's character,
by involving the community as a pledge for her good behaviour.
Dowry, we have argued, provokes a heightened interest by the
bride's family in the stability of her future union, and a greater
investment of time and effort in selecting a suitable partner. The
concern with moral discipline which has evolved in the process has
been of enormous significance in the religious and cultural history
of Europe over the centuries. To the exploration of that development
we must now turn.

5
The nature of passion

Of course, Kuku did not ask her: 'Will you marry me?' He only told her all the things they would do when they were married. But he looked so nice, so young, so charming ... that it was quite easy to imagine they were young lovers and their marriage of their own choosing. And he told her, 'Once I saw you at a wedding, and then I said to my father: "if you must arrange marriage for me, then please arrange it with this girl only."'

Ruth Prawer Jhabvala, *The Nature of Passion*

Some recent historiography of marriage has tended to dwell on the aspect of the union which is of crucial interest to us in the contemporary West, the possibility of emotional fulfilment for the man and woman. This is an important topic. It can be brushed aside too lightly with the argument that it is peripheral to the 'real business' of the arranged marriage, or that it is too hard to investigate scientifically, given the ambiguities of the evidence. Certainly there are smokescreens of language which have to be penetrated. What are we to make, for example, of this inscription on the tomb of a faithful wife in ancient Rome, as long ago as 80 BC: 'She whose chaste body went before me to the grave was my loving wife, one with me in heart'? When we learn that the woman in question had been married at the age of seven to the man, who must have been more like a father to her, we may feel that the conventional language of sentiment is masking a yawning gulf between the social structure of that period and our own (Grose-Hodge, 1946, plate IX). But rather than dismiss the historiography of sentiment as not worth doing, we should rather rise to the challenge of understanding the forms in which it is expressed, which have a changing significance over time. This is surely one of the great legacies of the French sociological school since Montesquieu, that moral behaviour is not an autonomous branch of human behaviour but requires to be related to its social context, to those economic and political structures which shape and constrain its development. Thus for de Tocqueville, Le

Play and Durkheim the rise of conjugal sentiment, particularly in the English-speaking countries and in the modern period, was no will-o'-the-wisp, but an interesting moral phenomenon which required explanation. It could not be understood on its own terms, and description of its expression, in the form of letters or memoirs, would not get us very far either. Language is, after all, a rather conventional currency: like money, which may circulate between countries while regulating quite different market conditions in each, words need to be related to their social context. It is largely with this problem of understanding moral behaviour, and the medium of its expression, in terms of social constraints that this chapter is concerned.

One of the great human dramas has always been the clash between what we want to do ourselves, and the social conventions. Marriage was a matter of economic and political strategy in pre-industrial society, but it was also concerned with the emotions. Where interest and emotion clash we have some of the great tragedies of a traditional world – one of the last portrayals of it, in the case of Europe, coming in the 1930s in Spain, in García Lorca's *Blood Wedding* and the *House of Bernarda Alba*. Where passion cannot be reconciled with the conventions of an arranged marriage, then it has to be represented as partaking of the nature of madness. The love philtre, which binds the will, has to be invoked as an explanation of the urge to self-destruction by lovers, from Carlo Levi's remote South Italian village (*Christ Stopped at Eboli*, set in 1936) back to the twelfth-century *Romance of Tristan*.

The drama of love, which is such an intriguing feature of Europe and Islam from the Middle Ages, has to be seen against the background of the arranged marriage. In societies where brides are transferred out of their families of origin, by purchase or capture, control of their sexuality is perhaps less important. In sub-Saharan Africa, where the great need is for manpower, illegitimate children may be incorporated in the mother's natal lineage if she is unmarried, or even into that of her dead husband (Goody, 1976, p. 43). In Eurasia, by contrast, the predominance of property over manpower has set up a certain tension between passion and interest from an early date. The marriage itself represents, we have argued in the previous chapter, a coming together of two family networks. Their concern is for the stability of an alliance which has involved a heavy material and moral investment, but which depends on something so fragile as the behaviour of two young people. The 'arranged marriage' is a particularly significant feature of Eurasian civilization, with its need to reconcile the emotions of the young with the long-term interests of the family.

The enormous complexity of the machinery set in motion to make this possible can be glimpsed in one marriage negotiation of later medieval Spain. In Seville in 1396 the first count of Niebla swore to the Master of Santiago, 'on a cross and on the Gospels', that his five-year-old son Enrique would wed Teresa, the Master's four-year-old daughter. He was to 'marry' her (*desposar por palabras de presente*) within a month of her seventh birthday. When she reached the canonical age of consent on her twelfth birthday, he would 'marry her under the veil, solemnizing the union in the face of the church'. He would 'consummate the marriage as soon as he was able', after Teresa's twelfth and his own fourteenth birthday. At what stage, the reader may ask, had Enrique and Teresa become man and wife, and in the eyes of whom? Technically what is happening on the girl's seventh birthday is a betrothal, but the words used by these laymen make it appear to be a binding marriage, an exchange of *verba de praesenti*, by which the two children declare that they take each other as man and wife. The veiling in church is an adaptation of an older Roman ceremony by which in Spain the head of the bride and the shoulders of the groom were covered while a priest pronounced a blessing (Dillard, 1984, pp. 62–3). Into the early modern period it symbolized the moment when the newly-weds were ready to face the community as man and wife, and assume the responsibilities of independent householders. This public, church ceremony might intervene a year or more after the actual marriage, the simple exchange of *verba de praesenti* in the home of the bride.

The count of Niebla and the Master of Santiago went on to draw up another document on the same day in 1396. It was an elaborate arrangement for the endowment of the young couple, significantly preceded by long Biblical references to the dignity and indissolubility of matrimony. The Master promised 500,000 *maravedís* in dowry, payable fifteen days before the 'veiling' (as always, this ceremony represented the moment of setting up house together and accompanied dowry contracts in Spain). The dowry was to be entrusted to the count in this case, given the youth of the pair, 'for their maintenance', but to be restored to the Master if the marriage produced no children. In 1399 Enrique, now count of Niebla in his own right through the death of his father, sent a deputation to claim Teresa from her father. In the latter's house, in front of a small assembly of

peasants, notaries and kinswomen, a priest conducted a simple ceremony, asking Teresa, in somewhat ambiguous language, if she 'gave
herself to be [*otorgarse por*] the wife' of Enrique, 'as the Holy Church
of Rome requires'. The affirmative replies of both parties were duly
recorded by the notary, but, significantly, no formula of union was
yet pronounced by the priest. Teresa, still only seven, went on living
with her father. On 20 February 1405 Enrique celebrated his fourteenth birthday, and on 4 March the question was put to him again
about accepting Teresa as his bride. On his affirmative response, the
priest from the young girl's parish took both their hands 'and married them'. But since it was in the time of Lent, there could be no
solemn 'veiling' in church, though it was specified that this was to
follow after Easter (Salazar, 1959, pp. 394–407).

What strikes the modern reader about this long drawn-out matrimony is the ambiguity of each of its stages. We like to distinguish
between marriage and betrothal; but the Spanish word *desposar*, true
to its medieval origin, will stand for both. The role of each of the
parties is not entirely clear. The match is clearly made by the
parents, and the first documents concern alliance and property. But
uncertainty about whether the agreement will hold after the children
are of an age to make up their own minds underlies the 'pledge'
which the count of Niebla has to make, of the lordship of three
villages, to the Master of Santiago, in case the contract is broken.
The word for the pledge, *arras*, is the same as for bridewealth, and
reflects an interesting shift of the latter in a society where the main
form of endowment has become the dowry. The *arras* seems to be
used increasingly, as here, to protect or acknowledge the honour of
the girl, a symbol that a groom is no longer merely taking away a
bride but entering upon a commitment to her family. The whole
question of sexual honour, and its significance for particular kinds of
society, we shall examine in a moment. But we may say for now that
the elaborate precautions of marriage contracts in later medieval
Europe were designed to guarantee the stability of a match in which
both families had a heavy investment.

This is where the issue of consent by the young couple themselves
becomes of great importance. At successive stages, at the age of
seven, then again at twelve or fourteen, Enrique and Teresa were
required to affirm their own agreement to the arrangement that their
parents had made on their behalf. The European 'arranged' marriage
was no unilateral transfer of brides; it was a commitment to an
enduring association between two families and demanded unusual

stability. We can sense this in the unease felt by parents at the time when it came to negotiating matches for their offspring. Luis de Requesens, later famous as governor of Flanders under Philip II of Spain, was only eight years old when a marriage was suggested for him in 1536 with a twelve-year-old girl of high lineage. His mother's reaction is interesting. The match was an excellent one, she wrote to her mother, but it would probably not work out because of the discrepancy in ages. Anyway, 'these marriages of children rarely take effect when they grow up' (March, 1941, vol. II, p. 304).

Consent had been the basis of marriage, at least formally, in ancient Rome, though, given the young age of many of the brides, one wonders what effect the doctrine can have had. That the Church should also make it the foundation of Christian matrimony was a natural development. For the men of the twelfth century no issue seemed more vital than establishing the lineaments of a stable union and distinguishing it from mere concubinage. This was the golden age of codification of law. The preoccupation of canon lawyers with clarity seemed to coincide with some trends among the laity. Repudiation of spouses, by contesting the validity of the marriage tie, had been tolerable when women carried little property to their husband; it was becoming less acceptable in the age of dowry, when the purpose of matrimony was to establish the friendship of two groups of in-laws. We have already examined the efforts to limit and clarify the prohibited degrees. Now we must look at the effort to distinguish a binding marriage from a more casual liaison.

Two great churchmen of the twelfth century laid the foundations for what is still, in many ways, the European concept of marriage. These were Peter Lombard, bishop of Paris, whose ideas were put across in his *Sentences,* and the Italian monk Gratian, author of the *Decretum* and master at the famous law-school of Bologna. Essentially the task before these men was to spiritualize and make official sexual relationships which up until then had been subject to considerable uncertainty. Both had, in their very different ways, to find some formula which would reconcile the weakness of the flesh and the social ambitions of the laity with the growing need for clarity and uniformity in the Christian life. They had to find some way of disciplining sexuality, while recognizing that not all liaisons between men and women could be made official, and that marriage had implications for property and social hierarchy. The formula which the Church arrived at was that of the intention of the parties – that is, marriage would be marked out, not by sexual behaviour or by transfers of property, nor indeed by overt signs as such (for these could be induced by fear or fraud), but by the state of mind of the man and the woman. On this fundamental point the agreement between Lombard and Gratian is more significant, it seems to me, than the differences which eventually drove them apart.

The problem which arose was that of interpreting 'states of mind'. Peter Lombard drew a clear distinction between a mere promise (*verba de futuro*) and an actual acknowledgement of marriage (*verba de praesenti*). By stressing that one could tell from the form of words used between the man and the woman what their intenions were, he was effectively making marriage into a contract like any other. It is misleading to suggest that he was attached only to a form of words: there was no single formula prescribed, and the words meant nothing without the intention, the mature consent freely given. From this point of view he was consistent with himself in allowing the consent to be given in private, without witnesses. But the drift of Lombard's thought, as far as I can interpret it through later Church legislation, was that marriage should become a proper contract, hence public and duly witnessed.

With Gratian we appear to be in a different world at first sight. For him the duly witnessed contract, the form of words, was of little account compared with the intention. Hence a promise to marry was nearly equivalent to marriage itself and binding on the parties. If sexual intercourse took place subsequently, then the betrothal was automatically converted into a marriage. Gratian seems to have been working with what one could call a 'sacramental' view of matrimony – that is, like all the great mysteries of birth, procreation and death, it required to be subsumed into a divine plan, if the miseries of the flesh were not to be seen as totally at variance with God's purpose. Though marriage was not formally defined as a sacrament until the Council of Florence in 1438, I think one can find much of the thinking which was to make it so foreshadowed in Gratian.

There is, no doubt, a more prosaic explanation too. Gratian was working in a Mediterranean environment, where the lineage and the dowry were always very important; Lombard in northern Europe where bridewealth and household had been traditionally the basis of marriage. In the south agreements between families, of the kind made between the count of Niebla and the Master of Santiago, often centred on two young people who were not yet fully autonomous, either economically or spiritually, of their kindreds. The ambiguity surrounding youthful betrothals in this milieu obviously suited aristocratic parents, who reserved marriage very much for the household rather than for the church. The Spanish situation recalls the descriptions given by Christiane Klapisch-Zuber for Renaissance Italy: a marriage in stages, which takes place fundamentally in the home rather than in a public place like a church. There is the exchange of consent between bride and groom in the presence of their parents, the signing of the dowry contract, then the very secular festivities when the man comes to take the woman from her father's house (1985, chapter 9). All this might take up to one year.

It is intriguing that the Lateran Council of 1215, source of most of the legislation on marriage in the Middle Ages, adopted fundamentally the views of Peter Lombard. Though agreeing that intention was the key, it wanted to see a public contract, with a form of words witnessed by a priest. This was a victory for the north European point of view, that of societies with autonomous households formed at marriage. It is a significant tribute in its way to the influence of French and English prelates in medieval Catholicism; at the Council of Trent (1545–63), as we shall see, this influence was finally surrendered to the Spanish and Italian Churches. But Peter Lombard's views were not completely victorious at the Lateran. In the first place secret marriages, though illegal, were still valid. Gratian's concept of sexual intercourse as converting a betrothal into a binding marriage continued to find a certain echo in the practice of the Church courts since 'intention' was the key to matrimony. Even where such intercourse had not intervened, Pope Alexander III had ruled in 1180 that the betrothed should be 'compelled' to honour their commitments, though his successor, Lucius III, had to issue a rider in 1181 that the degree of 'compulsion' should not be so great as to force an unwilling man into marriage.

Such caution was necessary because of the great power which the Church was beginning to acquire around this time through its network of diocesan courts. In the later Middle Ages we start to enter a different kind of territory in respect of marriage, one where ecclesiastical law begins to interfere more directly in the day-to-day life of the laity. Some of the earliest surviving records are for the diocese of Canterbury in the fourteenth and fifteenth centuries. Here the influence of Gratian also reached. Betrothal contracts had great force. Because so many 'marriages' were still contracted at home, sometimes without witnesses, it was hard to tell the betrothal apart from an exchange of *verba de praesenti*. Generally these cases came to court because one party regarded the 'marriage' as merely a promise to marry, which could be broken. The judges seem to have relied more on the intention than on the form of words (Helmholz, 1974, pp. 32–47).

But jurisprudence could vary a lot, and some of the German dioceses at the same time insisted on much more rigorous proofs of marriage – foreshadowing the controls which were to be introduced there, after the Reformation, on clandestine arrangements which lacked parental consent (Gaudemet, 1987, p. 236). There is a certain continuity in German marriage law between the fourteenth and nineteenth centuries, characterized by restriction on settlement and by community controls, which it might be worthwhile to explore further. In Spain the sheer ambiguity surrounding the *desposorio* – a semi-private arrangement between the parties, which might be either a betrothal or a marraige – continued down to the Council of Trent. The issue came up twice in as many generations in the case of the great Andalusian house of Guzmán, dukes of Medina Sidonia. The third duke, Juan (1466–1507), sought to marry his first cousin, Isabel de Zúñiga, 'and they say hc did marry her and treated her as his legitimate wife; but he soon abandoned her to marry doña Leonor de Zúñiga, that lady's sister' (Salazar, 1959, pp. 154–5). The offspring of Juan and Leonor was challenged as illegitimate, but managed to succeed to the title as duke of Medina Sidonia. However, this man further complicated the succession question by marrying the wife of his brother, 'while the latter was still alive'. Exactly what went on is not clear. The likely interpretation is that the brother, Alonso, fifth duke of Medina Sidonia, did not consummate his marriage. Knowing that he would die without heirs, he released his spouse, Ana de Aragón, to his younger brother, Juan, who went on to become sixth duke of Medina Sidonia. But the issue of Juan and Ana were soon challenged as illegitimate – by Juan's younger brother Pedro, created first count of Olivares in 1535. The bitterness between the counts of Olivares and the dukes of Medina Sidonia over this issue remained to poison the political atmosphere of Castile into the seventeenth century (cf. Elliott, 1986, pp. 8–9).

It is against this sixteenth-century background, of continuing uncertainty among the aristocracy over the status of *desposorio*, that one has to see the attempt at clarification by the Council of Trent. This assembly had long, difficult debates on the definition of a valid marriage, between 3 February and 11 November 1563. The French delegates wanted to make parental consent mandatory; they wanted a public ceremony in church, in front of a priest and three witnesses.

They were demanding something which was rather foreign to Mediterranean practice at the time, but more in line with that of northern France, and possibly of Germany. One senses in this area of debate at Trent more than an echo of the fundamental doctrinal cleavages over the nature of true religion: the discipline of the Germans against the community sense of Spaniards and Italians. The French prelates carried the voice of northen Europe to Trent, in more ways than one; but they were overruled by the Hispano-Italian majority. The decree *Tametsi*, which govened Catholic Europe down to the end of the old regime (until lay governments intervened to modify it increasingly in the eighteenth century), ruled that marriage was to be a public ceremony before a priest and at least two witnesses, preceded by the calling of banns on three prior holidays; but on the key issue of parental consent, it limited itself to expressing its 'detetestation and prohibition' of runaway marriages, while upholding their validity.

In some ways Trent made matters worse for the aristocracy. By specifying more clearly the difference between a betrothal (which did not require a priest) and a marriage (which did), it made the old, convenient confusion between both, which served the dukes of Medina Sidonia well, now impossible. At the same time, it deprived fathers of any control over either. The dilemma was highlighted by the case of the Constable of France, Montmorency, in 1556, which had motivated much of the French concern at Trent. The Constable's son, Francois, wanted to marry a lady-in-waiting to the queen, against the wishes of his father, who had arranged a match for him with an illegitimate daughter of the king. The exact status of the young man's commitment to the lady-in-waiting was typically ambiguous, because clandestine. When he was eventually persuaded to declare that he had not actually pronounced the ritual formula of marriage, but merely given a promise, he was released from his vows, and went on to marry the king's daughter (Gaudemet, 1987, p. 315). A near-disaster had been averted by a hair's breadth. It left the enduring legacy of the law of 1556, forbidding a man under thirty or a girl under twenty-five to contract a marriage without parental consent, on pain of disinheritance. There followed the draconian Ordinance of Blois in 1579, assimilating such runaway matches to abduction, which would entail the execution of the bridegroom and the priest. The French monarchy had effectively rejected Trent.

But it is not entirely clear how far these secular decrees actually modified Catholic marriage practice in early modern France. The memoirs of the duke of Saint-Simon recall one clandestine marriage of 1708, in which his brother-in-law was involved as a witness, which is open to several interpretations. The unruly 28-year-old son of the duke of Rohan was courting an actress, and 'his father lived in terror of his marrying her'. The expeditious remedy was to have the king place her in a convent. The young man, furious at first, was eventually reconciled to the idea of marriage with the eldest daughter of the duke of Roquelaure, whom his parents had chosen for him, and who 'despite her great expectations, was humped, hideous, and past her first youth'. The negotiations, however, stalled on the stinginess of the duke of Rohan, unwilling to allow his heir as big a settlement as the Roquelaures expected. The Rohan youth now demonstrated a lover's ardour, which the court of Louis XIV found comical, playing 'the passionate, despairing lover' and eloping with Mlle de Roquelaure, with the help of a 'vagabond and interdicted priest, a Breton', who married them. Saint-Simon, worried for the safety of his brother-in-law who had acted as witness, was advised by the Chancellor of France 'to provide for the escape of the priest and all other possible witnesses, the removal of signed documents, and an absolute denial in answer to questions'. The scenario was wholly pre-Tridentine, reminiscent in many ways of the Montmorency saga. Though the duchess of Roquelaure demanded the death penalty for young Rohan according to the law of 1579, a compromise was patched up on the main question of the property settlement, and a new marriage ceremony, in due form, ratified the accord (Saint-Simon, 1967–8, vol. I, pp. 356–60).

The whole affair prompts many questions about the relation between law and practice. In the first place, in spite of Catholic doctrine on the freedom of marriage, there was clearly not too much risk of a serious *mésalliance* between the son of a peer and an actress in the old regime, though the threat seems to have been there in the mind of the old duke. Secondly, amorous conduct seems to have been pressed into service at just the right moment to hasten on marriage negotiations between parents which had been sticking on financial details. And thirdly, a century and a half after Trent, the French aristocracy could still regard a marriage without banns as, in some sense, a true marriage – a popular attitude which put pressure on parents to come to some accommodation outside the courts. At a lower social level, the law of 1639, specifying that betrothals must be in writing if they were to have any force, seems not to have worried the diocesan court of Troyes, which continued to rely on oral evidence (Flandrin, 1981, p. 72).

The problem left by Trent for Catholic countries which were more respectful of ecclesiastical legislation was precisely that of betrothals. The Council had surrounded the act of marriage itself with the glare of some publicity, which would give parents a chance of persuading their offspring to mend their ways. But – even supposing that the bishop did not decide to dispense with the banns and keep the marriage secret, which he was allowed to do for good cause – could the young couple force the hands of their elders by contracting a betrothal? This was the issue which the parliament or Cortes of Castile drew to Philip II's attention as an abuse in 1579–82, and again in 1586–8. They seem to have had a *cause célèbre* in mind. During 1578 a lengthy investigation had taken place by Antonio de Pazos, bishop of Avila and President of the Council of Castile, into the matrimonial affairs of the great house of Alba. The heir to this title, Fadrique, was being sued by a certain Magdalena de Guzmán, daughter of a judge and lady-in-waiting to the queen, for enforcement of a betrothal made secretly in 1567. At a later stage in the proceedings she reinforced her suit by an allegation that sexual intercourse had subsequently taken place. But the initial demand rested on a secret *desposorio*, which Trent had just defined as no true marriage, but which lingered on in the lay conscience as very akin to one. As Philip II put it, Fadrique seemed to him 'obliged, both in conscience and as a gentleman, to marry the girl'. Fadrique's worried father, the great duke of Alba, then pre-empted further discussion by getting the young man to wed his cousin, María de Toledo, in due ecclesiastical form, albeit without letting the king know. Alba and his son were sent into detention, only to be released in February 1580 when the great general was recalled to court to lead the invasion of Portugal that year (Fernández Martín, 1980, pp. 559–638; Salvá and Sainz de Barranda, 1845, pp. 464–519).

Alba's fate, like that of Montmorency or Rohan, depended on royal favour rather than on canon law. Though Pazos had suggested referring the case to the Church courts, it was a committee of the Council of Castile – in which he himself as both a bishop and a minister had an ambivalent role to play – which handled the business. When Alba's star was in the political ascendant, in 1567 and 1580, there seems to have been little question of forcing his heir to contract a *mésalliance*. Nevertheless, if the law of marriage could be evaded it could not be ignored; and Trent does not seem to have resolved doubts about the force of clandestine betrothals. Tomás Sánchez, the Andalusian Jesuit, grappled with the problem in the principal guide to Catholic marriage doctrine in the early modern period, the *Disputationum de Sancto Matrimonii Sacramento Libri X*, (1602–5; originally published in Genoa in 1592, and still awaiting an English translation). Though sometimes denounced as scabrous, because of the place which sexual intercourse occupies in the discussion, it is really a traditional scholastic exercise, couched in the form of a 'concordance of discordant canons', which has echoes of Gratian. Like the latter, Sánchez is a lawyer–theologian, and the goal of both kinds of scholar is surely to reduce what they see as a 'mystery' or 'sacrament' – the union of flesh – to the discipline of a civil contract. Betrothal was a solemn obligation, particularly so where the girl's reputation was liable to be compromised by rupture (*lib.* 1, *disp.* 44). A man, indeed, could not be compelled to go through with a betrothal, though Sánchez allowed excommunication as one legitimate penalty in this case, since the degree of fear or compulsion required to constrain the will of a *vir constans* was assumed to be very great indeed. We know from the jurisprudence of the episcopal courts of Granada and Córdoba in the seventeenth and eighteenth centuries that men were held in gaol until they relented and agreed to go through with a marriage. The grounds required for proof of a betrothal were slender. As one author of the time commented, 'any woman', with a few witnesses, 'usually of doubtful character, and examined without informing the accused', could have a man gaoled by the bishop (Amorós, 1777, pp. 256–9). This was something of an exaggeration, but the records of the diocesan courts do show a willingness to interpret betrothal quite widely, and assimilate it to a binding contract. There is a clear difference here from the practice of the protestant states of Germany, and even of early modern France, which we shall have to explore in a moment.

The sanctity of betrothal in Mediterranean jurisprudence could be seen as a deference to local concepts of honour. More problematical are those cases where the Church upheld a certain right of 'abduction' by the male against a woman of higher social class. A typical example was where the girl's father refused the match, and where the boy appealed to the diocesan court to allow the girl to make up her own mind. These suits caused much unrest in early modern Spain, with canon law notionally upholding marriage as a free contract between a fourteen-year-old-boy and a twelve-year-old girl, and parents protesting that their children were too young to know their own minds. It was not until the eighteenth century that most Catholic states began to grasp the nettle, following the lead of the protestant states and of France, and require parental consent in all cases for the marriage of minors – Austria in 1753, Spain in 1776. Tomás Sánchez (1602–5), like the Council of Trent, was clear that children should ask their parents' advice about their marriages, but could not see why they should be compelled to follow it. Men are free, he commented, in an eloquent passage, and cannot be sentenced for life (*lib*. 4, *disp*. 23). As to whether parents might have recourse to the civil law and disinherit a wayward child in the interests of social order, he thought the 'more probable' opinion to be that they could not, since this might act as a deterrent to marriage. One may note that the discussion applied only to 'minors' under twenty-five years of age anyway. Basically the ecclesiastical literature of early modern Spain followed Sánchez's lead. Into the eighteenth century the assumption was that parents were often poor judges of the real interests of their children, that disputes were, of course, deplorable, but that where they arose they had better be adjudicated by the bishop than by a unilateral decision of one party.

How does one explain this tolerance of a kind of official elopement? Was the cannon law of consent ultimately at cross-purposes with the interests of lay society? We come back again to a fundamental conceptual point, which was with us in the different context of the law of incest: Do ideas have a life of their own, developing by a kind of inner logic in the hands of a professional class of holy men, or do they respond flexibly to social need?

For the first millennium of its history the Church had been inclined to look askance at the secular world. Spiritual perfection was sought through renunciation of lay life, in the withdrawal of monk or hermit. It would not be fair to say that there was hostility towards sexual relationships. Although the Fathers of the Church believed that the cares of a family hindered the spirit, they also maintained that marriage was inherently good, indeed a sacrament, though it was not formally defined as such until 1438. Much of our knowledge of clerical attitudes subsequently during the Dark Ages comes from the Penitentials of the seventh and eighth centuries. These books of punishment for sin come largely from Ireland and Britain, and are hard on the pleasures of the flesh. Perhaps the limited nature of the documents (and of the national temperament?) needs to be borne in mind when interpreting them. Probably there is more of a contin-

uity, at least in the Mediterranean, between classical civilization and
Christianity than we sometimes allow. The ancient Greeks liked to
distinguish man from the other animals by his use of reason, which
enabled him to control instinct and passion. The senses can make us
feel ashamed. They teach us what beauty is, but they cannot help us
attain it. The pursuit of beauty lies through the harmony of the
senses with reason. In the sexual sphere, this aesthetic balance is
called love (Foucault, 1979–85).

It is interesting that this concept was refurbished in the renaissance of Greek letters in the twelfth century, around the time the
canon lawyers were struggling with a new definition of marriage.
The lay model of love, one may say, was largely that of Ovid : the
sensuous pleasure of the chase, inegalitarian, self-centred. The classic redefinition, which has survived down to our own day, came from
the pen of a monk, Bernard of Clairvaux: 'Besides itself, love requires no motive and seeks no fruit. Its fruit is the enjoyment of
itself' (Leclercq, 1979, pp. 128–9). There is in Bernard a subtle
mixture of the sensual and the intellectual which was to become the
epitome of chivalry in the sexual sphere. One senses a return to
Greek sources, an acceptance of the urges of nature, a desire to
sublimate them rather than reject them. The acceptance of this
ecclesiastical model by lay society had its effect in enhancing the
status of women by making love a union of minds as well as of
bodies. It no doubt fitted in with the social changes among the
twelfth-century aristocracy which we have examined earlier, the rise
of daughters as heiresses at the expense of collateral males, the use of
marriage as a permanent alliance of two families rather than a surrender of a woman by one to the other. But Bernard's ability, here and
elsewhere, to capture the spirit of his age has to be seen against a
background of change in the Church itself. There appears to be an
increasing emphasis round 1100 on the humanity of Christ – no
longer the heroic, god-like figure of early medieval representation,
but the tortured man of the later medieval crucifix, the son of that
mother to whom the great Gothic churches after 1150 were now
dedicated, of that father, Joseph, whose apotheosis after Trent was
already prepared in the devotion of the fourteenth and fifteenth
centuries. An older dichotomy between the world and the spirit must
have seemed out of keeping with this outlook. The attempt of
Bernard to ennoble love, and of the Lateran Council of 1215 to
distinguish marriage from concubinage, surely corresponded to an
altered concept of the destiny of man. If the flesh was less sinful than

it had seemed to previous ages, then matrimony could be a valid option for a Christian seeking perfection.

As regards the emphasis of the medieval canon lawyers on the freedom of marriage, there may have been another influence at work. Goody has reminded us, in his history of the family in Europe (1983), of the tendency of powerful corporations to protect their own. One does not need to adopt a conspiratorial view of history to accept that there may have been a latent conflict, not always fully understood by the actors themselves, between the need of a family for married heirs, and that of a celibate clergy for recruits. St Teresa of Avila records one such incident among the high aristocracy of sixteenth-century Valladolid. After her elder brother and sister had entered the religious life, Casilda de Padilla was left as the last hope of her family for a direct heir. At eight years of age she was betrothed to her uncle, and went to live with the latter, in the house of his mother, her grandmother, for at least part of the year. 'When she had been with her husband (*esposo*) during the day, to her great contentment, and loving him more fully than her years required,' Teresa tells us, 'she would fall into a great sadness seeing how the day had ended, as all those to come must do' (1951, p. 62). This youthful awakening of the 1560s prompted her to run away to a convent before she was twelve years old. Persuaded to return home by her mother, the young girl ran away again, using an elaborate hoax to escape her guardians, and exhibiting both a child's sense of play and an adult's craftiness. Her 'uncle-husband' got a royal warrant to have her returned; but on her twelfth birthday, having reached the canonical age of freedom, Casilda was allowed to opt for the cloister. There are other examples in early modern Spain of this use of religion by children to flout the marriage strategies of their parents. There is also a reference to it in one of the great plays of the Golden Age, Lope de Vega's (1982) *El Caballero de Olmedo*. It is wrong to see nunneries as dumping grounds for the unmarriageable daughters of the aristocracy; they were that on occasion, but they were also an avenue of escape from parental pressure, a sanctuary where the individual could find herself. This helps us understand the refusal of the Tridentine Church to accept greater control by parents. As an eighteenth-century Jesuit, Matías Sánchez, put it, the requirement for parental consent to marriage in protestant countries stemmed ultimately from their rupture with the Catholic tradition of celibacy: since marriage was the only goal for children, it had to be carefully prepared (1792, p. 134).

But there is more to the problem of clandestine betrothal and the limitation of parental authority in Spain than the influence of the Catholic Church. Among the peasantry of the Mediterranean down to our own day there has survived a lively tradition of runaway marriages. Among Stirling's Turkish villagers (1965), one marriage in twenty is begun by elopement; among Lockwood's Bosnian Muslims (1975) it is nine marriages in ten; among the Sarakatsani shepherds of Greece, the bride will be abducted if her parents deny the 'reasonable' request of a suitor (Campbell, 1964). These elopements are often less romantic than they seem. Among the Bosnians the suitor is generally quite well known to the girl's family, and acceptable as a match; but negotiations may break down over the size of the dowry, in which case the young man forces the hand of the other side by running off with his intended – not unlike what happened in 1708 with the dukes of Rohan and Roquelaure. Elopement may be a good excuse for reducing the dowry, or denying it altogether; but the bad blood generally does not last. Sometimes, indeed, these abductions may be feigned. One typical case is recounted by the liberal politician Antonio Alcalá-Galiano in his memoirs of life in Cadiz at the end of the old regime. His widowed mother was 'very keen on her nobility' but poor as a church mouse; the hope of the family lay in a match between Antonio's sister and the helpful Señor Lassaleta, an agent in one of the counting houses of the city. Caught between a need for Lassaleta's money and horror of his low social standing, Antonio's mother asked that he should 'abduct' her daughter by an appeal to the diocesan court, alleging that the girl was being prevented from marrying by force. In that way, commented the mother, people would see that she had had no alternative but to let the marriage go ahead (1886, vol. I, p. 355). There is more than one example of the Machiavellian manipulation of the law of marriage in Alcalá-Galiano's memoirs, which makes us wonder how far elopement may not have served parental interests more generally. It was typical of the later Middle Ages and early modern period that they had to balance two systems of social stratification: one based on lineage, and the other on wealth. The great complaint of Italian and Spanish treatises of the period on marriage is that the pursuit of wealth has overridden the more noble concern with honour. May the canon law of consensual union not have provided parents with a convenient pretext for off-loading responsibility onto their children when a match was suitable but not honourable?

The tension, fictive or real, caused by abductions can really be understood only in relation to the high stakes involved in European, or Eurasian, marriage. Julian Pitt-Rivers has drawn attention to the peculiar role of sexual honour in the Mediterranean area. Interpreting Genesis, he suggests that the early Hebrews, like other pastoral peoples, practised exogamy, marrying their women off to strangers. Increasing concern for the purity of their faiths, accompanied by growing competition for land as settlement developed, led them to control their marriages more carefully. An incident in Genesis, where the sons of Jacob refuse the offer of the prince of Shechem (modern Nablus) to marry their sister, Dinah, and instead kill him for having seduced the girl, appears to signal, whether as myth or history, a turning point in Hebrew attitudes. The range of acceptable marriage partners has become restricted, and a new code of sexual honour has grown up to limit access to the women of the family by strangers (1977, pp. 126–71).

The need to control female sexuality corresponded to a situation where women were more likely to be heiresses, and to be endowed by their parents at their marriage. Where agriculture has become more complex, based on the plough rather than the hoe, there does seem to have been a tendency to lift women out of cultivation in the fields and guard them in the home. This is particularly true of households which have been able to build up a surplus of grain, with which they can then hire labourers to replace their womenfolk. Such a development might help explain the characteristic separation of women from the world of men in Eurasia, a separation which tends to increase as one moves up the scale of wealth, and into the town from the countryside. Anthropologists have noted that urban Muslims are more likely to veil their womenfolk than are their rural brothers, and that veiling tends to increase, in general, in proportion to female rights of inheritance (Goody, 1976, pp. 31–3; Tillion, 1966, pp. 24–5 and 178–9).

The separation of social roles by gender, combined with an emphasis on the interdependence of male and female, has been a characteristic feature of Mediterranean culture from classical times. It may have something to do with an early shift in this urbanized area from tribe to household, from cousins to brothers-in-law, as key units of social organization. From the time of Xenophon, management of the *oikos* or household has been the test of the good citizen. Xenophon's 'economy' means the allocation of separate but interdependent roles to men and women, within the context of the household: to the husband the care of the fields, to the wife the domestic domain. *Economía* continues to retain in the Spanish treatises down to the sixteenth century something of the Greek meaning: the proper management of a household through the ordered co-operation of its head, his wife and servants, in a manner akin to the functioning of estates in the commonwealth at large (e.g. Camos, 1592, p. 57). The word is linked to another which was developed in ancient Rome and which was to have a long history: *familia*, which meant not 'family' in our sense, but household, including servants (but excluding non-resident kin), and which was linked to the idea of patrimony. Both the *familia* and the *oikos* turned on the co-operation of a man and a woman in their respective spheres. This joint household enterprise was what Europe understood by 'economics' in the age of the peasant farm and the guilds – down, in fact, to the revolutionary changes of the eighteenth century, when, at the hand of Adam Smith (1776) and other writers, the word took on a new life of its own. That story we shall have to leave for our next chapter. But the Eurasian concern with the proper ordering of a household and its patrimony may help explain that peculiar emphasis in this culture on the withdrawal of women from the street and the field, and their reclusion in the domestic sanctuary or harem. One of the best-known Spanish works on marriage, *La Perfecta Casada*, was written by the great poet and mystic, Fray Luis de León, in 1583 to advise an aristocratic newly married couple. It spells out for the bride the separation of roles which underlies a good and prosperous marriage, understood as the management of a household. But the man cannot function as he ought in public affairs and about his business, unless the rumours coming from the hearth, in this small-scale commonwealth, enhance his reputation. His standing will depend to some extent on the decorum of his wife, and her ability to live up to her side of the partnership (1975, p. 119).

This question of sexual honour has tended to divide anthropologists working on peasant communities of the Mediterranean to the present day. In reaction especially to Pitt-Rivers, some have denied that honour has much autonomous force as a system of social ranking, maintaining that these communities are stratified essentially by wealth, and that the greater or lesser responsibility of one's womenfolk may only marginally affect status among near-equals. It would be difficult to deny that. But I do not think that this objection does full justice to the subtlety of Pitt-Rivers's argument. That relatively few men in Arab countries actually marry their parallel cousins, and relatively few Mediterranean peasants lose status because of the dishonourable conduct of their womenfolk, may be true at the descriptive level. The powerful or clever can always break the rules. But norms of conduct are interesting in themselves, even when breached. One wants to know why lip-service at least has to be paid to them, why they were devised in the first instance. What we are dealing with in these cases is surely the symbolizing of certain values which are perceived to be important for social relationships. Sexual honour is a widely diffused concept throughout Eurasia because it fits in so well with the nature of the arranged marriage in that area. Where in-laws are associated through the dowry system, as typically in this region, matrimony comes to assume a greater significance for social organization than in tribally orientated societies. Values of monogamy and permanence may come to be more prized, even in Islam, where polygamy is more strictly defined and limited than, say, in Black Africa. All this requires greater attention to be paid to the potentially disruptive effects of sexual passion; indeed, the ideal comes to be that of harnessing passion for the good of the arranged marriage, as a way of ensuring its stability and permanence. As the sixteenth-century Spanish humanist, Fray Antonio de Guevara, so neatly expressed it: 'For marriages to be enduring, loving and sweet, first the hearts of the man and the woman have to be joined before their hands are given to each other' (Ochoa, 1856–70, vol. I, p. 159). The powerful current of love poetry in medieval Islam, with its links with European chivalric romance, stems from a common Mediterranean legacy, paradoxical though it may seem, of the arranged marriage. The great problem for Mediterranean civilization has been that of cultivating passion, but within socially acceptable channels. Typically the issue arose in respect of courtship.

There were continual complaints during the early modern period in Spain about the excessive liberties allowed in courtship. Another Spanish humanist, the great Luis Vives, though thinking more of Flanders than of his native Valencia, wrote an extensive tract on the theme in 1524. He lamented the encouragement given by mothers to their daughters 'to go out, dress up, talk, sing and dance with any and everybody; to get to know, if they can, the man they are to marry, for people now believe that this is the way to find a husband and make a stable marriage' (1943, p. 162). While agreeing that women should not be forced into matrimony, he thought the liberty of courtship could be counterproductive, fanning 'amor' or passion at the expense of female 'shame', and thereby subverting the family. In

fact, Mediterranean societies since his day have tried to balance the
two concepts, not always successfully. In Andalusia, observers have
left us good descriptions of how appropriate suitors would be
allowed to get to know a girl, but at a safe distance, by being left
alone with her at night at the barred window of her parents' house,
in a rather ritualized and formal exchange of courtesies (e.g. Brenan,
1980, pp. 246–52). This is a continuation of a tradition which can be
traced back at least to the seventeenth century. In Lope de Vega's
play, *El Caballero de Olmedo*, to which we have alluded before,
there is a sensitive exploration of the misunderstandings which can
arise when a daughter is allowed by her father to court her future
husband for her attachment slips from the chosen suitor to another.
It is out of the ambivalence of Mediterranean courtship that the
typical institution of abduction is born. It was, no doubt, to facilitate
reconciliations and avoid feuds between families that the Catholic
Church developed its face-saving device of the legalized elopement.
But this institution could only flourish within defined limits.

As we have seen in the Alba case, no Catholic state seems to have
been prepared to countenance a *mésalliance*, whatever the provisions
of canon law about freedom and irrevocability of contracts. Runaway
marriages could enjoy ecclesiastical protection only if they did not go
too much against the social grain – if, indeed, they served (as we
have argued above) as a bridge between two rival concepts of social
hierarchy, an older one based on honour and a newer, focused on
wealth. Love, or passion, which defies this convention has had to
content itself with living beyond the law. This fact has had enormous
cultural implications. The relative tolerance of concubinage in the
Mediterranean – and the relatively easy integration of the offspring
into society – was to differentiate Catholic and Muslim states from
the protestant north in early modern times. The Council of Trent
had, indeed, launched a great campaign against sexual immorality.
The parish priests were to make regular reports on adultery or
fornication among their parishioners to the bishop, who, after warnings during three months, might expel the offending woman (not the
man). But the system never worked properly in Spain. The chapter
of Granada warned in 1565 that such legislation would stir up a
hornets' nest by publicizing liaisons which were best left discreet.
The diocesan courts rarely instituted *ex officio* proceedings for immorality; nor did the Inquisition, which limited its activities to
homosexuality, bigamy and blasphemy (including 'indecent proposi-
tions' that sex with a prostitute was no sin). But heterosexual rela-

tionships, providing they were discreet, went unpunished. They were either a matter for the criminal courts when they threatened public order, or for confessors. The indefatigable Jesuit missionary to Andalusia in the 1580s, Pedro de León, has left us a superb insight into how concubinage was dealt with, if at all. These affairs usually involved some risk of a *mésalliance*. Great tact was therefore required in persuading men to overcome their fear of the family, and this was achieved by omitting the banns and keeping the marriage a secret (Herrera Puga, 1981, pp. 90–3 and 110–11).

This discretion seems a world away from the public campaigns against immorality in protestant Europe at the time. The German courts after the Reformation began to discountenance the clandestine betrothal. Parental consent became virtually mandatory for girls and boys younger than about twenty or twenty-five who wished to marry. And the great *ex officio* proceedings of the Church courts against fornication in Tudor and Stuart England are well known. Why is there this great divide between northern and southern Europe, traceable back to the controversy between Lombard and Gratian, visible already in the jurisprudence of the fourteenth century, but certainly a major feature of the post-Reformation period? What seems to have been significant in the Reformation view of marriage was the discrediting of the idea of a 'sacrament' – that poetic sense of mystery which sublimated the union of bodies into a reflection of creation itself. The Reformers took a more practical approach in this as in other matters. Marriage was a secular vocation; it had to work through common sense. Like any other contract it could be established only between two responsible adults, and it might have to be revised (through divorce) if it did not seem to be working. There could no longer be any room for the ambiguities of the *Romeo and Juliet* world; clandestine betrothal and abduction were clearly wrong. As too was concubinage.

The particular drive of the Calvinists against sexual sins has to be seen as one part of a more general attempt to discipline a godless world. Though the truly godly were, of course, known to God alone, this world must show forth the glory of its creator. Predestination shifted the moral emphasis from the needs of man to the claims of God, and it was logical, therefore, to constrain unregenerate man from giving scandal through idleness, greed or lust. The godly zeal of the puritans required a new kind of commitment from lay society, a unilateral submission to exacting standards of moral behaviour. No other bridge with the Deity, such as prayer or sacrifice, made sense.

As Calvin told the Council of Geneva in 1541, 'I consider the principal enemies of the Gospel to be, not the pontiff of Rome, nor heretics, nor seducers, nor tyrants, but bad Christians ... I dread abundantly more those carnal covetousnesses, those debaucheries of the tavern, of the brothel and of gaming ...' (Ozment, 1980, p. 366). The subsequent enforcement of godliness on the lay population at large, in Geneva, Scotland or England, constituted a moral revolution which had no real equivalent in the Catholic countries.

It is true, indeed, that protestantism emerged out of ascertainable currents of spirituality of the later Middle Ages. The moral regulation of the lay life – as opposed to its redemption through prayer from behind monastery walls – was one of the great forces behind the coming of the friars, Franciscans and Dominicans, in the thirteenth century. The later medieval Church appears to have been moving towards an acceptance of the lay calling as a full means of attaining salvation, before Luther and Calvin clearly defined it so. The Augustinian friar Luis de León (1975), in his book of advice to *La Perfecta Casada* (*The Perfect Married Lady*), used the word *oficio* to define matrimony. In the context of the discussion the term has more of the overtones of vocation or calling than of estate in life. Through the fulfilment of the obligations of her *oficio* the married woman will please God better than if she neglects them in the pursuit of religious ritual. This practical, 'human' approach to marriage is reflected in the catechism of the Council of Trent which lists as the first function of matrimony, not procreation or the avoidance of fornication, but the companionship of man and woman, that 'hope of mutual aid, that each assisted by the help of the other may the more easily bear the ills of life, and support the weakness of old age'.

Catholic and protestant marriage doctrines were tending to converge, but each may have been better adjusted to its own kind of society. Clandestine betrothals and runaway marriages can probably be tolerated only in certain types of community. In the first place there would have to be some confusion about the true nature of the disparagement or mésalliance alleged by the parents of one of the parties. In the Mediterranean area there were two competing hierarchies of wealth and honour; this tension the action of the Church courts helped to ease, as in the Alcalá-Galiano case which we examined earlier. Secondly, and an allied consideration, there will tend to be some confusion over authority in a lineage society. The father, the head of the household, did not enjoy in early modern Spain the outright control vested in his Victorian successor. This point will be developed more fully in chapter 7; but it is worth recalling the influence of lineage and patrons in the Mediterranean.

This is illustrated by a case in Granada in 1542 when Leonor, eldest daughter of the lord of Castril, was married to Diego de Pisa, younger son of a royal judge. Closing the shutters of their house and refusing to have anything to do with the wedding, the Castril family alleged that their daughter might have made a much better match, for she was the grand-niece of the famous Francisco de los Cobos, secretary of the king. They had been forced to accept the marriage because Pisa had dishonoured their daughter by gaining secret access to their house at night during his clandestine courtship. The nature of that courtship had been typically ambiguous. Pisa's patron, the marquis of Mondéjar, governor of Granada, had been pleading his case with Leonor's mother – significantly, not with her father, for it was through the mother that the Los Cobos connection ran. The mother told him that 'she looked on [Los Cobos] as a father, that nothing could be done without his consent' – a convenient way of stalling the negotiations while not seeming to give an outright refusal to the powerful governor. The young lovers misread the signs; as young Diego wrote to Leonor, trying to reassure her that all would be well, 'My lady ... do but think that if your relatives were not happy with this match our side would not have stirred, nor yours either. Any resentment will only last a week' (Archive of the Chancery of Granada, 3/1102/2). In fact the resentment lasted considerably longer, motivating a bitter lawsuit over dowry, in which Leonor and Diego's love letters, confiscated by her irate parents, were entered as proof of her dishonour.

Clandestine courtship has traditionally tended to flourish in a culture which regards love as a passion, and passion as wild. The great love stories of medieval Europe, as Denis de Rougemont (1972) so perceptively remarked, are basically tragedies. As in Beroul's *Romance of Tristan*, the will is bound by a power higher than itself, symbolized often in both folk and literary culture by the love philtre, the magic potion which drives men – and women – mad. Even in *Romeo and Juliet*, where the passion is of great beauty, it is very much in the medieval tradition, a thing of overwhelming power which is ultimately destructive, and no model for social behaviour. All the more significant, then, is the revolution which began to sweep the European consciousness in the romantic era around 1800 – the notion that love is natural and gentle, hence something that can be transferred from poetry to life.

The way in which this revolution in sensibility occurred is still, perhaps, in need of further study. It can be related to the more general upheaval under way for a century or so before, which goes under the name of the Enlightenment. This complex movement began with a desire to apply reason to the governance of human affairs, emphasizing the self-contained nature of the universe as it was perceived by the senses. To study the actual working of creation, of the laws of nature, seemed a more worthwhile and reasonable ambition than to speculate on the unknowable, or accept, blinkered, the authority of tradition. The empiricism and flexibility of the eighteenth century were to make their influence felt in all spheres from politics and economics to private life. The mood of intellectuals corresponded in any case to changes in the family, which are not always easy to chart precisely. We could refer to the quest for intimacy in domestic architecture, most strikingly visible in the remodelling of Versailles after the death of Louis XIV. Before that, Mello (1923) had noted the growing desire for privacy in the re-building of Portuguese houses, and the new terms of endearments between husbands and wives: 'my companion', 'my old woman', 'my favour'. There is clearly a growing exclusiveness in the late seventeenth-century Portuguese noble family he describes. The extrusion of outsiders, whether patrons or lineage members, and the concentration on farming one's estate as the decisive mark of eminence through the income it generates, were general features of the eighteenth-century elite. They made the old canon law of marriage increasingly dysfunctional, and the only question could be: How long before the Catholic states broke with the Church on the matter?

In Austria in 1753 and in Spain in 1776, parental consent for the marriage of minors was introduced. A further Spanish decree of 1803 specified that this would apply to men under twenty-five and women under twenty-three, and that a father 'will not be obliged to give the reason or explain the cause for his refusal'; at most, a child might make a special, extraordinary appeal in cases of manifest oppression to the President of the local chancery court. Meanwhile laws of 1796 and 1803 made it illegal to gaol a man in enforcement of a promise of marriage, or regard any promise as a betrothal unless it were in writing. These rulings were adopted by the legislators of liberal Spain, whose spirit they fully encapsulated, after the fall of the old regime; at most, in 1862 the age of freedom for men was reduced to twenty-three and for girls to twenty. But the principles of the old canon law of marriage had been effectively interred. How had this

revolution come about? To classify it as part of the attack on the
Church by the Enlightened Despots of the eighteenth century hardly
takes us very far. The chief Spanish spokesman of the programme,
Joaquín Amorós, saw it as a defence of hierarchy, undermined, as he
thought, by a spate of runaway marriages. His apology of 1777 goes
beyond a defence of the new law into an analysis of societies based
on estates or castes, and bears some comparison with the writings of
his better-known German contemporary, Justus Möser. Both saw the
social structure of their day as reposing on the corporate pride and
sense of public responsibility of well-defined groups, whether guilds
or lineages, which (thought Amorós) should be endogamous.

This model probably had no longer much relevance to Spanish
society at the time. The new marriage laws of 1776–1803 seem
ultimately to be concerned less with safeguarding the purity of castes
than with strengthening the control of household heads over the
heirs to their property. As we have suggested above, the actual
operation of clandestine marriage and the jurisprudence of the diocesan courts in the old regime tend to show that purity of caste was
rarely imperilled, since young people could make their wishes felt
only where they enjoyed the support of kinsmen and the elders of
the community. Otherwise their tragic loves were readily aborted.
The canonical freedom of marriage had been allowed to survive as a
norm for so long in Catholic Europe because it helped ease the
transition from a hierarchy of honour to one of wealth. In old Spain
the well-born but indigent had been a numerous grouping, perhaps
10 per cent of the population, a veritable caste with its own ethic of
solidarity and man-to-man ties. By the eighteenth century this nobility was falling drastically in number, as social pre-eminence came to
be restricted more to those with financial leverage. We shall not go
over the reasons for this, already adumbrated in chapter 2 above.
But what seems clear is that the maintenance of elite status in the last
years of the old regime required greater attention to patrimony – and
hence to matrimony. It was no longer enough, as in twelfth-century
Catalonia, that one's son-in-law should be a 'trusty fellow'; he must
be a man of means.

One of the characteristic features of the Civil Codes of bourgeois
and liberal Europe of the nineteenth century was to reinforce 'patriarchy', the control of a man over his wife and children. The
intellectual arguments invoked would make an interesting study in
themselves, but can be summarized broadly as a need to reconstruct
hierarchy in a democratic society and a need to foster economic

development by affirming absolute rights of property. In his own contribution to the elaboration of the Spanish Civil Code, the lawyer, and later liberal prime minister, Sigismundo Moret was to argue (1863) that the regeneration of Castile could be achieved only through patriarchy, which he identified as an innovation at the time, a rupture with the medieval tradition of a rambling, federal family. Laws restricting the right of a man to trade with his wife's dowry were, he suggested, outmoded, a relic of the 'suspicion and fear' between lineages characteristic of the Middle Ages; laws specifying equal or near equal division of the inheritance among all the siblings were incompatible with the reward due to enterprise and industry (pp. 118–19 and 171). It is within this context of thought that one has to see the enhancement of parental control over marriage in liberal Europe.

In this whole area of the relationship of moral behaviour to social constraint, it is helpful to turn again to de Tocqueville. He was fascinated by what he saw in the 1830s of the difference in sexual relationships in America and France, and set about trying to explain the absence of clandestine marriages and the generally more stable 'homes' which he found across the Atlantic. 'There are hardly any premature alliances there. Americans marry only when their minds are formed and mature ...' Parental discipline was more relaxed, girls given greater opportunities of meeting members of the opposite sex in adolescence, without fear that a disastrous marriage would result. De Tocqueville thought part of the explanation lay in arrangements for control of property. Unlike France, where the married woman's dowry remained under her own control, though administered by her husband, America allowed a wife no separate property rights. 'In America the independence of the woman is lost for ever when she enters matrimony.' The 'abnegation' required of any woman under these circumstances would ensure that she would consider all the options very carefully before agreeing to marry (1963, Book 2, chapter 20). Elements of this discussion recall Le Play's admiration for the English 'home' with its cohesiveness guaranteed by the concentration of absolute property rights on the head of the household, who was thereby free to develop its prosperity and reward team effort. One senses in both descriptions a confluence of two streams: a Calvinist stress on moral discipline, and the greater turnover of property in an urban economy. As de Tocqueville put it: 'religiously orientated peoples and trading nations take a particularly serious view of marriage.' The growing centrality of marriage and the home in modern societies can be seen in yet clearer perspective if one considers the fate of the illegitimate.

The latter seem to have a more assured place in societies organized on principles of lineage rather than household. Among matrilineal peoples they can be accommodated without too much problem into the mother's tribe. Even among patrilineal populations, social rather than physical paternity may be the guiding rule for status, so that in Islam 'the child is reckoned to the bed on which he is born' – that is, he is treated as a full son of his mother's husband. On the medieval Spanish frontier, with its continual demand for manpower, the illegitimate appear to have enjoyed considerable rights of inheritance, even in competition with their legitimate half-siblings, in many municipal customs. But the thirteenth-century royal code, the *Siete Partidas*, marked a new restrictiveness in this respect, which was to grow with time. The Laws of Toro (1505) limited the bastard, where there was legitimate issue, to sharing in the fifth of the patrimony which testators were allowed to leave outside their family. He continued to be eligible for succession, however, if there were no legitimate children, and if the father so specified by will. In practice there continued to be some confusion on this issue. During the early modern period the chancery court of Granada heard many suits from the illegitimate alleging rights of succession to entails in preference to collateral kin. A thorough study is still needed of the whole issue; but my impression is that a change was taking place in the attitude of the judges to these pleas during the course of the seventeenth century. Instead of the presumption of succession being in favour of the illegitimate, these now had to establish clearly that their father wanted them to take precedence over the kindred.

Where the household and its property became the basic unit of society there was really little place left for bastards. Among the peasantry at any rate they had always been more of an embarrassment than among a lineage-conscious aristocracy; and entry to the guilds had frequently been denied to them. It was at the level of honour rather than property that they had a function. One of the great Counter-Reformation prelates of Spain, Juan de Ribera, is testimony to their role in certain spheres. Only son of the first duke of Alcalá, he was excluded from the succession as illegitimate and saw the title pass to his uncles. But he went on to a distinguished career as archbishop of Valencia (1569–1611), and sometime viceroy of that kingdom. His success may recall that of the more famous Pope Clement VII (1523–34), whose illegitimate birth counted for little compared with the fact that he belonged to the prestigious Medici lineage. But even in the sphere of honour one senses a change in the late medieval and early modern period, a growing investment of the word 'bastard' with those unpleasant moral overtones which it still has today. One can see it in Edmund's conduct in *King Lear*, perhaps, where there is some hint of an association between base birth and base deeds. In a play by José de Castro y Orozco, staged in Granada in 1838, *El Bastardo de Monteflor*, and designed to raise money for the local foundling home, the villain is doomed by the tragedy of his illegitimate birth to the perpetration of his treachery. 'Did I ask you for a life of reproach, a name of dishonour and shame?' he retorts to his father's upbraiding. 'Let the awful doom of my family run its course in me!' The rise of such attitudes in the late medieval and early modern period would make an interesting study in itself. I wonder whether part of the explanation is not to be found in the greater importance being attached during this time to the education of the young, about which more will be said in our concluding chapter. Certainly one of the leading pedagogues of Renaissance Spain, Pedro López de Montoya, writing in 1595, was convinced that a legitimate marriage was a necessary pre-condition of proper child-rearing. Fornication was forbidden not only on its own account but for 'the damage done to children born of it, who usually cannot be reared in a proper fashion' (Hernández Rodríguez, 1947, p. 262). Once again we are back, it seems to me, with the transition from a society organized round lineage to one based on household, a transition which may explain some of the stricter moral code introduced by the protestant Reformers.

The further history of illegitimacy can be touched on only briefly here. After a quantitative decline in both protestant and Catholic Europe in the seventeenth century, as revealed in parish registers, illegitimate births rose again steeply from the later eighteenth century. This process is part of that reorganization of property and employment under industrialization which we shall consider in our next chapter. But a few preliminary comments may be made here in relation to the particular topic of bastardy. In the first place it is clear that the phenomenon had become more typical, possibly for the first time, of the working class than of the elite. In the days of the peasantry and the guilds, jealous of the access to their scarce resources, and of an aristocracy counting its wealth in terms of retainers, the situation had been just the reverse. The apparent humanitarianism of the eighteenth century, opening the guilds to bastards for the first time, in Germany in 1731, for example, or in Spain in 1796, reflected changing attitudes to social structure. As Justus Möser, the great German political economist, pointed out in 1774, to admit the illegitimate to the guilds was to destroy the corporate pride of the latter and ultimately to undermine the whole basis of a society based on estates (in Forster and Forster, 1969, pp. 212–16). Indeed, the point was that the German governments were concerned to foment economic progress by broadening and cheapening the labour supply. It was precisely this new 'proletariat', lacking in any organized family structure, which Le Play was to identify as the worst social consequence of industrialization.

What one seems to be witnessing here is a growing differentiation of class in terms of moral behaviour, where a stable family environment, by permitting the careful husbanding of resources and the education of the younger generation, is becoming the very essence of elite status in a newly democratic society. Engels made a rather similar point. His whole analysis of the bourgeois family in the nineteenth century is worth re-reading for its attempt to situate moral attitudes in their economic context. Examining the development of marriage since the Reformation and the overseas discoveries, which he saw as the two decisive steps in the formation of capitalism, he explained the greater attention paid to conjugal love and freedom of the parties in terms of the general spread of the concept of 'contract' in bourgeois society. As inherited and corporate status counted for less, the family had to be accorded the same freedom to organize itself as any efficient business enterprise. The notion of a free contract between a man and a woman, though (which had impressed de Tocqueville about America), was an illusion, since control of property was vested in the woman's father or husband. Marriage might no longer be formally arranged in bourgeois northern Europe in the nineteenth century, but those who failed to respect the conventions of their class paid the penalty by falling into the proletariat – one of the definitions of which, as Le Play noted, was its lack of a formal family structure (Engels, 1884, pp. 505–8).

There are many apparent contradictions in the history of sexual attitudes and behaviour: the prevalence of passion and elopement in the Mediterranean area, where the arranged marriage and the subordination of women have been assumed to be very strong, the rise of patriarchy in Victorian England after a period during which English women seemed to enjoy much greater freedom than their continental sisters. This chapter has tried to suggest that such phe-

nomena are more than merely picturesque or superficial, that they do
have histories, that such histories can be reasonably documented,
and are worth taking seriously. They are worthy of study, not least,
because they relate to deep currents of change, economic and social,
within the society itself. Sentiment, like myth, is a profound expression of some of the underlying values of a culture, and a clue to its
structure. Durkheim summed up the connection with his usual
acumen, albeit in a slightly different context: '... if, as often hap-
pens, we see in the organisation of the family the logically necessary
expression of human sentiments inherent in every conscience, we are
reversing the true order of facts. On the contrary it is the social
organisation of the relations of kinship which has determined the
respective sentiments of parents and children' (1964, p. 349).

6

The economics of the household

> I am surprised that writers on society, now and in the past, have not accorded rules of inheritance a greater influence on the story of mankind ... They confer a godlike power over the fate of one's fellow human-beings.
>
> De Tocqueville, *De la démocratie en Amérique*

One of the merits of that pioneering anthropologist, Lewis Henry Morgan, was to draw attention to the role of property in the formation of the modern family. He pointed out that the primary meaning of the Latin *familia* was household and patrimony, not descent or kinship, which were associated with the *gens*. He suggested that the one gave way in importance to the other in the ancient world once a certain level of economic development had been reached. We have already noted Jack Goody's point that Eurasia poses different problems of analysis for the anthropologist of the family from those tribal peoples in the study of whom the discipline was pioneered. Agriculture here is based largely on the plough, which has permitted greater accumulation of capital than the hoe culture of Africa. This has led from an early date to the rise of the 'family', in Morgan's sense, at the expense of the clan. The shift poses a difficulty for the student, because the basic concepts of the discipline were worked out largely in relation to more economically backward peoples.

Since the Second World War, it is true, there has been a significant movement by anthropologists to understand the very different environment of an urbanized area like the Mediterranean. Case studies have multiplied, and a few idiosyncratic forms have become apparent. One can think, for example, of the valuable work done on abduction, and in highlighting the problem of sexual honour. But, whether because the individual case studies have been too localized, or because the cultural area falls too much within a relatively familiar European framework, there has been less conceptual advance in understanding family systems than the pioneering investigations of Africa and Polynesia yielded. There is, however, one big exception to this statement, and that is in the sphere of property. Because the Mediterranean lands have been settled and exploited for so long, a new kind of problem has confronted the student there, as indeed in Latin America and other 'urbanized' zones, the problem of capital accumulation and its influence on other social relationships. Unlike the tribal peoples of Africa, the peoples of the northern Mediterranean are 'peasants', liable for rent payments to landlords who control much of the property, and for service payments to outsiders like the clergy and the bureaucracy, who control the local culture, at least in part.

Historians of rural society have not tended to pay much heed, until recently, to the kinds of questions anthropologists were beginning to ask about the structure of the village. Our preferred, or more accessible, sources being of an econometric kind, registers of tithe yields or cadastral surveys, we worked with the assumption that land was a capital asset, whose size and distribution could be measured over time. We saw big and small landowners, or landholders (the difference was not always very clear to us), and the landless, and we were happy enough to call them social classes. It took the anthropologist to remind us that this is not enough. In Paul Stirling's *Turkish Village* (1965), as among William Lockwood's *European Moslems* (1975), the wealthier peasants tend to be the elderly. A man goes on acquiring land throughout his life; as his sons come of age to marry they contribute the labour and set up further consumption demands (since their brides are brought into the husband's family home), which make acquisition of more land both feasible and desirable. When the old father dies, his sons split the inheritance and, on the whole, go their separate ways; each of them will figure in the cadastral surveys in these middle years of life as only a small-scale landholder. In these peasant societies – which, admittedly, are those of Muslim peoples with extended households – the life cycle is a key factor in determining social stratification, possibly more so than the market economy.

It was the Soviet economist Chayanov who first systematically explored this link between family and landholding in his *The Theory of Peasant Economy* (1925). Societies which were organized by class were geared to a market economy. Those who held property in such an economy were engaged in a cycle of production for profit, the profit enabling them to pay the hired labour, at a sufficient discount to make the enterprise worthwhile. The rich peasant farmers of late Tsarist Russia, argued Chayanov, had shown few indications of involvement in such a cycle. Their production was geared fundamentally to satisfying the needs of their own households. As the number of mouths to feed grew, so the head of the household would expand his production by taking on more land, perhaps increasing the amount he sold on the market. But the labour for this process would come from within the household, growing in proportion to the consumer demand. A Russian *Kulak* who had several married sons, living with their brides under his roof, would have reached a natural limit of landholding and labour recruitment. He would be a 'wealthy' man, but his wealth would be related more to family structure than to the market economy; it had a significance at the level of the local community and its hierarchy of command, it had less relevance to social stratification at a national level.

There may be some features of the Chayanov theory which are peculiar to Russian conditions: the abundance of land down to a late date, the rotation of lands by the commune according to the needs of individual households until the Stolypin reforms of 1906–11. But it has a conceptual relevance to the analysis of peasant societies generally, forcing us to look at community structures where property-holding may be only one element in a wider framework of personal relations. Lockwood's study of the Bosnian mountain village of Planicia (1975) is a very neat illustration of the continued coexistence of the world of the market with that of the self-sufficient household down to the present day. The bigger the household in this area the more self-sufficing it will tend to be in respect of labour and ability to supply its own food and clothes. However, cash is vital in several significant ways. First, there are the taxes payable to the government, a problem which the cultivators of the soil throughout Europe had had to confront from at least the later Middle Ages, when kings began to recruit mercenary armies to replace the old feudal levy. Cash for this kind of emergency might often be found by the sale of a sheep (herds were a means of investment and display for the rich). Second, there are the luxury goods – coffee, tobacco (preferably supplied by smugglers in timeless fashion) – which have to be acquired. These are needed for the ritual exchanges of gifts and hospitality at marriages and funerals which maintain the prestige of a wealthy household. The surplus cash to purchase them may come from trading in the market. Each of these little mountain villages has its own special product – wool, cabbage, barrels, brushes – dictated as much by social tradition as by strictly economic considerations. One is reminded of the Spanish bishop's reply to the enquiry of 1782 about the reason for the lack of marriages outside the village: each community trained its girls from childhood in particular tasks (see above p. 80). These village products are traded rather irregularly at fairs, the proceeds being hoarded in the wife's dowry chest. The more ongoing exchanges take place within the community – work-sharing, barter, the occasional sale (but with the price fixed *ad hominem*, according to the social relationship with the purchaser). Money, however, will be used to regulate any big transfers of land or herds. As Lockwood suggests, the market economy can work, and has worked through much of European history, alongside a system of community obligations, enhancing the latter rather than disrupting them.

This is not an easy point to grasp for those of us who have lived in the West in recent times, in an economic system which is geared overwhelmingly to the market, whose exchange mechanism to a very real extent determines social standing. A fundamental problem in European history is determining how our present situation came about. Granted that land has nearly always been subject to economic exploitation and a source of income, at what stage did it become only or mainly that, losing its political and social functions? In the eighteenth century 'noble land' in Prussia was still theoretically not available for sale to commoners, since it was destined for the upkeep of an elite whose sense of honour and family tradition made them preferred servants of the state; in France in the same period the due known as the *franc-fief*, payable by commoners who purchased fiefs, reminded everyone that landholding had originally had a political function and was not just a capital asset. It is not just the significance of landownership which is being transformed in the eighteenth century, but the nature of urban work too. The guilds of the old regime were more than simple economic associations regulating production, but political institutions in a broad sense. Not only did one have to be a 'citizen' of the local town in Germany, through marriage to the daughter of a master craftsman if not through birth, in order to hold property or carry on a trade, but one had to meet certain social qualifications. The illegitimate, for example, and the sons of men in 'dishonourable' occupations (shepherds, skinners and others) were barred, until the Imperial edict of 1731. Defending the exclusion of the illegitimate, Justus Möser, as we have seen, elaborated a theory of orders in which the corporate pride of groups, whether craftsmen or nobles, was justified as the very basis of the state. In order to appreciate his view one has to remember that manufacture in

eighteenth-century Germany (and elsewhere) was geared to the out-
put of high-cost, labour-intensive articles. The exquisite detail and
care lavished on even routine pieces from this period, as we noted
when discussing 'caste' in chapter 2 above, remind us that the
economic criteria then were still pre-capitalist.

The connection between family and landholding has long fascinated historians of early Europe, concerned with the origins of place-
names, field-shapes, the evolution of landscape generally. Much
interest has centred on the meaning of terms like *hide* and *manse*,
which seem to refer to measures of land, but are something more
than that because of their link with social organization after the
Germanic invasions. The hide was not only the 'land of one family',
as defined by the Venerable Bede in the eighth century, but an
important administrative unit of Anglo-Saxon England because it
was grouped into the so-called 'hundreds'. It seems to be cognate
with a range of words in the Indo-European languages for matrimony (Charles-Edwards, 1972). But to what kind of family can the
hide have belonged, since it was a very large farm of 120 acres? Were
there joint families in the England of this period – that is, married
brothers with their wives and children living under the authority of
their father, as in Russia or the Balkans? The evidence suggests
rather that the homestead was cultivated by the peasant on his own,
with the help of his 'loaf-eaters', his hired men. The hide may have
been divided up, with each of the sons taking a piece of the holding
and making an assart in the nearby waste. But the importance of
solidarity with the kindred for the blood-feud would ensure continuing residence in and around the hide – not an inalienable patrimony, certainly, but nonetheless a significant anchor for a family in
an unsettled environment.

The *manse* probably served a similar function in the France of the
period. It is best conceived of as a large peasant homestead in the
wilderness, which may expand through land-clearance and subdivision into a hamlet. Bloch noted that hamlets of the mountainous
Limousin could be traced back to Carolingian *manses*. In the hill
country of the Languedoc some of these settlements, *mas* or *mazades*,
continued to exercise joint possession of the soil among their members down to the eighteenth century (1966, pp. 159–64). This process of segmentation seems to have continued wherever frontier
conditions merited, assisted by the tendency of the peasantry to
marry and settle locally where they had the chance. Alain Collomp
was able to trace five of the heads of households in the little Proven-

çal village of Les Chailans in 1730 back to their grandfather, Martin Chailan, who was a farmer there in the early seventeenth century. Indeed, fifteen of the twenty households in the community were headed by men called Chailan (1983, p. 90). As in the case of the hide, it is not necessary for us to posit inalienability of the land in order to appreciate the family solidarity of our ancestors.

Clearly, on the plain, in the regions of marsh and forest cleared by 'big men' who established their *villae* there – already in the days of Gregory of Tours, but decisively in the great age of colonization after 1000 – the manor (or villa) is more significant than the *manse*. But the latter continued to exist within the villa, as the plot assigned by a chief or colonizer to his dependant. Like the hide it seems to have been subject from an early date to morcellization. Gregory of Tours noted as early as the sixth century that the 'division of possessions' made it hard to levy the land tax; and Charles the Bald in 864 had to order that any portion of a *manse* alienated by *coloni* without the consent of their seigneurs must be restored. In Anglo-Saxon England a reasonably effective system of public taxation helped to keep the hide together as at least a notional fiscal unit; but the collapse of royal ability to tax in France during the tenth century removed even this barrier to disintegration. The manorial lords still took the *manse* – averaging now about thirteen hectares, though with an enormous spread around that mean – as the unit for the assessment of rents due to them. But then after 1100, with the growth of towns and money rents, the lords of France began to parcel out their great home farms among the peasantry and abandoned any attempt to keep the *manse* functioning.

Again, these developments in France can be seen best by contrast with what was happening in England. There the hide survived because it was adapted to the labour requirements of the manor, more geared towards high farming in the central Middle Ages than its French equivalent. The thirteenth-century court records speak of this ancient political unit as a convenient measure of land, 120 acres, which was the amount required to support a full plough team of eight oxen. It no longer corresponded to a peasant farm; rather, the substantial peasant of this period would have a quarter of a hide, a yardland, as it was called in the south of England, or an oxgang in the north, equivalent to 30 acres – which is intriguingly close to the area of the average *manse*. This was the 'ideal' peasant farm of the High Middle Ages, varying in superficial area according to the nature of the terrain perhaps, but capable of furnishing two oxen to the standard plough team of eight beasts. Such heavy ploughs may have been more necessary then than now, given the weakened state of underfed animals and the prevalence of the fallows. They required a considerable degree of co-operation among neighbours. Homans has observed, in his classic study of *English Villagers of the Thirteenth Century*, that men who held contiguous strips in one open field were often to be found as neighbours in the next (1975, p. 100). Such a system facilitated the grouping of plough animals for a team which could work all the holdings in a particular sector of the village at one time. The same team was also required to do ploughing on the lord's demesne. This need for co-operation would not prevent individual villagers exchanging or alienating their holdings, but it obviously was a constraining factor.

Like the Midlands and southern England, the 'plain' of north-eastern France was classic open-field or 'champion' country, where peasant farms were divided into strips which were scattered over the good and bad soils of the village. Bloch linked the formation of this system of landholding to the needs of the great wheeled plough, drawn as in England by its six or eight oxen, which was clumsy to turn and thus more manageable on elongated strips. The existence of the heavy plough made it necessary to keep the village fields few, long and open, capable also of fitting within the three-year cycle of fallow, spring barley and winter wheat. The existence of strips argued for some subdivision of an original patrimony like the *manse*, though this subdivision would necessarily be checked by the need for co-operation among neighbours in building up a plough team, and leaving particular fields fallow for grazing of the animals in any one year. It is misleading to set up too rigid a contrast between land which belongs to the family, and that which is available for purchase by individuals. Neither Bloch nor Homans would deny that land could be alienated, under certain conditions, in the manors of thirteenth-century England and France. Their point is rather that the constraints of a particular kind of farming system would make it difficult to do so. The superb cadastral surveys of French villages included in Bloch's book date from the eighteenth century, at a time when the accurate and standardized measurement of land was coming into vogue, contributing *inter alia* to complaints of a 'feudal reaction' or tightening of the fiscal screw by manorial lords on the eve of the French Revolution. Before that, measurement of land had been imprecise, not so much because the technology was missing as because the services of surveyors were not needed in a sluggish

market. Before the eighteenth century, land was assessed by customary criteria of significance to a community of local people – in Spain
usually by how many *fanegas* of wheat could be sown on it, in
medieval England by how many oxen could plough it in a year.
When such ways of measuring become redundant we can be sure
that a village community is beginning to break up through the
penetration of market forces. But before then it makes little sense to
ask if land was freely alienable or not, for the answer depends so
much on what one is trying to prove. Homans made the point once
with his usual acumen: of course thirteenth-century villagers bought
and sold land, but their frame of reference was a community built up
around obligations of status, age and family, to which such land sales
had ultimately to be subordinated. What men think they do, commented Homans, is as interesting for the historian as what they do
in practice; quantitative data on particular aspects of behaviour may
not capture the context in which that behaviour makes sense (pp.
195–6).

These points have to be borne in mind when assessing Homans's
account of the stem family in thirteenth-century rural England,
which has been much criticized. Land belonged to the family rather
than the individual, he suggested. In the open-field country, one son
would expect to take over his father's holding, possibly at marriage,
supporting his parents in their retirement either in the house or in
an annex. Non-inheriting sons might either stay celibate as wage-
labourers, or be placed in careers with the money which came in
from exploitation of the holding. There was considerable variation
from manor to manor, and great differences outside the open-field
country – partible inheritance in East Anglia, joint-holding by heirs
in Kent. But a general rule over the Midlands and the south of
England seems to have been that the land would pass to the eldest
son, a third or a half of the movables would go to the man's widow,
another third would be equally divided among all the children, and
the remaining third would be at the testator's free disposal, perhaps
for masses for his soul (pp. 134–5). The kind of 'stem family' which
Homans is here describing has nothing to do with co-residence.
Rather it is a flexible way of trying to safeguard the status of a
substantial peasant family in an intermediate stage of economic development where all the sons do not need to be accommodated
directly on the land. Homans speculates that Robert Grosseteste, the
famous thirteenth-century bishop of Lincoln, and reputedly a vil-
lein's son, may have been a classic product of this system, a younger

son launched on a career by the solidarity of the family (p. 135). It is a world which would have been very familiar to Le Play.

The old Anglo-Saxon hide may have had some connection with the 'joint family', where attachment to land as the unique source of wealth breeds some kind of co-residence, or, at least, neighbourhood settlement. But the stem family of the thirteenth century and later is a different concept, an adaptation to the greater challenges, perhaps, of a more complex society. Alain Collomp's beautiful portrait (1983) of the Provençal village of Saint-André (120 families) in the seventeenth and eighteenth centuries gives us one of the best insights since Homans into the subtlety of the relationship between stem families and peasant farming. Both men would agree that this type of family tends to grow organically (and imperfectly, always) rather than to a pattern imposed by a set of rules. It cannot be described adequately by standardized criteria such as the household co-residence of a married son with his father, but only seized as a way of living, through a comprehensive study of a local community as a whole. Though Provençal fathers were allowed by law to leave the bulk of the inheritance to one son, they rarely did so; yet they can be said in practice to have conducted a stem family strategy. How was this done?

The remote hill village of Saint-André, the subject of Collomp's study, set in the beautiful Gorges of the Verdon river in Provence, lived to a large extent by wool-working and muleteering as well as by some cultivation. From the mid-seventeenth century there was serious population pressure, with births regularly in excess of deaths. Emigration was an important safety-valve, with the apprenticeship of the sons of the richer peasants to trades in Marseille and Toulon down on the coast. But it still left the problem of accommodating many children who could not be so placed. The houses of this part of Provence were narrow and high, and rather cramped. On the ground floor was the stable or workshop, on the first floor a living-room overlooking the street, with a bedroom next door (this floor being reserved for the head of the household and his wife, together with any lodger), and on the second floor there would be two more bedrooms where adolescent children would sleep and fruit and grains be stored. At most one of these bedrooms on the second floor could be reserved for a married child and his wife . In principle one son would marry and bring in his bride during his father's lifetime, and he would be regarded as the heir. But many of these heirs got little more of the inheritance in real terms than their brothers. Where

THE ECONOMICS OF THE HOUSEHOLD

possible the land would be kept together. But this, while feasible for the richer peasants who could place younger sons in apprenticeships or in the church, and for the poor, whose cadet members had little to share anyway and a readiness to enter wage-labour, was dificult for the medium-scale peasants. Efforts had to be made in this social group to establish all the sons in houses of their own, bought or built for them by their parents. If necessary, the narrow family home could be subdivided, by placing partitions vertically so as to seal off the front rooms from the back, or horizontally, between the first and second floors. Some twenty of the 120 families of Saint-André lived in such 'half-houses' in the mid-eighteenth century. The process of subdivision could be read in the topography of the area: in the hamlets like Les Chailans, to which we referred earlier, created by a process of fission among the male offspring of the first generation of settlers, in the quarters of the bigger villages like Saint-André, where families with the same surname lived cheek by jowl. Rather as among Homans's villagers, the stem family here is not a rigorous prescription for conservation of the land and homestead, nor for co-residence necessarily, but a kind of nucleus around which the co-operation of siblings and cousins can be built up.

Even in the more orthodox stem family system of the richer peasants one notes the same emphasis on community. It is thanks to investment in the careers of younger sons that the future well-being of the main line is assured. From 1610 to 1711 the Simons, a family of local farmers and traders, succeeded one another, from uncle to nephew, as parish priests of Saint-André. The first of the line, Messire Honoré Simon, reared and educated his nephews, relieving the financial burden on his elder brother and preparing the clerical career of the next generation. At a slightly higher social level, the Férauds dominated the village during the seventeenth and eighteenth centuries as notaries and chaplains to a family endowment. The chapel of Sainte-Anne was a pantheon where the members of the clan were laid to rest; founded by a Féraud notary, its revenues allowed a member of the family to be ordained as priest at each generation and to say masses for the dead souls. What is fascinating about these families of the elite is their tendency to spread out and proliferate. The stem family did not work by restricting inheritance; rather it sought to put out more branches, subsidizing the careers of younger sons in the law and the church. The penalty of not doing so was biological failure or bankruptcy in a later generation.

Somewhat similar to the inheritance practices in Upper Provence seem to be those of the wealthy farmers of Burgundy, as recounted for us by Nicolas Rétif de la Bretonne in his famous *Vie de mon père* (1779). Nicolas set out to write an idealized account of family and community in the villages of Sacy and Nitry as he had known them as a child. The Rétifs were partly landowners, picking up plots here and there by purchase, and partly leaseholders; Nicolas's father, Edme, the protagonist of the story, held a position as seigneurial judge for a largely absentee Commander of the Order of Malta. Here, as in Saint-André, feudal controls on land transactions and feudal courts were still theoretically in operation, but were in practice exploited by the peasants themselves. Edme established most of his very large family away from the farm; Nicolas, for example, was apprenticed to the printing trade. It was the youngest son, Pierre, who took over the farm. In a sense, we have here a 'stem family system', though it would be misleading to define this too narrowly in terms of property (the Rétif farm was less a clearly defined unit of property than a patchwork quilt of rights and obligations, credits and leases). It would also not do to define it in terms of household structure: the Rétifs seem to have tried to establish their sons piecemeal in trade or in the Church or in farming with in-laws, recruiting outside labour to replace them. The stem family is, no doubt, better seen as a flexible response to certain kinds of economic challenge than as an 'institution' in its own right.

The survival of the stem family depended, no doubt, on a certain demographic equilibrium, a certain balance between population and resources. Demographic history has tended to develop recently on somewhat divergent lines from the study of the family. Its methodology is in great part closer to that of economics than to the other social sciences; nevertheless it cannot be neglected in any study of the family. One can detect several waves of population growth in Europe over the past millennium. The first, from the 'great age of clearing' after 1000 to a peak around 1300, underlay the expansive civilization of the High Middle Ages. This is the classic manorial period, the setting for some of the best-documented studies of the medieval peasantry, like those of Homans or Le Roy Ladurie (*Montaillou* 1980). There followed a great depression and readjustment. War, famine and bubonic plague dominate the history of the fourteenth century, reducing the European population by as much as a third. The recovery after 1450 was completed only by about 1650, when the landlocked villages of western Europe by and large returned to the population levels of the High Middle Ages, but hardly much beyond. Saint-André had reached a natural equilibrium by 1650: there were no further clearings to be made, and the old methods of farming could support no more mouths. Of course there were alternatives to the land: the working of wool, the cartage of goods between the booming towns of Provence. But further development here must ultimately destroy a particular kind of peasant civilization which had lasted, in one way and another, since 1300.

We know all too little of the demography of the Middle Ages which had made possible this first great expansion: low mortality? high fertility? Indeed, it is not often appreciated how little we know of the demography of the early modern period, in spite of a couple of decades of research. The problem is fundamentally that reliable and general series of parish records – baptisms, marriages, burials – are typical only of the period after 1650, when much of the drama is over. Nevertheless we can see something of how the demographic equilibrium of this period was achieved. The pioneering work of Pierre Goubert on the Beauvaisis (1968) still constitutes the basis from which any study of rural demography must start. He identified certain major constraints on the expansion of this northern French population in the age of Louis XIV: a high percentage of women, some 15 per cent, who never married; a late average age of twenty-five at marriage for the others; an extended interval between births of over two years (probably due to the inhibiting effects of wet-nursing on conception); the premature death of one of the partners to the marriage before the family was complete. These factors meant that the number of offspring produced by a peasant couple was much less than natural fertility would allow. The average was, in fact, 4.85 births; but of these only two or three survivors would be left at the age of twenty. Any tendency for the population to grow was further cut back by severe demographic crises, caused by a cycle of harvest failure, movement of grain, movement of rats with the grain, and spread of the deadly, rat-borne bubonic plague. Inhabitants of the Beauvaisis towards the end of the seventeenth century, Goubert tells us, would have seen several repetitions of this cycle in their own lifetime. Each time it meant the loss of 10 to 20 per cent of the local population, and a fall of conceptions by a third, cutting further into the meagre stock of youngsters available to marry at the next generation.

Goubert's picture of the early modern peasantry has occasionally been criticized (e.g., by Chaunu) as being too grim. Some studies of the same period, however, like that of François Lebrun, significantly entitled *Les Hommes et la mort en Anjou* (1975), are even bleaker. Whatever modifications we wish to introduce to the Goubert model will need to take into account variations in economic conditions as between the long-settled, crowded world of northern France and the frontiers of Europe. In the first place, where the land–labour ratio is more favourable, age at marriage is likely to be lower than that found by Goubert. This is the case of Tuscany in the wake of the Black Death, where we have unique information on the demography of such an early period. It is true at a later date of areas abutting on the last natural frontier of western Europe, the marshlands, only beginning to be reclaimed from the seventeenth century, thanks to improvements in technology. In one such part of Tuscany, the village of Altopascio, women were able to marry young, at just 21.5 years of age on average, though population pressure and consequent land shortage eventually pushed this up to twenty-four years by the later seventeenth century (McArdle, 1978).

One of the fullest explorations of the link between demographic and social structures is that of Delille on the kingdom of Naples in the early modern period (1985). Among the hill farmers of Campania traditional family holdings in *casali* were exploited essentially for subsistence. Land was scarce, the age at marriage was late, and alliances were contracted fundamentally within the community, with the sons or daughters of other farmers. The fertility rate was only about 20–25 per thousand, and the population grew slowly if at all. By contrast, down on the plain, in the grain-exporting region of Apulia, the peasantry had lost most of their land to the big estates of the aristocracy, and they had sunk to being wage-labourers or share-croppers or, at best, lease-holders. Controls on marriage and inheritance seemed, therefore, of little consequence, compared with the utility of producing extra manpower. The population married younger and had more children, the fertility rate being 40–50 per thousand; the small farms continued to be divided up at each genera-tion, with one or more siblings selling off his inadequate portion to go and find work on the big estates.

Demography, landholding and household structure are variables which are linked together in complex ways. Greater opportunities for employment in Apulia seem to have led to the peasant farm being treated as just one resource among several, fostering a trend towards equal inheritance, youthful marriage and nuclear family households. But such influences are rarely unilateral, because family structure is a variable in its own right and will feed back into the process of economic development. For example, the survival of peasant farms and communities in Apulia provided the landlords with a permanently cheap labour supply, which rendered mechanization unnecessary. Commercialized agriculture then ticked over at a very low level of productivity which one cannot understand in terms of economic theory alone. The relationship between the peasant and the land has to be studied also at the level of social values, and that brings us back to family structures.

In Sicily one finds a similar situation to that in Apulia. There the light dry soil could be worked with the Roman plough, which had not changed since antiquity. It was a simple piece of technology, consisting basically of a wooden shaft, shod with metal at one end and pulled along by one draft animal, typically from the later Middle Ages a mule. Subdivision of the inheritance had always been more feasible here than in the heavy clay soils of northern Europe, which required more elaborate machines capable of biting deeper into the earth and banking it up into high ridges for drainage. Those superb technological innovations of the Carolingians, the wheeled ploughs, needed six to eight oxen to draw, and a team of men to supervise them. The smaller, subdivided farms of the Sicilian peasantry made economic sense only in relation to the employment opportunities available on the great estates. Like Apulia, Sicily was a grain-exporting area, though we still know too little about how the big estates were actually farmed in the early modern period. In that age of bad communications and irregular markets it is better to think of these *latifundia* as holding companies, relying on their leaseholders and share-croppers, who were drawn from the ranks of the peasantry, rather than as big farms in their own right. They had the advantage of forming an ecological unit around which various peasant families could co-operate. Because the climate of Sicily was so drought-prone and the treeless landscape long eroded, cultivation had to be extensive, with only a third of the superficial area being sown in any one year. The remaining two-thirds was fallow, and part of the equally extensive pastoral system for which Sicily and the Mediterranean generally were famous. I am referring, of course, to transhumance, that once vast annual migration of sheep and men away from the scorched plains in summer up to the cool of the hills, of which the best known example is the Spanish *Mesta*. Much land had traditionally to be kept open and under-utilized in the Mediterranean, and the quarrels between arable farmers and pastoralists, between Cain and Abel, was one of the dominating features of social relationships throughout the area. Perhaps it is not too much to suggest that power in the rural Mediterranean lay less in property, which was too open to be fully exploited, than in personal relations, ties of family and of patronage which would provide the influence to keep the routes of transhumance safe (cf. Schneider and Schneider, 1976, pp. 74–9). There is a fascinating symbiosis in the latifundist areas of Apulia, Sicily and Andalusia between the nuclear family households of a small peasantry and the strong family solidarity of those who really hold power and wealth there.

What is becoming more apparent from recent studies is that we cannot properly understand the peasant family without a consideration of the feudal regime to which it was so intimately linked. In the fourteenth and fifteenth centuries plague and war, both occurring on an unprecedented scale, hastened the demise of classic serfdom over most of the urbanized areas of Europe. Something like a third of the population may have disappeared around this time, necessitating a drastic overhaul of the conditions of production. The abundance of empty land, combined with peasant insurrections against their lords, meant that in a broad swathe of territory, from Catalonia through western France and into England (where the extension of pastoral farming hastened the trend) the peasant became a free man, able to leave the manor and to subdivide or alienate his holding. He continued to pay rent to his lord, but this was fixed, and the land was largely his own. But this trend in the west was matched by an opposite movement in the east, which accelerated in the sixteenth century: the clamping of controls on the movement of a once free, frontier people, the rise of the so-called 'second serfdom' in Russia, Poland, and Hungary. There were several contributory factors to this process, which we can only summarize in barest outline here. One, in the case of lands along the Baltic coastline or the banks of the Vistula, with good access to shipping for western Europe, was the demand for cheap bread from the booming towns of the Atlantic sea-borne empires, especially Holland. In Russia, military centralization under the Tsars was probably a more decisive impulse, as part of the organization of a conscript army. In Austria, bureaucratic centralization under the Habsburgs seems to have led to a systematization of older, looser controls over the peasantry. Personal serfdom disappeared, i.e. old-fashioned, customary labour dependence, which must have grown out of service in the great households; but property rights were clarified, and those who opted to stay on the land had to accept more rigorous controls by their lords.

There is no single explanation of the 'second feudalism' which is such a characteristic feature of eastern Europe during the early modern period, nor is it necessarily a uniform thing. Generally, though, the cultivators of the soil seem to have lost a certain autonomy – autonomy as regards disposal of their tenures and as regards disposal of their labour. In Austria from the sixteenth century the peasant appears to have lost any right of dividing up his farm among his children; the unit had to be kept together in order properly to acquit the services due to the lord. A classic stem family system grew up in early modern Austria, centred on a cluster of dwellings in the countryside, a kind of solitary rural 'stronghold', as one author has put it, headed by a married couple, with a couple of rooms reserved for the retired parents (Rebel, 1983, chapter 2). To these households vagrant children could be attached by the authorities. The whole system depended on a tight control of marriage, so that younger children could neither split off part of the farm, nor alternatively establish themselves as cottagers elsewhere unless they had some employment. Labour was integrated into the stem family by a series of laws issuing from the royal authorities, though ultimately benefiting the feudal lords who drew rent from the peasant farms. In Austria the stem family was moulded by the increasing concern of the royal lawyers with maintaining rural order.

In the decentralized, aristocratic commonwealth of Poland a somewhat similar family system obeyed rather different dictates. Here the influence of a capitalist market for grain was more in evidence, and the requirement of labour from the peasantry more intense. Before the nineteenth century it was comparatively rare for big estates anywhere in Europe to be worked directly by wage-labour (even in the Mediterranean area they would tend to be parcelled out into several big leaseholds, at the very least). Rather the landlord would tend to encourage the growth of a peasantry on his estate – that is, a self-sufficient farming class, with enough land of its own to meet family needs. He would rely on jurisdictional or patronage controls to extract any labour which he himself might need, often on an irregular basis, since the market for grain (or for any other product) was itself so uncertain from one year to the next. Witold Kula (1976b) has noted how, in the case of Poland, the seigneurial domains would be worked according to the availability of labour: if the population was too small, much arable was left uncultivated, though if it was too big, then its surplus labour services might be sold off to a neighbouring seigneur. Revenue from the sale of grain, meanwhile, depended more on the actual volume of the harvest than on the price level in Danzig or Amsterdam. It was difficult in a bumper harvest year to stock the grain and wait for prices to climb. In any case the seigneur's prestige was determined more by the number of dependants he could feed than by his rent rolls. There was usually a horde of poor cousins at his castle in the seventeenth century, who had to be nourished. So, the bigger the surplus of wheat in a bumper harvest year, the bigger the gifts and waste. Agriculture in early modern Poland was 'producer'- rather than 'consumer'-led, and population was regarded as the basis of wealth (as it was indeed by all states before Malthus). There were laws against the emigration of serfs, inducements to local men to bring in wives from outside, permission for vagrants to settle down, so long as they accepted the obligations of serfdom. Essentially the feudal economy depended on a symbiosis between the needs of the seigneur for labour and the encouragement he could give to peasant families to build up that resource. The aim was always to avoid killing the goose that laid the golden eggs, by taking too much from the peasant at one time.

Inevitably such a strategy had implications for the structure of the serf family. It must be encouraged to be fertile, and so widows were often threatened with dispossession of the farm unless they remarried within the year. It must be in equilibrium with its holding, and so families which had lost the head or an able-bodied male might be allowed to sell off part of the land, or, more likely, be themselves transferred to a smaller holding. But, on the other hand, holdings must not be allowed to become uneconomically small through subdivision of the inheritance. Though we still know rather little about the actual structure of the Polish family, the estate regulations which Kula has assembled for the eighteenth century suggest a tendency on the part of the peasants themselves towards some kind of 'joint family household'. There are references to early marriages, to the crowding of fathers and brothers together in the same household, but also to the subdivision of farms. The last two phenomena are not mutually contradictory. We know from the work of anthropologists on the Balkans, where joint or multiple family households have survived down to the present, that these institutions are enormously hard to maintain. The quarrels of wives and jealousy over children put too great a human strain on such homes; they require the mediating hand of the grandfather, and once he dies the married brothers soon go into separate dwellings, though continuing to co-operate closely with one another, especially where herds are involved (see, for example, Campbell, 1964, pp. 72–9). One may assume that some such cycle also operated in early modern Poland. But by the eighteenth century the authorities were very keen to stop the subdivision of the farm, and to encourage something akin to the Austrian stem family. Can one suspect population pressure here? And may it be the absence of this deterrent which allowed the multiple family household to continue for so long among the Russian serfs? In the parts of Russia studied by Peter Czap (1978), for example, up to three-quarters of the residential units in the early nineteenth century contained more than one family, and girls were still marrying as young as seventeen or eighteen.

Population pressure by itself is not a good explanation, of course, for not only do we find these complex households on the eastern frontier but also in the long-settled lands of western Europe, typically among a share-cropping peasantry. As the same time as the 'second feudalism' was establishing itself in the east, a more subtle, less spectacular but ultimately no less significant revolution was under way in the western countryside. This was the accumulation of land round the big towns into the hands of a bourgeoisie – that is, a citizen class of diverse background (nobles, lawyers, merchants) whose distinguishing characteristic was that they had money to buy outright the property of the cultivator without the power to establish old-style feudal jurisdictions (though these often followed too, by purchase from the crown). It is a phenomenon which is under way round Florence in the fourteenth century, round Venice in the sixteenth, round Dijon in the seventeenth. For reasons which are exceedingly complex, this penetration of the countryside by bourgeois capital failed to alter radically the structures of economic life. As in Lockwood's Bosnia, two kinds of economy seem to have been in operation: at the formal level, one orientated towards contract and the market; at the base, a persistence of self-sufficiency and personal ties. These bourgeois estates were often farmed out to share-croppers, best defined as a category of wage-labourer who try to maintain a precarious economic autonomy as small farmers. As we noted earlier, large-scale farming with wage-labour is a feature of the nineteenth century; before then big estates were farmed indirectly, by settling some sort of colonist on them: a serf in Poland, a share-cropper in the early modern west (who would split his harvest fifty-fifty with his landlord). Share-cropping was a precarious tenure, often renewable annually. The lack of resources of the tenant ensured that he became, to all intents and purposes, the 'man' of his master, at his beck and call in all sorts of ancillary services.

One of the best descriptions we have of this kind of society concerns an estate of the Grand Dukes of Tuscany in Altopascio in the seventeenth and eighteenth centuries (McArdle, 1978). The duke owned the land, which he either rented out to substantial lease-holders for three or four lives at a time, or to poor share-croppers whom he supplied with seed. As in Poland at the time, the economy depended on the stimulus of cheap labour rather than of a buoyant market. Though the sharecroppers were nominally free men, they were constantly in debt to the duke, and the only way they could pay off thier obligation was by working for him. Such a captive labour supply was liable to be used wastefully. It could be invested in expanding the arable, typically through the building of dykes and the reclamation of the marshes. But, perhaps significantly, much of this work was done during the late seventeenth and early eighteenth centuries when, all over Europe, grain prices were low. It looks as though the duke was using his cheap labour to expand the volume of production at a time when the market was already saturated.

Labour was the key to the Altopascio economy, and it was reflected in family structures. The leaseholders were autonomous enough to pursue a strategy akin to that of Delille's Campanian peasantry, that is, establishing their children on separate farms and in separate households when they came of age to marry. By contrast, the share-croppers usually went on living together in the old family home after marriage, especially in the eighteenth century as land became scarce. Manpower was a source of wealth for them, a way of acquitting obligations to the landlord, and a way of staking a claim to a bigger farm from the available stock. The risk was that the labour supply would outgrow the resources of the farm, and then the duke would intervene to find work for the surplus members elsewhere. The ability of the landlord or his agent to intervene in the domestic sphere is, indeed, striking. An individual might have to be excluded from the family at his behest, for poor work, insolence or some crime, and his marriage would depend on permission from the same authority. It is an interesting reminder of how closely intertwined work and family were in the old regime. Also, as Kula has pointed out for Poland, the nature of labour requirements meant that it was not enough merely to have many bodies available, but that a balance of skills was needed as well. The head of the household was expected to keep enough land in his own hands to maintain a plough team, and also to have enough grown-up sons to send to reap on the lord's domain and enough smaller children to serve in the lord's kitchen or look after his small animals (1976b, pp. 194–5). Random demographic factors would determine whether he might have to recruit outside labour for this purpose.

One of the most detailed case studies of the link between labour requirements and the joint household is that of John Shaffer, *Family and Farm* (1982), which deals with the upland region of central France known as the Nivernais. The customary tenures of the later Middle Ages had been liable to escheat to the seigneur if there was not a clearly visible single heir at the peasant's death, a provision which encouraged married sons to stay on in their father's home, or at least to share the exploitation with him. But it was perhaps the development of share-cropping on the new 'bourgeois' estates built up in the early modern period which fostered the expansion of the multiple family household. Here, as in Altopascio, one had a peasantry lacking capital, whose single resource was manpower. On the heavy clay soils of the Nivernais, traditional agriculture made backbreaking demands, with typical plough-teams of six to eight oxen guided by two adult males, biting slowly into tough fallow. Most of the work had to be done in concentrated bursts, taking account of the weather – normally three ploughings of the fallow between harvest-time and the coming of the winter rains, in order to prepare the soil for sowing wheat or rye. The classic peasant autobiography of the Nivernais, Émile Guillaumin's *La Vie d'un simple*, suggests that an averagely large share-cropper's farm of sixty hectares would have required four males to work it (1980, pp. 223 and 242). What one notes in Guillaumin is the constant battle with time and the weather. Having labour resident on the premises is obviously an advantage because it can be drawn upon at short notice. A further factor in this upland region where cows are the chief source of cash is the haphazard labour demands of herding. Animals, in a sense, are like people, requiring urgent attention at certain unforeseen crises like sickness or birth, but for the rest mostly able to look after themselves. Pastoralism has been and is a perplexing industry when it comes to the management of labour, because the demand is relatively light over the year as a whole, yet intensive at points which cannot easily be predicted (a cow may drop her calf at midnight for example). Hiring labour on the open market to forestall these emergencies can be wasteful and expensive; pastoral farming is best carried on by some sort of extended family, where cheap labour, in the form of co-resident, married sons, is readily available.

The same result could probably be achieved by incorporating other kinds of dependants into the household, such as orphans or nephews. Extended families tended to grow naturally in the old regime, given the premature deaths of parents and the need to assign the bereaved offspring to a relative. Whether such relatives would take on the responsibility may have depended to some extent on the law: in the serf manors of eastern Europe such allocation of orphans seems to have been done by authority. In the freer lands of the west, much must have depended on the traditions of the area, and those, in turn, on a particular attitude to labour. In Altopascio not only did married sons live with parents, but orphaned relatives (or the widowed elderly) were quite regularly taken in as well. It is perhaps misleading to insist on biological kinship when determining the importance of extended families in a particular society. What seems more significant is the function which large households were able to play, so that servants would be brought into residence if kin were not available, and treated in a real sense as part of the family. Apart from Guillaumin, the most revealing printed source for French rural life is Rétif de la Bretonne's *My Father's Life* (1779 and 1986), a memoir of a wealthy Burgundian leaseholder. One sees here that balance of skills which Kula talks about for the Polish farm, the chief ploughman being the head of the household, assisted by a remote cousin, while hired labour looked after the vines, the oxen and sheep in descending order of age. The Rétif servants lived in and ate with the family, and listened to the father reading from the Bible after supper, or to stories told at the fireside in winter. They were local boys, known to the family anyway, 'and when their parents asked them why they were so keen to go into service in our house, they always mentioned the stories and the conversation in the evening' (p. 111). It was a recurring theme in the domestic conduct books of early modern Spain that the head of the household stood *in loco parentis* as regards the servants. Fray Antonio Arbiol (1715), in his treatise on the family, noted his obligation of instructing both children and servants in Christian doctrine in the free time after meals, for servants 'while they live under his roof have no other parents' (pp. 352–5). It seems to me that we should look more at the quality of relations within the household, rather than at the presence of biological kin, in order to understand traditional societies. The *familia* of old reflected an economic structure where cheap labour was more important than a buoyant market.

The end of this system, with the advent of a market economy in the nineteenth century, is charted for us by John Shaffer in his study of the Nivernais share-croppers (1982). From the 1840s improved communications allowed a shift from self-sufficiency in grain towards producing beef to sell in Paris. The consequent diminution of the fallows eased the pressure on labour at the autumn ploughing. Cash crops also permitted the tenant to accumulate reserves, and eventually move from share-cropping to leasehold, thus giving him greater autonomy. This complex interplay of factors, which we can broadly label an agricultural revolution, led to a decline of the old multiple-family households which had characterized the region in the past. The cheap, irregular labour which they had kept on hand was no longer adapted to the new conditions. It was a similar changeover from joint to nuclear family households which an agrarian enquiry of 1880 noted in the Emilia-Romagna area of Italy, formerly character-ized by the large homesteads of share-croppers. Here it was the reclamation of waste land and the spread of wage-labour in a more market-orientated economy which gave young people the opportun-ity of setting up for themselves after marriage, abandoning the old family farm. More intensive cultivation of the land also led to a fall in the size of the farms themselves; the concentrations of labour characteristic of the old extended families, as in the Nivernais, were just no longer adapted to the new economic conditions (Poni, 1978, pp. 201–21).

But the enquiry of 1880 also blamed a change in mentality for the collapse of the extended family: conscription into the army had become universal after the unification of Italy, leading peasant youths away from home and unfitting them, on their return, for the renewal of the parental yoke. It was this link between household structure and mentality which was one of the chief concerns of the school of Frédéric Le Play. Le Play's argument was that the growth of the economy in the nineteenth century created such a regular demand for labour that it made redundant the old family associa-tions. Children could afford to set up home for themselves at too early an age. This trend was encouraged by liberal legislation which specified more equal division of the family patrimony among all the siblings after the parents' deaths. Such independence for the young, argued Le Play, was illusory. The needs of the family would drive the woman to work; neglect of the children would follow. Alcohol-ism, 'the only relief from the fatigue of work and the cares of life,' and demoralization, 'habits of independence and promiscuity incom-patible with domestic order', would create a new phenomenon, pauperism. The poor of the old regime had ties of community to fall back upon; the pauper had none.

Le Play's ideas raise an immense agenda for discussion, and are fascinating because they try to grapple with the definition of a capitalist, class society in terms of family structure. Too much emphasis can be placed on that part of his argument which relates to inheritance, when this is only one part of his wider concern with how labour is recruited and remunerated under capitalism. But we may consider the changes in this area brought about by liberal legislation. The famous Civil Code of France (1804) made equal division of inheritance among siblings the norm, allowing, however, a parent to dispose freely of his or her estate in the following circumstances: up to a half if there was one child, up to a third if there were two, and up to a quarter if (as normal) there were three or more. The code did, in theory, limit the parents' options quite considerably, and some historians have seen it as influencing the marked restriction of births characteristic of French peasant families in the nineteenth century. The problem is that the Code did not automatically affect practice. As we have seen, in the Provence of the old regime, where the father could theoretically choose one main heir, he was reluctant to do so unless and until the other children could be set up in life. There is no reason to think that things changed much here after the Civil Code. Likewise, in the communities of the Béarn, where the pattern of economic life has changed little down to the present day, the farm is still disposed of to one heir, but on the same conditions as in Provence, that is, that the other children must be established in life. It was, as Le Play suspected and as seems to have happened in the Nivernais after 1840, where the market economy grows that the pressure to divide up the farm or to scatter the labour force will become irresistible. Rather than think of inheritance in terms of legal rules applied to property we should envisage it more as a set of guidelines for maximizing economic opportunity.

The Civil Code, Le Play believed, had been motivated by a new strain of humanitarianism. But there was another factor to which he paid less attention: the desire to prevent the re-emergence of an aristocracy. Rousseau, the Bible of the revolutionaries, made the point that democracy required an even spread of wealth. Indeed, for de Tocqueville and his contemporaries the very word 'democracy' carried connotations of egalitarianism which it has nowadays lost. No doubt the more restricted modern usage, in the sense of political representation, came in after the revolutions of 1848, as a reaction to the doctrines of socialism. The later civil codes – for example, that of Spain in 1889 – though modelled on the French, seem less concerned with establishing 'equality' than with laying the foundations of a liberal, bourgeois society. The old aristocratic menace had long gone; the new challenge of the later nineteenth century was to secure private property as a stimulus to the economy. Sigismundo Moret, who was later Liberal leader in Spain, as a young man attacked the forced equality of inheritance as retrogressive, preventing a father from handing on a functioning business or farm to his ablest son, and encouraging idleness and indiscipline in the home (1863). For him, as for Le Play, the English family, by giving a free hand to the father, was better adapted than the French to the challenges of liberalism and capitalism. In the event the Spanish code of 1889 marginally increased the father's freedom of manoeuvre, beyond the provisions of the old medieval laws, allowing him to advantage one child with a third of the inheritance (as under the old regime) and to dispose freely of another third (as against a fifth before). Sometimes, as Joaquín Costa discovered in Asturias, the peasant bundled the two thirds together as a consolidated advantage for one son (1885–1902, vol. II, pp. 102–3). More research is needed on this point; but it would clearly be a mistake to lump the civil codes of Europe together as favouring subdivision of the patrimony.

What they did do, of course, was to enhance the absolute property rights of the head of the household. Property in the old regime had been a way of ordering a political hierarchy, and carried with it troublesome social obligations. The great attack during the eighteenth century and subsequently on the entailed estates of the nobility and the Church as being economically wasteful reflected a fascinating revolution in the concept of wealth. One of the great commentators on the old laws of Castile in their final stage, the Galician Juan Francisco de Castro (*Discursos críticos sobre las leyes*, 1765–70), denounced the *mayorazgos* or entails for creating a miserable proletariat of younger sons who were costly to maintain for their elder brothers. The Spanish army did not need more officer cadets but more soldiers. One senses the transition from a society based on caste and patronage, where the younger sons were marked out as warriors because of their family background and were valuable as household retainers, to a world of cost-accounting and professionalism. The great estates in Spain, Italy and France, from being a prop of monarchy and a pillar of order in the countryside, came to be seen during the eighteenth century as a barrier to agricultural development. One of the reasons for this, frequently given in Spain, was that fathers were reluctant to invest too much in the *mayorazgo* since it would go to only one son, preferring to spend the money on establishing their other children in life (Castellano, 1984, p. 312; Sempere, 1805, pp. 348–64). One of the reasons for this phenomenon – which explains why so many aristocrats supported the liberal revolutions of the nineteenth century – must be a loosening of the bonds between siblings as political centralization rendered the old system of household retainers redundant.

The abolition of entails reflected a new attitude to property which we can see replicated in contemporaneous legislation against common lands of the villages and against copyhold or feudal tenures. There had been bitter controversy during the eighteenth century in Galicia about the status of the *foros*, three-life tenures which tenants maintained ought to be prolonged indefinitely by custom, and, in general, about the rights of landlords to take back land which had been leased out for so long that its 'ownership' was in doubt. Even in the rather somnolent Spanish countryside towards 1800 there was a growing desire for a clearer definition of 'property' and 'contract'. The older world of community ties and person-to-person relationships long survived, of course. But the liberal revolutions do not make sense without the tensions being generated by a new economic order.

What is happening is the transition to a class society. 'The bourgeoisie, wherever it has got the upper hand, has put an end to all feudal, patriarchal, idyllic relations. It has pitilessly torn asunder the motley feudal ties that bound man to his "natural superiors", and has left remaining no other nexus between man and man than naked self-interest ...' The famous words of the Communist Manifesto of 1848 (Marx and Engels, p. 38) could almost have been penned by Le Play. It was with 'proletarianization' that Le Play was ultimately concerned: the loss of social cohesion as economic opportunity generated a formless mass of individuals, impoverished, lonely and demoralized. It seems to have been particularly the cities which dismayed him. Urban growth in the early nineteenth century was, no doubt, a distressing phenomenon. The research of demographers suggests that mortality remained very high during this period, and that population increase depended largely on earlier, more frequent marriages, of the kind which worried Le Play.

The problem was that employment in the early nineteenth century remained so largely traditional. The trades of Paris or London, for example, were still those of the old regime – food preparation, textiles, building – though on a vastly expanded scale. So much of the labour was ill-prepared socially for its new environment, retaining strong links with the rural milieu from which it had recently come. Like the workers in Russian towns down to the early twentieth century, or the Turkish *Gastarbeiter* in modern Germany, the building labourers of Paris under the July Monarchy (1830–48), as memorably described by one of their number Martin Nadaud in his memoirs (1895), were peasants on loan to the city, who fully intended to go back to their villages. They came to Paris to work for a year or two at most. They took up residence in lodging houses behind the Place de Grève, near the town hall and the markets, or on the outskirts of the city, beside the walls. They constituted an all-male, violence-prone society, a breeding ground for crime and prostitution. This society was just beginning to settle down (in particular through the immigration of women) by the time that Zola captured its lineaments for ever in *L'Assommoir* (1971, first published in 1877). But what one notices still in the 1860s is the artisanal quality of the work – laundering, roofing, blacksmithery, provisioning; and its back-breaking, labour-intensive nature. For example, hauling drinking water up to the flats still had to be done by hand, while starching of shirts was one of those myriad, time-consuming tasks of a world both more vulnerable to dirt and more concerned to keep up appearances than our own. All this meant that abundant labour – male, female, child – was required to be on hand, but was never fully utilized or remunerated. In Zola's Paris the classic problem was the under-employment of the small trades, their lack of reserves, their petty borrowing, and ultimately their demoralization, symbolized in the tavern called *L'Assommoir*. At one level the story is about alcoholism; but for Zola, as for Le Play, this is but the most visible symptom of a deeper social problem. The tavern is the place where contacts are made and jobs found, a centre of sociability on which the workers will have to call when they are sick or out of work. Investment in friendship, which might be stigmatized as idleness by middle-class observers, was indeed just that: an investment against hard times.

What is striking about Zola's Paris is that it is less anomic than Le Play, with his focus on a traditional hierarchy, would lead us to believe. The family is no longer orientated around the defence of a patrimony, and no longer able to ensure the welfare of its offspring on its own; but the poor immigrants of the faubourgs have managed to recreate a small-scale community of mutual help, which recalls the solidarity of the village. After all, as Anderson has suggested for

Preston in the 1850s, immigrants were often to be found living alongside people from the same rural community as themselves. There was less anarchy and more 'structure' to the working-class family than one might expect. But its focus was now the earnings of its members through labour, rather than the defence of patrimony. This seemed to observers like Le Play to lead to a dangerous upward pressure of population through thriftless marriages. In his major study of the big industrial town of Lille, Pierre Pierrard noted: 'There is never any question in the folk literature of betrothals: at a dance or a party the man and the woman meet and size each other up, aware that each will bring to the marriage more courage than money' (1965, p. 121). This ease of meeting between the sexes could also lead to those casual liaisons which seemed to aggravate the problem of proletarianization. Illegitimacy, at which we had a preliminary look in the last chapter, was intimately associated with the economic growth of the nineteenth century, at least in its first half.

We need, before looking again briefly at this problem in the present context, to distinguish between country areas, where the illegitimate were in some sense the 'excluded' – the victims of a system of landholding which had no room for them – and the towns, where they were fully welcome as labour on the same terms as the legitimate. In those areas of Europe where some kind of stem family system continued to operate, like north-western Portugal or southern Germany, bastardy rates tended to be very high indeed during the nineteenth century, averaging one in five births in places. Since these were often very Catholic societies, with no evidence of anti-clericalism or a fall in religious observance, the trend is intriguing. Demand for labour in conditions of restricted inheritance must have something to do with it, though the exact connection perhaps requires further exploration.

But this problem of rural illegitimacy seems of a different order from that prevalent among the working class of the big towns like Paris. Again, Émile Zola's novel of life under the Second Empire, L'Assommoir, casts a penetrating, if partial light on the pressures at work. Here concubinage seems to have been a fairly stable arrangement. Its incidence seems to have grown alongside, rather than as an alternative to, an increasing frequency of marriage. For the heroine of L'Assommoir the civil registration of her second union is of little more practical consequence than the non-registration of her first. Since there is no property in either case the legal situation of the children hardly matters. Since patronage ties with employers, seigneurs or priests have been replaced by community ties within the neighbourhood, the culture of respectability has been replaced by one of loyalty. Marriage becomes a partnership, subject to the informal constraint of satisfying the other party. One should neither over-idealize the union, nor underestimate its stability. The role of women in the nineteenth century, as employment opportunities diversified, has generated a large literature and some controversy, and has become a growth area in family history. Terms like 'emancipation' perhaps miss the point – that though the working-class woman was earning more in a capitalist economy, and often not shackled to a husband (at least before 1850) by formal ties, her union was in some ways more stable than it had ever been. The reason lies in the changing nature of employment.

In many trades the old skills of the master craftsman became partly redundant as mechanization in the nineteenth century led to a subdivision of the manufacturing process into a series of routine operations which could be handled by less skilled operatives. In *L'Assommoir* we find the Lorilleux working together as man and wife, in a garret which is both workshop and home, forming the links for gold chains. In the days of the guilds such an operation would have been part of the goldsmith's trade, carried on as an all-male craft, with its hierarchy of producers and sellers. The rise of the 'putting-out' industry here, with the consequent specialization and simplification of operations, had given women a new economic role, reinforcing the family as a work-team. Such examples can be found in other trades as well.

Even the early factories represented less of a disruption here than used to be thought, since the employers preferred to deal with family groups. Until the 1830s cotton spinners and weavers would hire their own assistants, and these would often be their own children. It was only the introduction of power looms around that time which led the factory owner to recruit his operatives directly as individuals (cf. Anderson, 1971, pp. 114–18). Family employment was typical also of the coal-fields of northern France in the 1860s, as captured in another of Émile Zola's classic novels, *Germinal*. This well researched book shows us a system of payment by piece-rates, with employees of the company being assigned a part of the coal-face to work and allowed to recruit the assistants they needed, these being normally their own children. The wife would generally not accompany her husband if enough of their children were of an age to make up an adequate work-party.

The question of family structure is, as Le Play suggested, at the very heart of the transition to a capitalist economy and society. There is a new awareness of this among social historians of the period generally. Interesting attempts are being made to link working-class movements to the context of life at the time, trying to understand them less as precursors of socialism and more in their own terms as struggles to refashion a threatened artisanal and community-orientated life-style. The work of Louise Tilly and Joan Scott (1978), for example, by ranging over both family structure and the labour struggle, promises to shed new light on both. It would be a pity if family historians, in their legitimate concern with laying firmer, quantitative foundations for their own discipline, were to forget this wider dimension.

After all, the collapse of a feudal society cannot really be understood without the accompanying transformation of household, marriage and inheritance, for it had been through the family that labour was provided under feudalism. Taking up the point made by Kula and Chayanov again, a feudal economy operates with regard to the supply of labour rather than to the stimulus of the market. It is a world lacking the modern distinction between 'public' and 'private': instead of the categories of employee or citizen there is a single relationship of obligation which may be summarized in the phrase, 'the man of another man'. Regulating marriage, on the farm as in the guilds, was consequently of greater interest to the community than would be the case at the present day. Equally the patrimony of the household is best conceived of under feudalism as a network of obligations, to neighbours, family members and the seigneur, rather than as property in the modern sense. It would be misleading to set up too rigid a contrast, though, and to substitute legal ruling for the subtle nuances of everyday life. We might consider the implications of a story recounted by Rétif de la Bretonne in this regard. His father, as village judge, was forced on one occasion to award the land of a local inhabitant to an outsider. The latter had the better documentary title, but the former was known and liked in the community. The judge told the victor of 'his doubts concerning the legitimacy of the man's victory, with such force that he shook him', and used his influence to have another piece of land assigned to the loser. The latter, grateful for the the apparent change of heart by his opponent, thanked him 'with a small gift of game and poultry', went on to become 'the friend and protégé of his opponent in law, who constantly helped him thereafter' (1986, p. 105). Though some of the details of the story are obscure, the main thrust is clear enough: in mid-eighteenth-century Burgundy the freedom to buy and sell land was still informally constrained by consideration of persons. As in the Middle Ages, in the heyday of feudalism, wealth was reckoned as much in terms of friendship as of property. The separation of the two is one of the characteristic features of capitalism. It made possible the rise of domestic privacy which is the hallmark of the nineteenth century.

7
The rise of domesticity

In America there is nothing that we could call adolescence.
De Tocqueville, De la démocratie en Amérique

... as to American boys who are men at fifteen – I find them simply repulsive
Alexander Herzen, Childhood, Youth and Exile

The political stability and economic efficiency of the Anglo-Saxon world fascinated French observers like de Tocqueville and Le Play in the early nineteenth century. Part of the explanation, they thought, lay in the successful differentiation that had taken place there between public and private space. They admired what they saw as an intimate bonding of husband and wife and children, which taught the self-discipline required by a democratic society. Partly through the vesting of absolute rights of property in the head of the household, and partly through other cultural influences, the Anglo-Saxon family appeared to function as a team. It had cut itself off from those troublesome, particular obligations to patrons and allies, and adapted itself better to the impersonal exchanges required by a capitalist economy and the impersonal duty needed in a liberal polity. In short, the development of the 'home' was the necessary counterpart to the wider transformation associated with democracy.

The puzzlement of de Tocqueville and Herzen at some aspects of this new family, as reflected in the quotations which head our chapter, related basically to the rise of discipline. Youth in traditional France or Russia was a stage in the cycle of responsibility which an individual owed the community, a rather glorious time of communally sanctioned riotousness and wildness. Youths were those who could take risks because they had not yet the responsibility of a wife and children; in Greece they were those who were expected to bear the brunt of any feud. Youth passed away not with the years but with the assumption of a new responsibility before the community as a married man, heading a household. One of the striking features of youth in the old world is that it was a separate stage in life, not a preparation for what was to come. In one of Cervantes's short stories, 'La Fuerza de la Sangre', there is a fascinating insight into this problem. A young aristocrat callously rapes a girl, forgets about her and goes off to the wars. In a contrived sequence of coincidences which appealed more to a seventeenth-century audience than our own he is reunited with the girl and her baby, recognizing them as his own. He has done the right thing by the community, assumed his responsibility for a new household, become an adult. There is no hint of what we find troubling: that his conduct as an adolescent may have flawed him fatally for adulthood. It was precisely this rise of adolescence as a period of preparation rather than as an autonomous stage in the life cycle which seems to have marked the America observed by de Tocqueville and Herzen. Its new seriousness intrigued them.

The Victorian family was characterized by discipline and by patriarchy, and it is appropriate that the early anthropologists of the time, McLennan and Robertson Smith, should have spent their lives showing their contemporaries how novel a phenomenon this was. They attacked the notion that patriarchy was the original model of society, and the prototype out of which civilized states developed. Rather, in earlier times authority lay with a wider group. We may remind ourselves of Robertson Smith's words: 'There cannot be a greater mistake than to suppose that Arab society is based on the patriarchal authority of the father over his sons: on the contrary there is no part of the world where parental authority is weaker than in the desert' (1903, pp. 68–9). Fundamentally our modern family has grown up around concepts of household autonomy and discipline, which are the creation of a particular civilization, a man-made artifice rather than a natural legacy. There are many ways of approaching this particular theme, but one of the most significant is through the history of childhood. It is in the demands made of young people and in the training given to them that we can glimpse part of the adjustment which Europe had to make to 'democratic' society. This was the problem which called forth one of the most innovative historical books of our time, Philippe Ariès's *L'Enfant et la vie familiale* (1973).

It is the fate of classics that, after a time, they become worn, because their central ideas pass into common currency and their context is forgotten – rather like a bed or a path losing its shape when only the middle bit is used. Something of that sort has overtaken Ariès's pioneering work. The book is about the discovery of childhood around the time of the Renaissance, but surely not about childhood as such. It uses evidence about child-rearing as a way of exploring changes in the role of the family and in social hierarchy with the advent of modern times. Its concern is with the rise of that peculiar phenomenon of the West, the domestic, nuclear family household, rather than with the experience of growing up. Ariès pre-empted some of his critics by pointing out that he was not really exploring the quality of personal relationships, and not saying that a greater interest in childhood from the time of the Renaissance corresponded to a greater interest in children. The problem of love between parents and their offspring was a separate issue, and one, he thought, which probably lay outside the domain of the historian (p. 414).

There are two separate, though intertwined, strands to Ariès's analysis: one is the rise of domesticity, and the other the rise of the school. They are two parts of the same process, which is about educating the young for an increasingly professionalized, non-hierarchical society, in which status has to be achieved rather than being ascribed by inheritance. Ariès is, in fact, though not directly, working through the old preoccupation of de Tocqueville and Le Play with the Anglo-Saxon 'home'. We shall start by looking at some of the evidence he uses for tracing the spread of domesticity, and then go on to consider the implications of educational changes. His framework, I believe, is sound enough, but there may be some things to be said about the materials used to build it.

A considerable part of his documentation is a richly textured analysis of changing art forms. He notes that it is not until the twelfth century that Western painters began to depict the child Jesus not as a little adult but as a human infant, demonstrating a new awareness of the distinctive anatomy of the child. This development gathered pace in the later Middle Ages. It was accompanied by a parallel emphasis on the Virgin Mary as a mother, and on St Joseph, rather later (particularly after the Counter-Reformation of the sixteenth century), as a father. These artistic shifts are intriguing and convincing, perhaps less in themselves than against the background which we have already explored in previous chapters. The twelfth century was the great age of chivalry, among whose manifold features was a new cult of love between men and women, and a new emphasis on the human dimension of the Gospel story. Not only was there a delight in portraying the birth at Christmas, but an increasing attention to the sufferings of Christ in Holy Week. The

God of the early Middle Ages is a figure of power and majesty, somewhat remote from this world; the God depicted by later medieval painters is the bloodstained man on the cross. No doubt there was a deliberate reaction here by artistic patrons, churches and monasteries, to the growing threat at this time from the Albigensians, who stressed the sinfulness of man and the created world, and argued that the spirit must be freed from the body. A similar reaction against Calvinism, which also posited such a gulf, though in a more sophisticated way, might explain the iconography of the Counter-Reformation, which stressed that God had shared the hopes and fears of ordinary mortals. The sixteenth century, for example, witnessed a new emphasis on the celebration of Holy Week and the Eucharist (Corpus Christi).

This humanization of sacred iconography, at a time when religion established the norms of personal behaviour, must be of interest to the family historian, though its interpretation is not always easy. Less significant, perhaps, is the next step in the artistic revolution: the taking of the Holy Family as a model for depictions of the laity. From the Renaissance, those who give money to build burial chapels wish to be portrayed in paint or stone along with the saints, and with their human family beside them. There is a new concern to immortalize in this way even very young children. After 1600 these pictures begin to come out of the churches and are increasingly to be found in private houses. Simon Schama has recently explored this astonishing popularity of the child in Dutch painting of the seventeenth century (1987), but it can be found on a lesser scale in French art too. The implications of this shift – domesticity, laicization especially in protestant cultures – can be seized upon too quickly. Some of the most delightfully intimate pictures of parents and children at this period actually come from a Mediterranean setting, from the brush of the great Spanish painter Bartolomé Esteban Murillo (1617–82). The least interesting part of his production in many ways are those pictures for which the Victorians loved him, the sentimental but carefully observed portraits of children, cheerful young ragamuffins from the streets of Seville. Significantly, in view of Schama's recent study, the market for this work seems not to have been Spain but Flanders and England, whose merchants were well represented in Seville. Murillo, like most Spanish artists, avoided the subject of the lay family as such. The tombs and burial chapels of Spain, which generated some demand, continued to be dominated by the saints and by the coats of arms of lineages. There are, no doubt, special reasons for this, which remain to be explored: a reluctance to admit secular representations of the person within the sacred space, the occasional refusal, such as that of the synod of Granada in 1565, to allow funerary sculpture which might divert attention from the altar to the tomb. There may be an aftertaste of Muslim iconoclasm here. More likely there was a feeling that, while reverence for the ancestors was pious, and could be expressed through the arms of the lineage, depiction of individuals was vain hubris. Yet religious iconography continued to open for the Spaniards, as for the artists of the later Middle Ages, a marvellous way of emphasizing human values. Surely there can be no more intimate expression in seventeenth-century art of the domestic setting than Murillo's *Holy Family with the Little Bird* (1983, plate 8). The art of Catholic Europe is less obviously a social document than that of the protestant North; but for that reason it is all the more intriguing. It raises once again the question of the link between those two supreme manifestations of moral values, religion and family.

Art forms may reflect social values, but the equivalence is not direct. The same caveat applies to other kinds of evidence about domestic relationships. The greater personal expressiveness, for example, in letters and memoirs of the early modern period, particularly from the eighteenth century, does reflect a certain social change, but one which cannot be adequately assessed by taking the documents themselves at face value. Middle-class observers of nineteenth-century peasants were often shocked by their apparent callousness towards their wives. Even so level-headed and knowledgeable an investigator as Joaquín Costa who lived from 1846 to 1911, could write of the peasantry of Upper Aragon, among whom he was born, 'they are more concerned by the sickness of their plough animals than by that of their wife, because replacing a wife does not cost them money ...' (1885–1902, vol. II, p. 284). He went on to explain how comprehensible this attitude was, amid a rural poverty which would force a farmer to sell a field in order to get a new ox. This is not to say that genuine affection could not grow between a man and a wife in these circumstances, even after an arranged marriage, but rather that the function of marriage was different from that in a modern, urban society, and loyalties to the household as an enterprise overrode the more particular tie between the sexes. The evidence for parent–child relationships is not so much one of indifference – that varied from home to home as at the present day – as of a culture where childhood meant something different from its modern equivalent.

It is obvious that affection for offspring has been a constant feature of the human condition, even in the most adverse circumstances. The sheer proliferation of infant deaths everywhere before about 1850 should not mislead us into thinking that the bonding between parents and children was any less than today. Some of the most vivid evidence on this score comes from the letters of Estefania de Requesens, wife of the tutor to the future King Philip II of Spain, to her mother. From April 1535 we can follow Estefania's new pregnancy, her preparations for the lying-in, her joy at the birth of little Caterina in August, her fondling of the babe, who was, however, suckled by a wet-nurse. But six weeks later the child experienced a sudden spasm and died in her mother's arms, in one of those sudden infant deaths of the old regime, whose cause is not much clearer to us than it was to contemporaries themselves. 'This has brought back the pain I had for the others I lost,' Estefania told her mother, 'though I know I should thank God for everything, for I have three little angels now in heaven' (in March, 1941, vol. II, pp. 269–71). There may have been a problem here and elsewhere of lack of simple hygiene: the infant was crowded into a narrow apartment (there being not enough room in the palace) with its mother, the wet-nurse and its seven-year-old brother Luis, future governor of Flanders, then sick with measles.

The question of wet-nursing has sometimes been taken as an indication of parental indifference towards little children. As in the Requesens case, it need not have stopped a close bonding between mother and baby. It has to be remembered that breast milk was almost the only safe food for a baby in the first couple of years of life, and breast-feeding lasted for eighteen months to two years on average. A renewed conception during that period would cause the supply of milk to dry up, with potentially disastrous consequences for the suckling. Though ecclesiastics since the Middle Ages had been urging women to breast-feed their own children, this was hardly realistic advice for most middle-class mothers before the possibility of either contraception or earlier weaning in the nineteenth century. Tomás Sánchez, in his discussion of this problem (1602–5, lib. 9, disp. 22), noted that abstinence from sex during the two years of breast-feeding was not a sensible proposition. The reasonable alternative was wet-nursing. The Basque gentleman Esteban de Garibay (born 1533), tells us in his memoirs (1854) that his mother suckled him 'until she felt herself to be pregnant with my brother', when she handed him over to a wet-nurse. The fact that his mother often used to talk with him about it, and that both were very

close throughout life, seems to tie in with the evidence from the
Requesens case that wet-nursing did not interfere with the bonding
between mother and baby. It is true that we are dealing here with
aristocratic families, which could afford to bring wet-nurses into the
home. In the case of the artisan families of Lyon in the eighteenth
century, described so vividly by Maurice Garden, there was a massive exodus of babies out to the countryside, to peasant surrogate
mothers. Many did not return, and the whole nature of the parent–
child relationship was clearly different in this context (1975, pp.
59–84).

But our sources speak generally of a delight in children. The
memoirs of the Basque gentleman Garibay are full of concern at the
sickness of his offspring, the diary of the Cadiz merchant Raimundo
de Lantery (1949) for a somewhat later period (1673–1700) speaks of
his desolation at the sudden death of his eighteen-month-old son
Nicolás. It is not necessary to regard this as a particularly middle- or
upper-class phenomenon: the peasants of that well-documented
fourteenth-century village *Montaillou* were given to great expression
of grief at the death of their children (Le Roy Ladurie, 1980, p.
210). Among the Sarakatsani shepherds of Greece children are thoroughly spoiled at the present day. At the age of ten they mingle
freely with the adults and are surprisingly outspoken (Campbell,
1964, pp. 154–72). One is reminded here of some passages from the
letters of Estefania de Requesens describing the delights of both
parents in the cheeky retorts of their six-year-old son Luis to his
father: 'you are not well informed, sir'; or his scraps with the
Castilian pages in the royal palace, who ganged up on the Catalans –
'no milksop, but as much a man as if he were fifteen' (March, 1941,
vol. II, p. 196). What we seem to witness here is a pride in the
young as embodiments of the lineage. Indulgence of children in
traditional society was at least as common as in the modern West,
but it had a different function and context. We can see this in the
sphere of discipline.

Corporal punishment was certainly applied to children in the old
regime, but it fitted only with difficulty into an aristocratic, hierarchical society. Philip II was whipped when he was about four, in
spite of the tears of women about the palace 'at seeing so much
cruelty'. Our source, the Requesens correspondence, also contem-
plates a beating for Luis, because 'he cries very quickly if things are
not done just as he wants' – but in this case the father thought it
proper to consult his mother-in-law first to see if she had no objec-

tion (March, 1941, vol. II, p. 110). In fact, the rod seems generally to have been spared for aristocratic children. The sixteenth-century pedagogue Pedro López de Montoya, writing in 1595, observed that it was more suited to 'low, servile sorts', and that noble spirits were better corrected with 'honour and shame' (in Hernández Rodríguez, 1947, p. 374). A little later, Diego Gurrea, tutor to the future duke of Cardona, warned that corporal punishment should be applied only as a last resort to the sons of the nobility once they had reached the age of reason (seven years), 'for they are now little men, with their touch of pride' (1627, pp. 22–4 v). These attitudes persisted down to the end of the old regime. Chateaubriand recounts for us in his memoirs (1976, pp. 82–4) his fury and successful resistance when a school teacher tried to beat him for climbing a tree to rob a bird's nest; he was then aged about twelve. His near-contemporary, the Cadiz aristocrat Antonio Alcalá Galiano, was about seven or eight when he was threatened with a beating by his schoolmaster for not knowing his lesson. 'My father flared up in anger ... and believing that his own honour and that of all his family was damaged in my person ... took his hat and grasped his sword, determined to go and break the latter on the venturesome school teacher's back' (1886, vol. I, p. 39).

These anecdotes are, like so much of the evidence for the history of childhood, picturesque but puzzling. When set alongside the evidence given by Lawrence Stone (1979) and others for the prevalence of corporal punishment of the young in England – a growing phenomenon over the early modern period – we feel that it is inadequate to talk simply of indulgence or severity, but that these attitudes have to be related to some kind of social context. Like Campbell's (1964) Sharakatsani shepherds, the Spanish aristocracy often refused to whip their children, because they regarded the latter more as the embodiment of the lineage and less as apprentices preparing for careers in a competitive and professionalized world. Ariès (1973) noted that youths in traditional society were introduced very quickly to the world of adults. This could be seen, for example, in recreations, which were shared by young and old, before special games began to be devised for, or abandoned to, children in the course of the seventeenth century. When Luis de Requesens was only nine we find him tilting at the ring with a lance, though he was not yet able to mount a horse (March, 1941, vol. II, p. 329). And the following year he became a knight of Santiago, a royal favour which was perhaps not yet quite the sinecure it later became, but reflected the early induction of the young noble into the world of men. His contemporary, St Teresa, who was born in 1515, tells us in her autobiography how she and her brother read the lives of knights errant and saints (could they tell the two apart?) when they were youngsters: 'we made up our minds that we would go to the land of the Moors', she recalled with quiet irony, 'begging our way for the love of God, so that they could cut off our heads there . . . Having parents seemed the biggest obstacle in our path' (1980, p. 22). The literature for children, which was to develop in eighteenth-century England, was slower in affecting the more hierarchical societies of the continent. Antonio Alcalá-Galiano, born in 1789, was taught to read with fables, though it is a moot point at what stage Aesop and La Fontaine came to be regarded as specifically children's literature. His father, a naval officer, gave him a copy of *Don Quixote* when he was six, but then withdrew it, thinking there were passages unsuitable for tender minds. In fact, Antonio tells us in his memoirs that he used to read the popular romances circulating in the servants' quarters, like *Charlemagne and his Twelve Peers* (1886, vol. I, pp. 26–7). It would be difficult to distinguish this fare from the usual diet of the peasantry at the time, known to us from studies of the so-called *Bibliothèque Bleue* in France, or *Literatura de Cordel* in Spain, cheap ballads and fabulous tales hawked by pedlars.

There was, then, a certain shared culture of adults and young people in traditional society, which helped to break down barriers between social classes. In spite of this, youth was recognized as a category of life in its own right. Philosophers had long written of, and engravers depicted, the popular theme of the 'ages of man', the cycle of development through infancy, childhood, youth, maturity and senility. Our ancestors were aware of these stages; but Ariès is surely right to suggest that their function was quite different in a hierarchical society. It is a way of apportioning social responsibility, by drawing the person into the community. It is the equivalent of those depictions of society in medieval illustrations, thought Ariès, where one sees the man at his trade, because the social hierarchy is conceived of in terms of fixed groups and their occupations. There is no separation of public and private space; men in traditional societies belong to the community which confers upon them their roles through rankings of age and social responsibility. It is all very different from an industrial world where the exchange of professional services through the mechanism of the market renders redundant such a strict hierarchization of roles. Campbell describes the youth culture of the *pallikari*, an age-set among the Sarakatsani shepherds. They are young men who have done military service but are not yet married. Marriage and the headship of a household (which may have to wait until after the death of the father) are the real marks of adulthood here as in other traditional communities. These create new obligations towards the society at large, irrespective of age or biological development. The youth among the Sarakatsani are similarly defined mainly in terms of such responsibilities. They are the unattached young males, capable of bearing arms and unencumbered with a wife and children, hence more suitable for acts involving some personal heroism or danger, like avenging a wrong done to their family (1964, pp. 278–82). In French and Spanish villages of the old regime such 'youth groups' also had a fairly defined existence, though it is possibly unwise to invest them with too much institutional significance.

If youth approximated more to the category of an 'age-set', of the kind which anthropologists have observed among African tribes, with definite social responsibilities, this was no doubt due to their early removal from the home and induction into employment. From Rétif de la Bretonne (1986, first published in 1779) down to Émile Guillaumin (1980, originally 1904) we have testimony that the substantial peasant households of western Europe continued to have many non-family members sharing their sleeping and eating space – that is, servants, who were often young people from the neighbourhood, assimilated to foster-children. The Spanish word for a servant, *criado*, comes from the verb to rear, *criar*; and given that ten was the age at which service often began in the households of seventeenth- or eighteenth-century Granada, one can see why. Such people were no longer children in our sense, but not adults either. It is, above all, the apprentices who most resemble the status of the *pallikari*, with a clear group identity as tough and turbulent young men: their closure of the gates of Londonderry in 1689 against the army of King James II is a reminder of how different the role of the young then was from that which we expect of them today. Modernization seems to have brought with it a greater, not a lesser disciplining of the young. It is no less real for being subtle and informal, and those who cannot accept it are marginalized as hooligans.

The old world of hierarchy and age-sets began to give way, Ariès suggests, around the time of the Renaissance. One can see in the iconography a shift from portrayal of social status in terms of trades to an emphasis on the individual in the setting of his family group:

the wife is introduced in the fourteenth-century illustrations, working alongside her husband; then in the sixteenth century the child makes his appearance, as the scene shifts in these popular almanacs or *calendriers* from the street to the home. A change was taking place in domestic architecture, Ariès reminds us, which enhanced the dignity of the interior. From the seventeenth century the great households of the aristocracy began to get rid of their retainers and page boys and esquires; the servants who remained were in a different category of professional employees (no longer *criados*!), separated from the family by the invention of the back stairs and the specialization of rooms, with the bedroom becoming more private.

The 'privatization' of domestic space is a fascinating topic in its own right, and a few words may be in order here. Richard Goldthwaite has charted the rebuilding of Florentine homes in the fourteenth century, with a decline of the open loggia fronting onto the street and a rise of the enclosed courtyard as reflection in stone of the diminishing role of the clan and a new emphasis on the nuclear family (1980). At the same time these patricians began to move their banks and cloth shops away from their main residence in an interesting quest for domestic privacy. Florence was precocious, as Goldthwaite acknowledges, and it may be no accident that in this home of the Renaissance the individualized autobiography also begins to appear about this time. Genoa began rebuilding only in the sixteenth century, and even then the patrician palaces continued to cluster near one another in well defined districts; in Venice the home long continued to be a warehouse too. The separation of workshop and domestic residence was a long-drawn-out process over Europe as a whole. In mid-nineteenth-century Lübeck, as Thomas Mann describes it for us in his semi-autobiographical novel *Buddenbrooks* (1975), the great merchants kept their counting-houses on the ground floor of their own residences, and even stocked their wares there too. At a lower social level, as we have seen in the Guillaumin memoirs, servants continued often to live in with the substantial peasantry of nineteenth-century France. Nevertheless, one can hazard a guess that this overlap between work and home was beginning to decline in western Europe generally during the seventeenth and eighteenth centuries. One senses the movement, without being able to pin it down, in changes overtaking apprenticeship. After 1700 apprentices are less and less mobile, more and more either the sons of craftsmen fathers or their neighbours, living at home (at least in southern Spain) with their own parents and coming to work during the day. The increasing restriction of access to the guilds about this time, combined with higher life expectation, may explain some of the growing localism of recruitment. One may speculate that the Apprentice Boys of Derry would have received a good hiding from their parents had the great siege begun much after 1689.

A tighter family discipline may have accompanied the remodelling of interiors at this time, at least among the upper classes, as parents and children retreated within a suite of rooms increasingly separated from the servants. Mark Girouard has traced the process back to the fourteenth century in England, when lords began occasionally to withdraw, for dining or entertaining, from the great hall into their private 'chamber' (1980). But the life of the noble household was still dominated essentially by its public functions, and a numerous presence of kin and retainers prevented any real domesticity. The Civil War period (1640–60) really marked the turn of the tide, the disbanding of the last retainers, the rise of the 'cabinet' at the expense of the hall. Stronger central government throughout western Europe after this period seems to have led to parallel developments in architecture. The great Portuguese general and essayist Francisco Manuel de Mello commented in 1651, 'now it is a mark of distinction to run up private rooms and apartments ... and there are those who live as privately from their wives as they do from their neighbours' (1923, pp. 61–2). We may speculate that the search for privacy by the French kings in the eighteenth century, symbolized by the construction of the *petits appartements* at Versailles, marked the breakdown of the patronage system on which government in the old regime depended. Louis XVI's political problems stemmed not least from his personal unhappiness at having to live in public; more than a trait of character, it was a symptom of a crisis in the role of the household and its head.

What was passing away was a type of open household where subjects and apprentices were integrated into a patronage relationship with the master, approximating to that of fosterage. In that old world, as Ariès observed, the child stands in a special relationship to the community rather than to its own parents. One of the features of the old regime which impressed de Tocqueville was the young age at which people could assume positions of power, being elevated thereto through family background or patronage, whereas in a democracy such men would require longer training and greater competition in order to arrive (1963, pp. 336–7). The point is that status was apportioned to the individual according to the needs of the social hierarchy (stability, honour) rather than according to his professional capacity. The third duke of Alcalá became effectively an 'adult' at the age of fourteen, when he married in 1597 the daughter of the powerful minister Cristóbal de Moura. As his tutor commented, 'thereupon he left behind him the agreeable domain of letters and the sweet rule of his mother to go into the world of politics and the ups and downs of married life' (González Moreno, 1969, p. 59). Such precocity was, however, coming to be seen as a spoiling of the fruit before it was ripe. The assumption of responsibility according to status rather than preparation was at odds with the needs of a more sophisticated society. The Count-duke of Olivares was to set up the Royal College in Madrid to provide this foundation for the future governors of Spain. The foundation charter noted that it was no longer good enough that the nobility 'have no care or wish for anything other than getting by, so that they can carry on the past greatness of their families' (Fuente, 1884–9, vol. III, pp. 61–2).

It was one of the great merits of the Ariès thesis to have directed attention to the importance of schooling for the creation of a modern concept of childhood as a period of moral preparation. He noted that in the Middle Ages the school had a largely vocational bent, as a training ground for clerics. By the fifteenth century the spread of colleges, where the students lived a collective life under moral supervision, suggested that a new concept of education was abroad. Ariès drew attention in this respect to the writings of Gerson (1362–1428), Chancellor of the University of Paris and an influential exponent of the idea that a student was not just acquiring a professional qualification but learning to be a man. Education was becoming more diversified at this period, and literacy for its own sake an increasingly valued asset for the laity. Renaissance educators were concerned that their charges should acquire not just book learning but an experience of the human condition. The classics were to be studied for the (largely) secular morality which they would inculcate. Not all of this is new; but there probably is an increasing awareness of the complexity of social relationships in a more diverse, urban environment. The search for political legitimacy and for conditions of trust in one's fellows posed itself with a new acuteness in the urban republics of fourteenth- and fifteenth-century Italy. Here the principle of hierarchy based on orders of priests, knights and workers, and of theocratic government which had, in part, sustained the feudal monarchies, was first called seriously into question. What we know as the Renaissance was closely bound up with a quest for the foundations of a broader political order in the turbulent, anomic world of the city.

If one can see a single trend in humanist education it may be an emphasis on prudence and control of instinct, as a preparation for the role of citizen. Contrary to the norms of feudal society, where the impetuosity of the youthful warrior is valued, the ordered states of the Renaissance require self-control and dissimulation. The young must be trained in the hard school of discipline, and the precocious cheek of a youthful Requesens could no longer be countenanced. Diego Gurrea, tutor to the duke of Cardona, stressed the value of an ordered timetable of tasks throughout the day, so that the child learned to control his fatigue and frustration from an early age (1627, fos. 72–5 v). He noted that games, too, must become a source of instruction. Bowls, hand-ball, horse-racing, fencing, hunting were good in themselves, but sometimes dangerous in the hands of grown men, when honour or bets were at stake. 'When these considerations intervene, men ignore their health, wear themsleves out, and lose all moderation of time and effort' (fo. 72 v). Exercise here is coming to be invested with a new meaning, as a school for character. Ariès noted how adults began to abandon certain kinds of game to rustics and children in the seventeenth century. Wrestling, playing with the hoop, primitive rugby and many other sports had attracted all ages and classes of Frenchmen in the Middle Ages, but came to be considered 'unseemly' – pending their reclassification under new rules in the nineteenth century.

Ariès's 'small contribution to the history of games' has still been too little developed. But it does seem to be part of that general process of self-discipline which he saw as being under way from the Renaissance. The influence of humanist theory was less in this respect, he thought, than more routine changes at the level of home and school. From about 1650 the children of the gentry were no longer required as retainers in the big households. Order was guaranteed instead by a more professional army and bureaucracy, which recruited its members increasingly through the military academies or the lawschools. A regular pattern of entry to schools, and a more standard system of promotion through the various grades, consequently became the norm. It was still a curiously mixed career, though, where patronage and family connections continued to secure posts for the young aristocrat. Chateaubriand was educated for the navy in the 1770s, but obtained an army commission through the influence of his brother at Versailles; his Spanish contemporary

Alcalá-Galiano was enrolled in the elite Guards regiment at seven, and his regular schooling was virtually over by the time he was thirteen or fourteen. Nevertheless there does seem to be a greater regularity about the careers of the elite in the eighteenth century: fewer children accompanying their parents to war at thirteen, more of that slow grind through set classes in school and fixed rungs on the ladder of promotion which de Tocqueville saw as a feature of democratic societies. Careers like that of Thomas Platter, a Swiss peasant's son born in 1499, who learned to read only when he was eighteen after a vagabond existence, and then went on to study Latin, Greek and Hebrew in three years, before becoming rector of a big school in Basle, became unthinkable (Ariès, 1973, pp. 272–7).

The eighteenth-century Enlightenment, with its enthusiasm for education, its sense of individualism and competition, helped ease the transition from the hierarchical structure of the old regime. But Ariès is surely right to see this society as more stratified in terms of class than the old. The reasons are twofold. In the first place the greater standardization of the curriculum and of the age of entry to school meant that those children who did not come from homes which had prepared them for education by the age of ten stood little further chance. The Thomas Platter model was no longer applicable by 1800. In the second place, the household was turning in upon itself. The main difference between a 'bourgeois' and a 'noble' by 1800, one is tempted to say, was not so much one of pedigree, for that could be usurped, as of an attitude to life. The world of the nobility was that of patronage, through the personal ties of the great households, reaching down from Versailles itself. When those ties were clipped, as they were in the eighteenth century, one had an elite which, regardless of pedigree, had to compete for power, status and wealth through the exercise of its talents. The Revolution of 1789 did not so much abolish the nobility as register the demise of a political and economic system in which nobility made sense. The bourgeois home of the nineteenth century – self-contained and competitive – was not only a picturesque feature of the new age, it was the very precondition of liberalism itself. But with that new political and economic system went a greater distancing in terms of language and culture between rulers and ruled.

The twin revolutions around 1800, industrial and political, have causes which go beyond the scope of the present study; but surely the contribution which the family historian might make to their understanding should not be ignored. There was a transformation of the relationship between the individual and his fellows, which had enormous implications in the sphere of moral values. The Breton aristocrat Chateaubriand, at home in two worlds, recalls in his memoirs the subtle impact of school and church in disciplining the young warrior and preparing him for the new age. The 'sound of bells', marking out the time of tasks, accustomed him to the regularity needed in a democratic society. But it was the moral supervision of the young mind which is perhaps most striking. The preparation for first Holy Communion, at the age of twelve, had become something more than a 'rite of passage' into the world of men. By Chateaubriand's day, thanks to a century and more of Counter-Reformation preaching and teaching, it had become a delving into the mind. Chateaubriand gives us a vivid portrait of his own examination of conscience, his temptation to hide his shame, then his final coming to terms with his own weakness. 'I have not told you all', he manages to blurt out to his confessor. And he adds, as a commentary on the incident: 'I would say that day made a gentleman of me' (1982, vol. I, pp. 87–8). The words which I have translated as gentleman are *'honnête homme'* in the original; they seem to be used by the author as a comment on the contrast between the pre- and post-Revolutionary worlds, between the aristocrat whose word is law because of who he is, and the gentleman whose word is taken because of what it is. It sums up the shift from the hierarchy of the *ancien régime* to the hegemony of the nineteenth-century bourgeoisie.

I was reminded, reading Chateaubriand, of the suggestive analysis of Philip Greven about child-rearing and politics in eighteenth-century North America (1977). It attempts to link the revolutionaries of 1776 to a certain kind of personality: 'republican' or 'commonwealth man', god-fearing, individualist, self-assertive. Such men were the New England puritans. What is interesting about their background is that they tended to grow up in nuclear family households where the authority of the father and his capacity for moral supervision were very strong. The puritan child was disciplined from an early age by close scrutiny of his activity. He was invited to reflect upon his behaviour, growing up with an awareness of his own weakness, for which he had to assume full responsibility. Compare this, suggests Greven, with the experience of the Virginia planters, men who found the transition to a democratic society after 1776 in general more difficult. This Anglican gentry had grown up in extended family households where parental supervision was weaker, and where the moral tone was set by a numerous servant body. As children they had been accustomed to being whipped, like the servants, if found out. Their values tended, when they grew up, to be those of 'honour' – that is, putting a good face on things – rather than conscience. They had an unselfconscious loyalty to their own caste and an unquestioning acceptance of hierarchy.

With Greven we are entering the realm of what is sometimes called 'psycho-history', which has aroused more controversy than most branches of the discipline. The idea that the 'child is father of the man' has been enormously influential in our own century thanks to the work of Sigmund Freud. The link with history came through one of his disciples, Erik Erikson, who stressed that the way a child is reared is not the arbitrary choice of its parents but is to some extent conditioned by the culture of which they themselves are a part. 'I think that the psychoanalytic method is essentially a historical method,' commented Erikson, '. . . it throws light on the fact that the history of humanity is a gigantic metabolism of individual life-cycles' (1977, p. 14). The most celebrated attempt to apply the theory, Erikson's *Young Man Luther* (1959), has not met with unqualified approval from historians. Apart from the difficulty of using Luther's scattered table-talk to reconstruct his supposed *Angst* with a demanding father, there is the question of whether all this really helps us understand Luther's struggle with the pope and God. No doubt it is a useful contribution in its own right; but while the domain of the historian is essentially social relationships, investigation of the individual psyche must seem rather peripheral. The better approach for the historian, as another psychoanalyst has suggested (Hunt, 1972), is to sketch in the framework of social values which influence, and are influenced by, particular patterns of child-rearing – much as Greven has tried to do for early America. In this regard much more needs to be known about the transformation of personal relationships with the coming of capitalism – the separation of public and private space, the rupturing of ties of patronage, the enhancement of the autonomy of the home and of the father's authority within it.

This impersonality of social relationships was one of the features of America which struck de Tocqueville in the 1830s. Gone were the networks and kin groups of the old world; here nothing stood between the individual and the mass of his fellow citizens. Here there was no call for the values of altruism, honour and loyalty which had served the *ancien régime*; rather the emphasis was on '*une morale de l'intérêt bien entendu*' (enlightened self-interest), 'which forms a multitude of citizens who are disciplined, temperate, moderate, thoughtful and in control of themselves ...' (1963, p. 277). One is reminded here of the systematic self-discipline which Benjamin Franklin practised on himself for a while as a young man in the 1730s, as he tells us in his *Autobiography* (1948, pp. 74–7). He drew up a list of the virtues he wished to cultivate, such as temperance, honesty, diligence, discretion, determining 'to give a week's strict attention to each of the virtues successively'. He noted down in a diary the results as a way of monitoring his progress. Such systematic self-discipline was not completely unknown at the time or before. The Florentine merchant Gregorio Dati tells us in his diary how he made a resolution in 1404, at the age of forty-two, 'to advance by degrees along the path of virtue' by imposing a certain restraint on his activity: to abstain from business on solemn church holidays, to abstain from sexual intercourse on Fridays, to make a habit of prayer or almsgiving. 'I have written this down,' he tells us, 'so that I may remember my promise and be ashamed if I should chance to break it' (in Brucker, 1967, p. 124). There is a different quality, of course, about the moralities of Dati and Franklin; the former seems scarcely aware of that '*morale de l'intérêt bien entendu*', that utilitarian ethic, which dominates the writings of the latter – the consideration, as he tells us in one place, that certain actions were bad not because religion had prohibited them but because they damaged the perpetrator himself in the long run. Nevertheless, the quiet introspection of Dati is a sign of a coming revolution, the breaking of those exclusive loyalties and of that concern with outward honour which are the requisites of a caste society.

We might speculate about the conjunction of influences which made this growing individualism possible. The cut and thrust of urban life had, no doubt, something to do with it – more in a town of manufactures and modest fortunes like Florence than in the aristocratic trading empires of Venice or Genoa. Max Weber drew attention, of course, to protestantism. The Reformation undermined that collective approach to salvation which had found expression in indulgences – that is, the application of the merits of Christ and the saints to the community of the undeserving. Luther's famous protest against indulgences (1517) struck at the very heart of the medieval church; the rest of the Reformation, in a sense, was merely the working out of the logical consequences of that action – the abolition of special priestly intermediaries with God, justification of the unworthy individual through his own faith, the working out in fear and trembling of one's own salvation with the instruments to hand in creation. To do one's duty competently and honestly was the best that man could do, as a husband and father, as a peasant or merchant. Weber perhaps underestimated the late medieval legacy on which Luther drew here. Some of this spirituality would have been familiar enough in fifteenth-century Florence or Bruges, among the Brethren of the Common Life more particularly, and it also influenced the work of the friars, whose function, from their thirteenth-century foundations, had been precisely to enhance the dignity of the lay life, particularly of those merchants and artisans among whom they chiefly moved. Fray Luis de León, as we mentioned in an earlier chapter, was working with something close to the Lutheran concept of the lay calling, when he reminded the *Perfect Married Woman* that her prayer to God must be essentially through proper fulfilment of her *oficio* or state in life.

Nevertheless, Weber was probably right to suggest that the Calvinist legacy went some way beyond this, and was the real key to the fashioning of the Western 'individual'. Calvin's God was an inscrutable power beyond the ken of man. By breaking essentially with anthropomorphic concepts of God, Calvin threw man, to all intents and purposes, back on his own resources. The doctrine of predestination, that God out of all time and for no human 'reason', had elected certain men for salvation, had a terrible, compelling logic about it, which must have shaken old concepts of hierarchy and community to their foundations. Since there was no visible guide to salvation, the old Christian commonwealth effectively disintegrated, and each individual was left to plough his own lonely life course. Godly conduct became, indeed, the necessary but not sufficient sign of belonging to the Elect. Somewhat paradoxically, Calvin was committed, as we saw earlier, to the creation of a godly commonwealth on earth; but, again, this was a necessary sign of the striving of the chosen, not a sufficient means for redemption of those coerced into such a spiritual community. Calvin's community rested on discipline, not charity as that word had been understood in the medieval Church. This discipline, voluntary or imposed, took the form of attacks on idleness, fornication and dishonesty (as R. H. Tawney reminded the readers of his *Religion and the Rise of Capitalism*, 1926, the Elizabethan puritans attacked usury and enclosures with unparalleled venom). This moral austerity had no real equivalent in Catholicism, though there were echoes of it in the tighter parish discipline imposed by the Council of Trent (1545–63) and in the training of the young in schools. But what the Calvinists seem to have imposed on society at large, on both the saints and the sinners, was a new concept of social obligation, divorced from expectation of spiritual reward, ethically neutral (one might almost say), and applicable to all men alike. Is it too much to say that the very concept of society as we know it, as an integrated and egalitarian community, overriding particular bonds of family and favour, is, in fact, born around the time of the Reformation? The work ethic for Max Weber was this kind of scrupulous fulfilling of duty by the individual, without regard to persons, which made the tightly integrated and ultimately self-fuelling market economy possible. What Weber called the 'spirit of capitalism' is close to what Durkheim understood by the 'division of labour' and de Tocqueville by a 'democratic' society: it is an economic and political framework within which competition for status is regulated by universal and standard rules, free of the patronage and corruption which characterize less highly integrated societies. Ultimately it is the precondition of the modern 'home'.

Conclusion

I shall not attempt to summarize here the arguments of this book. To do so, I fear, would create a misleading impression that the history of the family had more of a unity of theme than it does in fact possess. Rather, my aim has been to suggest the complexity, but at the same time the fascination, of a subject which touches on so many areas of human experience. Like a torch-light or a litmus paper, the family is perhaps less interesting in its own right than for what it can tell us about social relationships generally.

The problem ultimately for the student of the family is that of remembering that he is dealing with a concept, a creation of men's minds and of their culture, rather than with a material thing. As a way of understanding social structure it can be as helpful or as problematical as its sometime rival, class. To pretend that the family is something else, a biological relationship or a household, is to risk impoverishing the investigation. It is natural that we should want to know a little more about where our Western family, centred round the conjugal couple and its offspring, came from. But to take the categories which are familiar to us – the household, the husband–wife and parent–child relationship – and order the data of the past round them may be to pre-empt the terms of the enquiry. To understand the past demands more of an effort on our part to understand it on its own terms.

There are two dangers in this respect. The first is that we treat family history as a discrete area of enquiry, divorced from a sensitive feeling for the religious ideals or political structure within which families belonged. It is the danger of specialization, so common a feature of the modern academic community, against which Ariès acutely warned. The second problem, related to this, is that we substitute quantitative precision for methodological rigour. Statistics are no doubt necessary for the social scientist, on whose findings about age at marriage and household formation governments may be expected to take action in all our interests. The 'lowest common denominator' of human behaviour is important to calculate in a mass,

democratic society. It is less certain that that figment of the calcula-
tor's imagination, the 'man in the street', who marries at twenty-five,
lives alone with his wife and two children, and probably by the year
2020 will divorce at forty, is helpful for that branch of learning
known as the humanities. Statistics have helped the historian in all
sorts of ways to capture better the profile of the ordinary man in the
past, and for that we must be grateful. But they are an approxima-
tion to the truth. They create an 'ideal type', with which government
planners may be forced to work, but which the academic community
should surely, if it is to justify its existence, call constantly into
question. The point is simply that quantification creates a two-
dimensional frame of reference; it should be the aim of the family
historian to provide the missing third dimension.

Traditionally this has been done by the novelist, alive to the
infinite nuances of individual behaviour and particular situations.
The technique of the historian, particularly in such a sensitive area
as that of the family, may have to approximate more to that model.
It was once done, rather brilliantly, by the social anthropologists in
the course of their observations in the field. The trend in that
discipline, however, in recent years, has been towards more theoretical, comparative studies. The resulting mathematical models of
human behaviour, though neat, leave the historian feeling uneasy. In
order to understand why one society operates with dowry at marriage
and another with bridewealth, why in one cross-cousins marry and in
another parallel cousins, the matching of a fixed list of variables is
probably no substitute for a less ambitious attempt to study just one
of those societies in the round. Some anthropologists have, indeed,
been proponents of a 'thick description' of human behaviour, which
would leave more of the options for later interpretation open. History has traditionally been good at description but poor at theory.
The family, perhaps more than other themes, now faces it with the
stark challenge of doing both, if it wants to advance.

The family historian, like others in the discipline, has been hap-
piest when working close to his sources, close to what he can
measure. Much of the historical material on the European family is
to be found in censuses of the population and in registers of births,
marriages and deaths. Both kinds of document are organized, by and
large, in terms of household, and it has been round the structure of
the household that most good historical studies of the family have
centred in recent years, at least in the post-medieval period. We have
had classifications of household by type – complex, stem, nuclear,

joint (see glossary) – and attempts to compare across cultures and over time as a way of understanding social process. A certain unease with the limitations of this methodology has become apparent in some recent publications, with scholars seeking to explore ties beyond the household – and, indeed, seeking to redefine the *familia* in terms of the servant body as well as of co-resident kin. We are reaching the point, it seems to me, where analysis of the household in its own right, as an institution, will give diminishing returns on the investment of effort by the student. The point is, surely, that the household or the family are merely heuristic concepts which help us explain the economic and political structure of a particular society; they are not self-contained entities which can be studied in themselves. One cannot build a house by piling one brick on top of another; one cannot understand an economy or a polity by multiplying studies of household organization. There has to be an architect's plan, an ability to grasp the totality of the finished structure, first and foremost.

Braudel once said that history starts with a problem. The family, to the nineteenth-century pioneers of the discipline, seemed to provide a central core from which one could explore the changing structure of entire civilizations. The ambition of their successors is clearly much more modest, and they have been willing to accept the greater specialization, with its consequent limitations, of modern social science. The problem with this is that the family, as a discrete field of research, is of somewhat marginal relevance to European history. All the studies which have been published in recent times, emphasizing the predominance of the nuclear family household or the continuity of conjugal sentiment in the past, have rather tended to strip away the romance or exoticism once surrounding the supposedly more barbarous life of our ancestors. The quest for truth is admirable, but the European family has become more prosaic and dull – which poses more acutely the old question: Why bother studying it? The answer is, surely, the same as Le Play or de Tocqueville might have given, which is that the family was a way of ordering social and political life, and generated a set of values, which marked the very distinctive culture of the pre-industrial world. It was a substitute for the bureaucracies and the markets which now rule virtually all our lives in the West; it was a principle of conduct, of the kind more familiar to us from ancient Rome where piety was equivalent to reverence for ancestors. There is surely a tremendous agenda for co-operation here among historians of the Christian religion, of feudalism and of the advent of capitalism. '"It is fear of history on the grand scale which has killed history on the grand scale" ... May it rise again!' Braudel's words in the preface to his classic study of the Mediterranean (1972–3) sound both a warning and a challenge for the history of the family.

Suggestions for further reading

Chapter 1   The meaning of family

One will want to start with the Victorian pioneers, who laid the
foundations of the subject and who are still immensely stimulating to
read. Lewis Henry Morgan (1974; originally published 1877) marries
theory and description in his study of clan among the Iroquois and
the ancients. John F. McLennan (1970; originally published 1865) is
more schematic and less attractive. The problems he raises about
matriliny and exogamy are better approached through W. Robertson
Smith (1903; originally published 1885).

Claude Lévi-Strauss (1969), dedicated to Morgan, is the most
ambitious attempt since that time to reduce the variety of family
forms to a system. Its flavour can be captured in Robin Fox (1967),
an interesting overview, avowedly more concerned with the 'mecha-
nics' of family structures than with their function, which perhaps
thereby limits its usefulness for the historian. The 'mechanical'
model, tending towards the abstract, is combated by Pierre Bourdieu
(1977), which stresses that family systems are less rule-based and
more flexible responses to local ecologies. This emphasis on understanding the 'function' of the family in its local setting comes
through in the classic A. R. Radcliffe-Brown and Daryll Forde
(1987, originally published 1950). I have used, rather, Radcliffe-
Brown's collected essays (1952).

Changes in family structure as a historical problem really began to
excite the European imagination in the early nineteenth century.
French thinkers, confronted more acutely than most of their contemporaries with the problem of refashioning social hierarchy and political legitimacy in a period of democratic upheaval, were pioneers
here. Some of the finest insights into the links between family and
social structure are still to be found in Frédéric Le Play (1864),
much more sophisticated and nuanced than the better-known *L'Organisation de la Famille* (1871), and the equally subtle N. D. Fustel
de Coulanges (1984; originally published 1864), of which there is an
old English translation (Boston, 1900).

The best single introduction to the history of the family, because of the sheer range and diversity of its approaches, must be R. Forster and O. Ranum (1976). Good overviews of the ancient and medieval periods are to be found in David Herlihy (1985) and Jack Goody (1983), while for the early modern period there is Jean-Louis Flandrin (1979), and for the more modern, Michael Mitterauer and Reinhard Sieder (1982). There is a considerable literature on England, of which in some ways still the most stimulating, because of its imagination and breadth, is Peter Laslett (1965; third edition, 1983). A good, up-to-date survey is Ralph Houlbrooke (1984).

I read the comprehensive and attractive F. and J. Gies, *Marriage and the Family in the Middle Ages* (New York 1987) too late for incorporation in the text.

Chapter 2   The role of the ancestors

My approach to the question of the role of family and of caste in the organization of traditional society was stimulated by reading Émile Durkheim, (1964, originally published 1893), and Alexis de Tocqueville (1963; originally published 1835–40), of which there are several English translations. The most stimulating case study of a clan society must still be E. E. Evans-Pritchard (1969). The essays of Meyer Fortes (1969 and 1970) are also fundamental on concepts of lineage. Perhaps the most useful case study of kinship in the European domain, an infertile field for the anthropologist, is the beautifully written J. K. Campbell (1964). Many of the writings of Louis Dumont turn on the question of individualism, hierarchy and caste. See especially his *Homo hierarchicus* (1966; English translation, 1980) on caste in India.

In medieval Europe the intertwining of lineage and caste can be followed in studies of the nobility. Two classic introductions, on which I have drawn here and elsewhere in the book, are Marc Bloch (1965; original French edition, 1939–40) and R. W. Southern (1987; originally published 1953). A more specific focus on family is provided by Georges Duby (1981; English translation, 1984) and by J. C. Holt's recent study of the evolution of primogeniture among the English baronage after 1066 (1982–5). Particularly helpful on the concept of lineage among the continental nobility are Timothy Reuter (ed.) (1978) and Léopold Génicot (1982). For the Hispano-Arabic frontier and potentially diverging structures of descent, see Pierre

Guichard (1977). On the bilateral kindreds of the Germanic peoples I have found informative Alexander C. Murray (1983).

On the more modern period I have found contemporary memoirs of noble lineages very enlightening. I have drawn heavily in the text on Gonzalo Argote de Molina (1957) and on Martín de Viciana (1972), especially volume II. On France there is much still to be learned about the self-definition of the elite from biography and autobiography. Particularly useful are Charles de Ribbe's edition (1879) of the memoirs of Jeanne de Laurens, and François-René de Chateaubriand, (1976), *Mémoires de ma vie* (the manuscript of 1826) which seem a little richer than the polished version delivered for publication as *Mémoires d' outre-tombe* (1982; originally published 1848–50), of which there is an English translation. Almost any good study of the aristocracy of the period has considerable information on family structure. This literature can be approached through Jonathan Powis (1984).

On religion and the family, the editor of this series has drawn my attention to Constance B. Bouchard, *Sword, Miter and Cloister: Nobility and the Church in Burgundy 780–1198* (1987). And I feel I ought to have made greater use of the superb H. S. Maine, especially his *Ancient Law* (1861), a worthy complement to Durkheim.

Chapter 3   The politics of family

A fundamental introduction to the role of the family as the hub of political institutions in simpler societies is provided by Evans-Pritchard (1969). Much of the best ethnographic work in this domain has centred on the more complex societies of Islam, where there has been an intriguing interplay between city, state and tribe. Still thought-provoking is Robert Montagne (1973), partly modified by Ernest Gellner (1969). One of the most impressive of these studies of feud, faction and 'feudalism' in a tribal setting is Fredrik Barth (1965). But the interested reader will want to turn also to Ibn Khaldūn (1967) for an unrivalled fourteenth-century insight into the political sociology of complex tribal societies. The best commentary on Ibn Khaldūn's approach is Ernest Gellner (1981).

I have drawn heavily on a couple of epics for an insight into feuding and feudalism in the medieval period, particularly *The Song of Roland* (1957) and *The Nibelungenlied* (1965). These can be set in context by looking at J. M. Wallace-Hadrill (1962) and the classic

Bertha Phillpotts (1913). Alexander C. Murray (1983) provides a careful textual criticism of the Barbarian codes, informed by anthropological insights.

Family history can throw light on the problem of political authority in medieval Europe, as Andrew W. Lewis demonstrates with his study of royal dynasticism (1981).

The distinctiveness of European forms of political order was one of the preoccupations of Max Weber, whose *The City* (1960) raises many questions for the historian of the family. That Weber overestimated the distinctiveness and cohesion of the urban community in Europe is becoming apparent from research on the northern shore of the Mediterranean, where family groupings often carved out town space among them in a way more reminiscent of Islam or China. For the role of lineages in the Italian cities of the Middle Ages and Renaissance, see Hughes (1975), Heers (1977) and Kent (1977). Richard Goldthwaite (1968) takes a different line, emphasizing the 'individualism' of the Florentines, particularly in the field of business. Clearly it is important in this area to distinguish the context: lineage may have more relevance in some spheres than others – more, for example, in the struggle for power in a 'republican' and competitive political system than under the Medici, more in building up a party following than in conducting a successful trading enterprise.

Renaissance Spain, like Italy, was fertile in feuds, still too little explored. The fascinating contemporary account by a Basque noble, Lope García de Salazar (1884; written c.1471), has been studied by Julio Caro Baroja (1956). But it is really in the competitive 'democracies' of the communes – rather like those of Italy in being dominated largely by an aristocracy with strong rural ties – that the vendetta flourished. There are some useful insights in Juan Moreno de Guerra (1929), but more particularly in the stimulating study of Marie-Claude Gerbet (1979), which pays great attention to family structures. On the way in which these lineages adapted to the coming of absolutism in Spain much remains to be done. One of the best explored dynasties is that of the Mendoza, on whom there are most informative studies by Angel González Palencia with Eugenio Mele (1941–3) and by Helen Nader (1979).

On feuding generally, the works by J. Black-Michaud (1975) and Stephen Wilson (1988) ought to be cited for their contributions to methodology and to the understanding of Mediterranean family structures.

Chapter 4   The arranged marriage

On the definition of marriage and its function in tribal societies one
cannot do better than go back to McLennan, Robertson Smith and
Morgan (see section for chapter 1). More sophisticated and nuanced
approaches, based on a greater range of field research, will be found
in those I would describe as their intellectual heirs, Claude Lévi-
Strauss and Robin Fox, whose key works have also been mentioned
above. One will want to add to the list of theorists Jack Goody,
(1976), which is perhaps the most useful of that author's many
contributions in the key area of female inheritance in Eurasia and its
consequences for matrimony. Linked to this topic is the question of
endogamy, of which anthropologists have made heavy weather.
Their work is sampled and criticized in Jean Cuisenier (1975) and
Pierre Bourdieu (1977).

   The historical conundrum of Europe, where female inheritance
did not lead to endogamy, has been explained by Jack Goody in
terms of Christian influence (1983). A key study of the Christian law
of matrimony and of its relation to social practice is Jean Gaudemet
(1987).

   On the actual practice of the Germanic peoples I have relied much
on Gregory of Tours (1974) and on *The Nibelungenlied*, cited in the
section for chapter 3. These should be set in context with Suzanne
F. Wemple (1981). They may be contrasted with the trend towards
greater endogamy in urban societies, when the dowry becomes the
typical form of marriage prestation. One of the richest insights into
medieval families anywhere, and particularly good on marriage, is
S. D. Goitein (1978).

   The link between dowry, lineage and monogamy is the main
theme of Georges Duby's study (1981) cited in the section for
chapter 2 above. Also useful here are Pauline Stafford (1983) and,
particularly on property, David Herlihy (1978). Fascinating questions about the role of dowry in relation to the hypergamy of women,
breaking with older forms of vassalage and hierarchy, are raised by
The Poem of the Cid (1984). The context of this document is now a
lot clearer in some respects thanks to Heath Dillard (1984), though
she deals with a different social layer from that of the Cid. The
relationship of marriage forms to social hierarchy is explored in the
pioneering article of J. E. Ruiz Domenec (1979). Finally there is
useful information on the shift in marriage prestations at this time in
Diane Owen Hughes (1978).

For the more modern period, Alan Macfarlane (1986) is an interesting attempt to link marriage with forms of property and inheritance. Much of the best work on this period concerns this kind of link, often in the form of case studies of the peasantry, and may best be left for discussion in the section for chapter 6 below.

Chapter 5   The nature of passion

This most delicate area, concerned with the construction and control of sexual roles, requires some understanding of the cultures to which they relate. The anthropology of honour, that particularly Mediterranean institution, helps us set relationships between the sexes in a broader social context. Important here are Germaine Tillion (1966) and Julian Pitt-Rivers (1977).

Michel Foucault (1979–85) adopts a philosophical approach to the history of human relationships, and provides an important insight into the nature of discourse. He asks us to see sexuality less as a biological urge which has to be restrained by law and more as a set of variable norms which mould human culture. This relativist approach, as applied to the literature of chivalry, has deepened our understanding of the medieval mentality. Independent of Foucault, though sharing his interest in sexual expression as a key to social values, are Denis de Rougemont (1972) and Jean Leclercq (1979). Sensitive reconstruction of family rituals of the past may lay bare latent meanings, and help us take these societies more on their own terms instead of measuring them by the values which we hold important. This seems to me one of the great virtues of the investigations developed by Christiane Klapisch-Zuber (1985) and, for the nineteenth century, Martine Segalen (1983).

Surveys of court records are somewhat more problematic when it comes to reconstructing sexual behaviour in the past (historians of crime have faced similar questions about their own work), and the same reservation would apply to the legalistic literature on the subject written by canonists and theologians. The fare may be sampled in Jean-Louis Flandrin (1981) and Guido Ruggiero (1985). Somewhat wider in scope is Robert Wheaton and Tamara K. Hareven (1980). The interpretation of legal records requires much attention to the way the courts themselves worked. Inspiring in this respect are R. H. Helmholz (1974), Alain Lottin (1975) and John T. Noonan, Jr. (1972). One of the problem areas, the significance of clandestine marriage, cannot be tackled without an awareness of the social context. Fundamental here is Verena Martínez-Alier, (1974). Luis Martín (1983) is one of the few studies of the role of women in the Hispanic domain in the early modern period.

The rise of protestant discipline is best approached through Steven Ozment (1983), an important survey of the attitudes of the German Reformers. More insight into the working of marriage courts under protestantism is provided by Thomas Max Safley (1984). The English experience is perhaps now best approached through R. B. Outhwaite (1981). On the allied problem of illegitimacy, its fall in the seventeenth century and subsequent revival on the threshold of modern times, see P. Laslett, K. Oosterveen and R. M. Smith (1980). On the medieval period, there is much information on the continuing honour accorded to the illegitimate in Chris Given-Wilson and Alice Curteis (1984). One of the fundamental issues about illegitimacy, already adumbrated by Engels and Le Play from different perspectives, is its relationship to the growth of a class-rather than estate-orientated society in the nineteenth century. That is, the very definition of the industrial or rural proletariat was coming to be its lack of a stable home environment. This issue has been raised again very interestingly by Brian J. O'Neill for rural Portugal in the late nineteenth and early twentieth centuries (1987).

It would be churlish to end without mentioning two nice case studies illustrating different aspects of men–women relationships in the Renaissance: Gene Brucker and Steven Ozment (1986). But surely the richest of such portraits is that of the fourteenth-century Florentine, Francesco di Marco Datini, whose voluminous correspondence constitutes the nucleus of Iris Origo's classic book, *The Merchant of Prato* (1963).

Chapter 6   The economics of the household

The key contribution of anthropology in this area has been to demonstrate that property in pre-industrial society is less a capital asset and more a strand in community networks. The concept comes across forcefully in Paul Stirling (1965), J. Davis (1973) and William G. Lockwood (1975). Jack Goody (1976), already cited in the section on chapter 4, is the best introduction to the problem of inheritance as it affects family structures. The whole topic depends on an understanding of how pre-industrial economies work, and the best intro-

ductions here seem to me to be A. V. Chayanov (1966) and Witold
Kula (1976).

The most delightful case study of the relationship between the
peasant economy and the family is surely still George C. Homans
(1975). The attack on its main thesis by Alan Macfarlane (1978) is
stimulating in its own right, because it tackles the important question of the transition from feudal to capitalist economy from the
novel angle of family structure. But it rather overshoots its target by
setting up an unrealistically rigid model of a peasant economy, and
does not do full justice to the subtlety of Homans's argument.
Barbara Hanawalt's recent book on the English peasant family of the
fourteenth century (1986) is a lively, if essentially descriptive, survey
based on her deep knowledge of coroner's court records. There has
been an abundance of research into the topic of the medieval English
peasant household and economy, which is best approached through
Richard M. Smith (1984).

For early modern Europe, an older collection of articles on family
and inheritance edited by Jack Goody and others (1976) still re-
tains its usefulness. But the best approach may now be through
particular case studies. First, one should read the sensitively written
Alain Collomp (1983), a little gem on the stem family of one community in early modern France. Then there is Gérard Delille's
rigorous comparison of demographic structures in two contrasting
regions of the old kingdom of Naples, linking these to differing
patterns of landholding and inheritance (1985). On the particular
ecology of the peasant joint family, one will want to consult Frank
McArdle (1978) on an early modern Tuscan village, and John W.
Shaffer (1982) on the Nivernais in east-central France. Shaffer is
particularly instructive on the impact of modernization in the
nineteenth century. His work should be complemented from the
'inside', as it were, by the 'autobiography' of an autodidact of
peasant stock from the same area, Émile Guillaumin (1980). More
romanticized but nonetheless illuminating on peasant family life and
work in eighteenth-century France are the memoirs of Nicolas Rétif
de la Bretonne (1986). One of the most vivid insights into this topic
comes from a somewhat unusual source, the record of the persecution of the Cathar heresy by the local bishop in the Pyrenean village
of Montaillou in the early fourteenth century. Le Roy Ladurie's
study (1980) of this now famous community will, I hope, be set one
day in the context of a fuller exploration of the peasant economy of
the area at the time. Giovanni Levi also makes interesting use of

judicial, alongside notarial records, in order to explore the nature of social relationships in a seventeenth-century rural community in Piedmont (1988).

For the more modern period, and for the nature of the household economy in the transition to capitalism, there is Peter Kriedte et al. (1981), a difficult but useful book, with a significant theoretical orientation. The relationship of family and work in the pre-industrial town can now be explored through the case studies of Martha C. Howell on fifteenth-century Leiden and Cologne (1986), and David Nicholas on fourteenth-century Ghent (1985). For the adjustment of the household to industrialization, Michael Anderson (1971) is fundamental. An important approach to this topic has been through studies of the working lives of women. There is a growing literature in this area, but one can familiarize oneself with the terms of the debate by consulting Louise Tilly and Joan Scott (1978).

Demography is at the heart of household economics. The most thorough reconstruction of a pre-industrial population is probably that of E. A. Wrigley and R. S. Schofield for England. They have summarized their findings and suggested some implications in a symposium edited by R. I. Rotberg and T. K. Rabb (1986). Wrigley's collected articles (1987) make an important link between demography and economic development, as does the more schematic David Levine (1987). For the continent, there is now the massive collective work of Jacques Dupâquier and others on French demography from prehistory, of which the first two volumes, taking the story down to 1789, have appeared to date (1988). For the more modern period, an early work of Philippe Ariès (1971; originally published 1948) is still enormously stimulating on the link between geography, economy and French population movements – surely a minor classic by a master better known for his books on other topics. On the late medieval period, the important reconstruction of Tuscan families by David Herlihy and Christiane Klapisch-Zuber, based on the outstanding data in the Florentine census of 1427, can be approached through the summary in Herlihy (1985).

The topic of household structure, part of the understanding of how a pre-industrial economy works, has tended to emancipate itself as a discrete area of research. The basic introductions here are the collections edited by Peter Laslett and Richard Wall (1972) and Richard Wall (1983). An attempt to see the household in more dynamic terms, as a flexible set of relationships, underlies the symposium of historians and anthropologists edited by Hans Medick and

David W. Sabean (1984) and the essay by Andrejs Plakans (1984), drawing on his Latvian research. Perhaps the whole concept of the household as the basic unit of enquiry needs to be questioned more thoroughly. One aspect which is likely to prove fruitful, though, is the exploration of the partnership of husband and wife, and the increasingly subordinate role of the woman in the Victorian home. An interesting insight into the reality of patriarchy as the foundation of a liberal society is provided by three geographically dispersed yet complementary studies of nineteenth-century women – that of Leonore Davidoff and Catherine Hall on England (1987), of Bonnie G. Smith on France (1981), and of Silvia M. Arrom on Mexico (1985). On peasant households, by contrast, see Segalen (1983) and Zonabend (1984).

Chapter 7   The rise of domesticity

The concept of domesticity or the home is probably best approached through the classic study of de Tocqueville on America in the early nineteenth century. What one is really trying to explore here is the ending of a patronage society and the rise of the professional. Both topics are the twin themes of Max Weber's controversial and splendid work, *The Protestant Ethic and the Spirit of Capitalism* (1985; originally published 1904–5). Complementary to Weber is that other classic, Philippe Ariès on childhood (1973), which grapples with much the same problem from a different angle, that of the inculcation of discipline in the school.

Ariès is something more than a chronicler of domesticity, but much of his argument depends on an interpretation of the sources for the latter. Useful insights into the problem of iconography are provided by Diane Owen Hughes (1986) and Robert Wheaton (1987). An enormous amount can be learned from architecture about the evolution of family life. I have found Richard Goldthwaite (1980) stimulating in this and other respects. The multi-volume series edited by Philippe Ariès and Georges Duby, *The History of Private Life*, of which volume I on the ancient and early medieval world has appeared to date in English (Harvard University Press 1987), promises to be a rich mine for historians of the family.

A systematic survey of English diaries and autobiographical sources is to be found in Linda Pollock (1983). Her argument that children were not a 'forgotten' category in the old regime is, I think, less a riposte to Ariès than to more incautious exponents of the theme. Standard accounts of the rise of the 'companionate' family can be seen in Lawrence Stone (1979), and in Edward Shorter (1976). While all these books have their merits, they do raise problems of interpretation, not so much at the level of the sources used, which seem reliable and representative enough, at least of certain social groups, as at the level of context. If one wants to abandon Ariès's high ground, his grasp of broader social structures, and focus on the quality of relationships within the family, then one probably has to move more deliberately into the discipline of psycho-history.

A fundamental introduction to this discipline is Erik Erikson (1977). His case study of *Young Man Luther* (1959) has been followed up by Elizabeth W. Marvick (1983), which is also informative on the historical context. The psycho-analyst David Hunt has suggested that historians might do better to fill in the context within which certain child-rearing practices make sense, rather than focus too precisely on individuals, on whom documentation from such remote epochs is likely to be unsatisfactory. His book (1972) is an interesting demonstration of this broader approach. So too is Philip Greven on child-rearing in relation to political orientation in colonial America (1977).

My ideas on childhood in the old regime have been shaped by reading Chateaubriand's memoirs, cited in the section on chapter 2, and some Spanish autobiographies: Esteban de Garibay (1854), written in the late sixteenth century, and Antonio Alcalá-Galiano (1886), for the late eighteenth and early nineteenth centuries. Perhaps the best source for Spanish childhood is the Requesens letters of the early sixteenth century, published in José M. March (1941). The pedagogical literature of Spain is surveyed in Juan Luis Morales (1960).

On the question of adolescence and the rise of discipline in the modern period a fine introduction is provided by John R. Gillis (1974). Finally, on the Spanish household, see F. Chacon (ed) *La Familia en la España Mediterránea* (Barcelona, 1987).

Reference list of works cited in the text

Dates in brackets after titles indicate original publication, where of interest.

Aksakov, Sergei 1917, *A Russian Gentleman*, London.
Alberti, Leon Battista 1969, *The Family in Renaissance Florence* (1438–41), ed. Watkins, R. Columbia, South Carolina.
Alcalá-Galiano, Antonio 1886, *Memorias*, 2 vols., Madrid.
Amorós, Joaquín 1777, *Discurso en que se manifiesta la necesidad y utilidad del consentimiento paterno para el matrimonio de los hijos* ..., Madrid.
Anderson, Michael 1971, *Family Structures in Nineteenth-Century Lancashire*, Cambridge.
Arbiol, Fray Antonio 1715, *La Familia regulada con doctrina de la sagrada escritura*, Zaragoza.
Argote de Molina, Gonzalo 1957, *Nobleza de Andalucía* (1588), Jaén.
Ariès, Philippe 1971, *Histoire des populations françaises et de leurs attitudes devant la vie depuis le XVIIIe siècle* (1948), Paris.
Ariès, Philippe 1973, *L'Enfant et la vie familiale sous l'ancien régime* (1960), Paris.
Arrom, Silvia M. 1985, *The Women of Mexico City 1790–1857*, Stanford, California.
Artigas, Miguel 1925, *Don Luis de Góngora y Argote: biografía y estudio crítico*, Madrid.
St Augustine 1972, *The City of God*, Harmondsworth.
Barth, Fredrik 1965, *Political Leadership among Swat Pathans*, London.
Bermúdez de Pedraza, Francisco 1981, *Antigüedad y Excelencias de Granada* (1608), Granada.
Beroul 1970, *The Romance of Tristan*, Harmondsworth.
Black-Michaud, J. 1975, *Cohesive Force: Feud in the Mediterranean and the Middle East*, Oxford.
Bloch, Marc 1965, *Feudal Society* (1939–40), 2 vols., London.

Bloch, Marc 1966 *French Rural History: an Essay on its Basic Characteristics*, London.

Bonnassie, Pierre 1976, *Le Catalogne du milieu du xe à la fin du xie siècle: croissance et mutations d'une société*, 2 vols., Toulouse.

Bouchard, Constance B. 1981, 'Consanguinity and Noble Marriage in the Tenth and Eleventh Centuries', *Speculum*, 56, pp. 268–87.

Bourdieu, Pierre 1977, *Outline of a Theory of Practice*, Cambridge.

Braudel, Fernand 1972–3, *The Mediterranean and the Mediterranean World in the Age of Philip II*, 2 vols., London.

Brenan, Gerald 1980, *South from Granada*, Cambridge.

Brucker, Gene (ed.) 1967, *Two Memoirs of Renaissance Florence*, New York.

Brucker, Gene 1986, *Giovanni and Lusanna: Love and Marriage in Renaissance Florence*, London.

Camos, Fray Marcos Antonio de 1592, *Microcosmia y govierno universal del hombre christiano*, Barcelona.

Campbell, J. K. 1964, *Honour, Family and Patronage: A Study of Institutions and Moral Values in a Greek Mountain Community*, Oxford.

Cárdenas, Francisco de 1884, *Estudios Jurídicos*, 2 vols., Madrid.

Caro Baroja, Julio 1956, *Linajes y Bandos*, Bilbao.

Castellano Castellano, Juan Luis 1984, *Luces y Reformismo: las Sociedades de Amigos del País del Reino de Granada*, Granada.

Castro, Juan Francisco de 1765–70, *Discursos críticos sobre las leyes*, 3 vols., Madrid.

Cellini, Benvenuto 1956, *Autobiography* (1558), Harmondsworth.

Cervantes, Miguel de 1967, *La Fuerza de la Sangre* (1613), Madrid.

Charles-Edwards, T. M. 1972, 'Kinship, Status and the Origins of the Hide', *Past and Present*, 56.

Chateaubriand, F. R. de 1976, *Mémoires de ma vie* (1826), Geneva.

Chateaubriand, F. R. de 1982, *Mémoires d'outre-tombe* (1848–50), vol. I, Paris.

Chayanov, A. V. 1966, *The Theory of Peasant Economy* (1925), Homewood, Illinois.

The Poem of the Cid 1984, Harmondsworth.

Collomp, Alain 1983, *La Maison du Père: famille et village en Haute-Provence aux xviie et xviiie siècles*, Paris.

Costa, Joaquín et al. 1885–1902, *Derecho Consuetudinario y Economía Popular de España*, 2 vols., Barcelona.

Cuisenier, Jean 1975, *Économie et parenté: leurs affinités de structure dans le domaine turc et dans le domaine arabe*, Paris.

Cuisenier, Jean 1976, 'Kinship and Social Organisation in the Turko-Mongolian Cultural Area', in Forster and Ranum, pp. 204–36.

Czap, Peter 1978, 'Marriage and the Peasant Joint Family in the Era of Serfdom', in D. L. Ransel, pp. 103–23.

Davidoff, L. and Hall, C. 1987, *Family Fortunes: Men and Women of the English Middle Class 1780–1850*, London.

Davis, J. 1973, *Land and Family in Pisticci*, London.

Davis, J. C. 1975, *A Venetian Family and its Fortune 1500–1900: The Donà and the Conservation of their Wealth*, Philadelphia.

Delille, Gérard 1985, *Famille et propriété dans le royaume de Naples* (XVe –XIXe siècle), Paris.

Dessert, Daniel 1987, *Fouquet*, Paris.

Dillard, Heath 1976, 'Women in Reconquest Castile', in S. M. Stuard (ed.), *Women in Medieval Society*, Philadelphia.

Dillard, Heath 1984, *Daughters of the Reconquest: Women in Castilian Town Society 1100–1300*, Cambridge.

Duby, Georges 1976, 'Lineage, Nobility and Chivalry in the Region of Mâcon during the Twelfth Century', in Forster and Ranum, pp. 16–40.

Duby, Georges 1981, *Le Chevalier, la femme et le prêtre: le mariage dans la France féodale*, Paris.

Duby, Georges 1984, *Guillaume le Maréchal ou le meilleur chevalier du monde*, Paris.

Dumont, Louis 1966, *Homo hierarchicus: essai sur le système des castes*, Paris.

Dupâquier, Jacques et al. 1988, *Histoire de la population française*, 2 vols. to date, Paris.

Duque de Estrada, Diego 1860, *Comentarios del Desengañado* (c.1642), Madrid.

Durkheim, Emile 1964, The Division of Labor in Society (1893), New York.

Einhard and Notker 1969, *Two Lives of Charlemagne*, Harmondsworth.

Elliott, J. H. 1986, *The Count-Duke of Olivares: The Statesman in an Age of Decline*, New Haven and London.

Engels, Friedrich 1968, *The Origins of the Family, Private Property and the State* (1884), in his *Selected Works*, London.

Enríquez, Alonso 1886, *Vida 1518–43*, in Colección de Documentos Inéditos para la Historia de España, vol. 85, Madrid.

Erikson, Erik 1959, *Young Man Luther*, London.

Erikson, Erik 1977 *Childhood and Society* (1950), London.

Escolano, Gaspar 1878, *Décadas de la Historia de ... Valencia*, 3 vols., Valencia.

Evans-Pritchard, E. E. 1969, *The Nuer: A Description of the Modes of Livelihood and Political Institutions of a Nilotic People* (1940), Oxford.

Fernández Martín, Luis 1980, 'La marquesa del Valle: una vida dramática en la corte de los Austrias', *Hispania* 143 (1980), pp. 559–638.

Flandrin, Jean-Louis 1981, *Le Sexe et l'Occident: évolution des attitudes et des comportements*, Paris.

Flandrin, Jean-Louis 1979, *Families in Former Times: Kinship, Household and Sexuality*, Cambridge.

Forster, Robert and Forster, Elborg 1969, *European Society in the Eighteenth Century*, New York.

Forster, Robert and Ranum, Orest (eds) 1976, *Family and Society: Selections from the Annales*, Baltimore and London.

Fortes, Meyer 1969, *Kinship and the Social Order: The Legacy of L. H. Morgan*, London.

Fortes, Meyer 1970, *Time and Social Structure*, London.

Foucault, Michel 1979–85, *The History of Sexuality*, 2 vols., London.

Fox, Robin 1967, *Kinship and Marriage: An Anthropological Perspective*, London.

Franklin, Benjamin 1948, *Autobiography*, London.

Froissart 1978, *Chronicles*, Harmondsworth.

Fuente, Vicente de la 1884–9, *Historia de las universidades, colegios y demás establecimientos de enseñanza en España*, 4 vols., Madrid.

Fustel de Coulanges, N. D. 1984, *La Cité antique* (1864), Paris.

García de Salazar, Lope 1884, *Las Bienandanças e fortunas* (c.1471), Madrid.

Garden, Maurice 1975, *Lyon et les Lyonnais au xviiie siècle*, Paris.

Garibay, Esteban de 1854, *Memorias* (c.1533–92), in *Memorial Histórico Español*, vol. VII, Madrid.

Gaudemet, Jean 1987, *Le Mariage en occident: les moeurs et le droit*, Paris.

Gellner, Ernest 1969, *Saints of the Atlas*, London.

Gellner, Ernest 1981, *Muslim Society*, Cambridge.

Génicot, Léopold 1982, *La Noblesse dans l'occident médiéval*, London.

Gerbet, Marie-Claude 1979, *La Noblesse dans le royaume de Castille*

1454–1516, Paris.

Gillis, J. R. 1974, *Youth and History: Tradition and Change in European Age Relations*, New York.

Girouard, Mark 1980, *Life in the English Country House*, London.

Given-Wilson, C. and Curteis, A. 1984, *The Royal Bastards of Medieval England*, London.

Goitein, S. D. 1978, *A Mediterranean Society: The Jewish Communities of the Arab World as Portrayed in the Documents of the Cairo Geniza*, vol. III, *The Family*, Berkeley and London.

Goldthwaite, Richard 1968, *Private Wealth in Renaissance Florence: A Study of Four Families*, Princeton.

Goldthwaite, Richard 1980, *The Rebuilding of Renaissance Florence*, Baltimore and London.

González Moreno, Joaquín 1969, *Don Fernando Enríquez de Ribera, tercer duque de Alcalá de los Gazules 1583–1637*, Seville.

González Palencia, Angel (ed.) 1932, 'La Junta de Reformación', in *Archivo Histórico Español*, vol. V, Madrid.

González Palencia, Angel 1941–3 (with Eugenio Mele), *Vida y Obras de Don Diego Hurtado de Mendoza*, 3 vols., Madrid.

Goody, Jack 1972, 'The Evolution of the Family', in Laslett and Wall, pp. 103–24.

Goody, Jack 1976, *Production and Reproduction: The Domestic Domain*, Cambridge.

Goody, Jack 1983, *The Development of the Family and Marriage in Europe*, Cambridge.

Goody, J., Thirsk, J. and Thompson, E. P. (eds) 1976, *Family and Inheritance: Rural Society in Western Europe 1200–1800*, Cambridge.

Goubert, Pierre 1968, *Cent mille provinciaux au XVIIᵉ siècle: Beauvais et le Beauvaisis de 1600 à 1730*, Paris.

Gregory of Tours 1974, *The History of the Franks*, Harmondsworth.

Greven, Philip 1977, *The Protestant Temperament: Patterns of Child-rearing, Religious Experience and the Self in Early America*, New York.

Grose-Hodge, H. 1946, *Roman Panorama*, Cambridge.

Guichard, Pierre 1977, *Structures sociales 'orientales' et 'occidentales' dans l'Espagne musulmane*, Paris.

Guillaumin, Emile 1980, *La Vie d'un simple* (1904), Paris.

Gurrea, Diego 1627, *Arte de enseñar hijos de príncipes y señores*, Lérida.

Hanawalt, Barbara 1986, *The Ties That Bound: Peasant Families in*

Medieval England, Oxford.

Heers, Jacques 1977, *Family Clans in the Middle Ages: A Study of Political and Social Structures in Urban Areas*, Amsterdam.

Helmholz, R. H. 1974, *Marriage Litigation in Medieval England*, Cambridge.

Herlihy, David 1978, *The Social History of Italy and Western Europe 700–1500*, London.

Herlihy, David 1985, *Medieval Households*, Cambridge, Mass.

Hernández Rodríguez, E. 1947, *Las Ideas Pedagógicas del doctor Pedro López de Montoya*, Madrid.

Herrera Puga, P. 1981, *Grandeza y miseria en Andalucía 1578–1616*, Granada.

Herzen, Alexander 1980, *Childhood, Youth and Exile* (1852–3), Oxford.

Holt, J. C. 1982–5, 'Feudal Society and the Family in Early Medieval England', *Transactions of the Royal Historical Society*, vols. 32–5.

Homans, George C. 1975, *English Villagers of the Thirteenth Century* (1941), New York.

Homer 1980 *The Odyssey*, Oxford.

Houlbrooke, Ralph 1984, *The English Family 1450–1700*, London.

Howell, Martha C. 1986. *Women, Production and Patriarchy in Late Medieval Cities*, Chicago.

Hughes, Diane Owen 1978, 'From Brideprice to Dowry in Mediterranean Europe', *Journal of Family History*, 3, pp. 262–96.

Hughes, Diane Owen, 1986, 'Representing the Family: Portraits and Purposes in Early Modern Italy', *Journal of Interdisciplinary History*, 17.

Hughes, Diane Owen 1975, 'Urban Growth and Family Structure in Medieval Genoa', *Past and Present*, 66.

Hunt, David 1972, *Parents and Children in History: The Psychology of Family Life in Early Modern France*, New York.

Ibn Khaldūn 1967, *The Muqaddimah: An Introduction to History*, London.

Kent, F. W. 1977, *Household and Lineage in Renaissance Florence*, Princeton.

King, P. D. 1972, *Law and Society in the Visigothic Kingdom*, Cambridge.

Klapisch-Zuber, Christiane 1985, *Women, Family and Ritual in Renaissance Italy*, Chicago and London.

Kriedte, Peter et al. 1981, *Industrialization before Industrialization*,

Cambridge.

Kula, Witold 1976a, *An Economic Theory of the Feudal System: Towards a Model of the Polish Economy 1500–1800*, London.

Kula, Witold 1976b, 'The Seigneury and the Peasant Family in Eighteenth-Century Poland', in Forster and Ranum, pp. 192–203.

Lantery, Raimundo de 1949, *Memorias 1673–1700* (ed. Alvaro Picardo y Gómez), Cadiz.

Laslett, Peter 1965, *The World We Have Lost* (3rd ed., 1983), London.

Laslett, Peter and Wall, Richard (eds) 1972, *Household and Family in Past Time*, Cambridge.

Laslett, Peter, Oosterveen, K. and Smith, R. M. (eds) 1980, *Bastardy and its Comparative History*, London.

Laurens, Jeanne de, see Ribbe, Charles de.

Lebrun, François 1975, *Les Hommes et la mort en Anjou aux XVIIe et XVIIIe siècles*, Paris.

Leclercq, Jean 1979, *Monks and Love in Twelfth-Century France*, Oxford.

León, Fray Luis de 1975, *La Perfecta Casada* (1583), Madrid.

Le Play, Frédéric 1864, *La Réforme sociale en France déduite de l'observation comparée des peuples européens*, 2 vol., Paris.

Le Roy Ladurie, Emmanuel 1980, *Montaillou: Cathars and Catholics in a French Village 1294–1324*, London.

Levi, Giovanni 1988, *Inheriting Power: The Story of an Exorcist*, Chicago & London.

Lévi-Strauss, Claude 1969, *The Elementary Structures of Kinship* (1949), Boston.

Levine, David 1987, *Reproducing Families: The Political Economy of English Population History*, Cambridge.

Lewis, Andrew 1981, *Royal Succession in Capetian France: Studies on Familial Order and the State*, Cambridge, Mass.

Llorente, Juan Antonio 1809, *Colección diplomática de varios papeles ... sobre dispensas matrimoniales*, Madrid.

Lockwood, William G. 1975, *European Moslems: Economy and Ethnicity in Western Bosnia*, New York.

Lottin, Alain 1975, *La Désunion du couple sous l'ancien régime: l'exemple du nord*, Lille.

McArdle, Frank 1978, *Altopascio: A Study in Tuscan Rural Society 1587–1784*, Cambridge.

Macfarlane, Alan 1978, *The Origins of English Individualism: The Family, Property and Social Transition*, Oxford.

Macfarlane, Alan 1986, *Marriage and Love in England: Modes of Reproduction, 1300–1840*, Oxford.

McLennan, John F. 1970, *Primitive Marriage: An Inquiry into the Origins of Capture in Marriage Ceremonies* (1865) (ed. P. Riviere), Chicago and London.

Mair, Lucy 1972, *An Introduction to Social Anthropology*, Oxford.

Maltby, William S. 1983, *Alba: A Biography of Fernando Alvarez de Toledo, 3rd Duke of Alba 1507–82*, Berkeley and London.

Mann, Thomas 1975, *Buddenbrooks* (1902), Harmondsworth.

March, José M. 1941, *Níñez y Juventud de Felipe II 1527–47*, 2 vols., Madrid.

Martín, Luis 1983, *Daughters of the Conquistadores: Women of the Viceroyalty of Peru*, Albuquerque, New Mexico.

Martínez-Alier, Verena 1974, *Marriage, Class and Colour in Nineteenth-Century Cuba*, Cambridge.

Marvick, Elizabeth W. 1983, *The Young Richelieu: A Psycho-analytic Approach to Leadership*, Chicago.

Medick, Hans and Sabean, David W. (eds) 1984, *Interest and Emotion: Essays on the Study of Family and Kinship*, Cambridge.

Mello, Francisco Manuel de 1923, *Carta de Guía de Casados* (1651), Oporto.

Mitterauer, M. and Sieder, R. 1982, *The European Family: Patriarchy to Partnership from the Middle Ages to the Present*, Oxford.

Montagne, Robert 1973, *The Berbers: Their Social and Political Organisation* (1931), London.

Morales, Juan Luis 1960, *El Niño en la Cultura Española*, 4 vols., Madrid.

Moreno de Guerra, Juan 1929, *Bandos en Jerez: los del puesto de abajo: estudio social y genealógico de la Edad Media en las fronteras del Reino moro de Granada*, Madrid.

Moret, Sigismundo 1863 (with Luis Silvela), *La Familia Foral y la familia castellana*, Madrid.

Morgan, Lewis Henry 1974, *Ancient Society, or Researches in the Lines of Human Progress from Savagery through Barbarism to Civilisation* (1877) (ed. E. B. Leacock), Gloucester, Massachusetts.

Mousnier, Roland 1967, *Fureurs paysannes: les paysans dans les révoltes du XVIIe siècle*, Paris.

Murillo 1983, *Bartolomé Esteban Murillo 1617–82*, Royal Academy of Arts Exhibition Guide.

Murray, Alexander C. 1983, *Germanic Kinship Structures: Studies in Law and Society in Antiquity and the Early Middle Ages*, Toronto.

Nadaud, Martin 1948, *Mémoires de Léonard, ancien garçon maçon* (1895), Paris.

Nader, Helen 1979, *The Mendoza Family in the Spanish Renaissance 1350–1550*, New Brunswick, NJ.

The Nibelungenlied 1965, Harmondsworth.

Nicholas, David 1985, *The Domestic Life of a Medieval City: Women, Children and the Family in Fourteenth-Century Ghent*, Lincoln, Nebraska.

Noonan, John T. Jr. 1972, *Power to Dissolve: Lawyers and Marriages in the Courts of the Roman Curia*, Cambridge, Mass.

Ochoa, Eugenio de 1856–70, *Epistolario Español: colección de cartas de Españoles ilustres antiguos y modernos*, 2 vols., Madrid.

O'Neill, Brian J. 1987, *Social Inequality in a Portuguese Hamlet: Land, Late Marriage and Bastardy 1870–1978*, Cambridge.

Origo, Iris 1963, *The Merchant of Prato*, London.

Outhwaite, R. B. (ed.) 1981, *Marriage and Society: Studies in the Social History of Marriage*, London.

Ozment, Steven 1980, *The Age of Reform*, New Haven and London.

Ozment, Steven 1983, *When Fathers Ruled: Family Life in Reformation Europe*, Cambridge Mass.

Ozment, Steven 1986, *Magdalena and Balthasar: An Intimate Portrait of Life in Sixteenth Century Europe Revealed in the Letters of a Nuremberg Husband and Wife*, New York.

Pérez y López, Antonio 1781, *Discurso sobre la honra y deshonra legal*, Madrid.

Phillpotts, Bertha 1913, *Kindred and Clan in the Middle Ages and After: A Study in the Sociology of the Teutonic Races*, Cambridge.

Pierrard, Pierre 1965, *La Vie ouvrière à Lille sous le Second Empire*, Paris.

Piferrer, Francisco 1857–60 *Nobiliario de los Reinos y Señoríos de España*, 6 vols., Madrid.

Pineda, Juan de 1963–4, *Diálogos familiares de la agricultura cristiana* (1589), 5 vols., Madrid.

Pirenne, Henri 1939, *Mohammed and Charlemagne*, London.

Pitt-Rivers, Julian 1971, *The People of the Sierra* (1954) (2nd ed), Chicago and London.

Pitt-Rivers, Julian 1977, *The Fate of Shechem or the Politics of Sex: Essays in the Anthropology of the Mediterranean*, Cambridge.

Plakans, Andrejs 1984, *Kinship in the Past*, Oxford.

Plato 1906, *The Republic*, London.

Plato 1960, *The Laws*, London.

Pollock, Linda 1983, *Forgotten Children: Parent–Child Relations from 1500 to 1900*, Cambridge.

Poni, Carlo 1978, 'Family and "Podere" in Emilia-Romagna', *Journal of Italian History*, 1, pp. 201–21.

Powis, Jonathan 1984, *Aristocracy*, Oxford.

Radcliffe-Brown, A. R. 1952, *Structure and Function in Primitive Society*, London.

Radcliffe-Brown, A. R. and Forde, Daryll (eds) 1987, *African Systems of Kinship and Marriage* (1950), London.

Ransel, D. L. (ed.) 1978, *The Family in Imperial Russia*, London.

Rebel, Hermann 1983, *Peasant Classes: The Bureaucratisation of Property and Family Relations under Early Habsburg Absolutism 1511–1636*, Princeton.

Rétif de la Bretonne, Nicolas-Edme 1986, *My Father's Life* (1779), Gloucester.

Reuter, Timothy (ed.) 1978, *The Medieval Nobility: Studies on the Ruling Classes of France and Germany from the Sixth to the Twelfth Century*, Amsterdam.

Ribbe, Charles de 1879, *Une Famille au XVIIe siècle d'après des documents originaux*, Tours.

The Song of Roland 1957, Harmondsworth.

Rotberg, R. I. and Rabb, T. K. (eds) 1986, *Population and History: From the Traditional to the Modern World*, Cambridge.

Rougemont, Denis de 1972, *L'Amour et l'occident* (1938), Paris.

Roussel, Denis 1976, *Tribu et cité: étude sur les groupes sociaux dans les cités grecques aux époques archaïques et classiques*, Paris.

Ruggiero, Guido 1985, *The Boundaries of Eros: Sex Crimes and Sexuality in Renaissance Venice*, Oxford.

Ruiz Domenec, J. E. 1979, 'Systèmes de parenté et théorie de l'alliance dans la société catalane, env. 1000–env. 1240', *Revue Historique*, 261, pp. 305–26.

Safley, Thomas Max 1984, *Let No Man Put Asunder: The Control of Marriage in the German South-West 1550–1600*, Kirksville, Missouri.

Saint-Simon, Duc de 1967–8, *Historical Memoirs: A Shortened Version*, ed. L. Norton, 3 vols., London.

Salazar y Castro, Luis de 1959, *Historia Genealógica de la Casa de Haro*, Madrid

Salvá, Miguel, and Sainz de Barranda, P. (eds) 1845, *Colección de Documentos Inéditos para la Historia de España*, vol. VII (the Alba marriage), Madrid.

Sánchez, Matías, 1792, *El Padre de Familias*, Madrid.

Sánchez, Tomás 1602–5, *Disputationum de Sancto Matrimonii Sacramento, Libri X*, 3 vols., Madrid.

Schama, Simon 1987, *The Embarrassment of Riches: An Interpretation of Dutch Culture in the Golden Age*, London.

Schneider, Jane and Peter 1976, *Culture and Political Economy in Western Sicily*, New York.

Scott, Sir Walter 1952, *The Heart of Midlothian* (1818), London.

Segalen, Martine 1983, *Love and Power in the Peasant Family*, Oxford.

Sempere, Juan 1805, *Historia de los Vínculos y Mayorazgos*, Madrid.

Shaffer, John W. 1982, *Family and Farm: Agrarian Change and Household Organisation in the Loire Valley 1500–1900*, New York.

Shorter, Edward, 1976, *The Making of the Modern Family*, London.

Las Siete Partidas del Rey Don Alfonso el Sabio 1807 (facsimile reprint, 3 vols., 1972), Madrid.

Smith, R. M. (ed.) 1984, *Land, Kinship and Life Cycle*, Cambridge.

Smith, W. Robertson 1903, *Kinship and Marriage in Early Arabia* (1885), Boston.

Smith, Bonnie G. 1981, *Ladies of the Leisure Class: The Bourgeoises of Northern France in the Nineteenth Century*, Princeton.

Southern, R. W. 1987, *The Making of the Middle Ages* (1953), London.

Stafford, Pauline 1983, *Queens, Concubines and Dowagers: The King's Wife in the Early Middle Ages*, London.

Stirling, Paul 1965, *Turkish Village*, London.

Stone, Lawrence 1979, *The Family, Sex and Marriage in England 1500–1800* (abridged edition), London.

Tawney, R. H. 1926, *Religion and the Rise of Capitalism*, London.

St Teresa of Avila 1951, *Libro de las Fundaciones* (c.1573–80), Buenos Aires (English translation, 1913, London).

St Teresa of Avila 1980, *Su Vida* (c.1565), Madrid (English translation, 1957, London).

Tillion, Germaine 1966, *Le Harem et les cousins*, Paris.

Tilly, Louise and Scott, Joan 1978, *Women, Work and Family*, New York.

De Tocqueville, Alexis 1963, *De la démocratie en Amérique* (1835–40) (abridged edition), Paris.

De Tocqueville, Alexis 1967, *L' Ancien Régime et la révolution* (1856), Paris.

The Romance of Tristan, see Beroul.

Vega, Lope de 1982, *El Caballero de Olmedo* (1606), Madrid.

Viciana, Martín de 1972, *Chrónica de la Inclita y Coronada Ciudad de Valencia* (1564) vol. II, Valencia.

Villadiego, Alonso de 1766, *Instrucción política y práctica judicial . . .* (1626), Madrid.

Vives, Juan Luis 1943, *Instrucción de la Mujer Cristiana* (1524), Madrid.

Vovelle, M., 1973, *Piété baroque et déchristianisation en Provence au XVIIIe siècle*, Paris.

Wall, Richard (ed.) 1983, *Family Forms in Historic Europe*, Cambridge.

Wallace-Hadrill, J. M. 1962, 'The Bloodfeud of the Franks', in his *The Long-Haired Kings*, London.

Weber, Max 1960, *The City*, London.

Weber, Max 1985, *The Protestant Ethic and the Spirit of Capitalism* (1904–5), London.

Wemple, Suzanne F. 1981, *Women in Frankish Society: Marriage and the Cloister 500 to 900*, Philadelphia.

Wheaton, Robert and Hareven, Tamara K. (eds) 1980, *Family and Sexuality in French History*, Philadelphia.

Wheaton, Robert 1987, 'Images of Kinship', *Journal of Family History*, 12, pp. 389–405.

Wilson, Stephen 1988, *Feuding, Conflict and Banditry in Nineteenth-Century Corsica*, Cambridge.

Wolf, Eric 1982, *Europe and the People Without History*, Berkeley and London.

Wrigley, E. A. 1987, *People, Cities and Wealth: The Transformation of Traditional Society*, Oxford.

Zapata, Luis 1859, *Miscelánea* (c.1580–90), Memorial Histórico Español, vol. XI, Madrid.

Zola, Emile 1968, *Germinal* (1884), Paris (English translation, 1974 Harmondsworth).

Zola, Emile 1971, *L'Assommoir* (1877), Paris (English translation, 1970 Harmondsworth).

Zonabend, F. 1984, *The Enduring Memory*, Manchester.

Glossary of kinship terms
used in the text

Affines One's relatives by marriage.

Agnates, agnatic Relationship traced through the male line only, as typically in ancient Rome.

Arras A 'pledge'; significantly the word comes to be applied to the endowment of the bride by her husband in Castile in the early modern period. Cognate with *donatio propter nuptias*.

Bilateral (kindred) A grouping of relatives who trace their common identity through the ancestry of both mothers and fathers. Akin to the Germanic *Sib*, and a relative rarity in world cultures, at least among tribal peoples.

Bridewealth Endowment of either (a) the bride's family, or (b) the bride herself by the groom. The former, sometimes called the brideprice, is typical of *unilineal descent groups*, which are compensated, as it were, for the loss of their women. The latter, more common among the people of the Mediterranean and Europe, seems to testify to a certain breakdown of tribal structures, and an emancipation of the household, being akin to the later English *dower*.

Clan A Gaelic word, defined by the *Oxford English Dictionary* as 'family, stock, race'. Loosely applied to *unilineal descent groups*; distinguished from a *lineage* by some authors because of the multiplication of branches whose exact relationship with the main stem is either not known or not a matter of great moment (i.e. inheritance of property is less important than solidarity of numbers).

Cognates, cognatic One's relatives as traced both through one's father and one's mother, considered as a homogeneous group – therefore the opposite of *agnates* or *agnatic*.

Collateral kin Relatives beyond the *stem family* and its patrimony, or more loosely, beyond the conjugal family and its household.

Consanguines Relatives by blood.

Cross-cousins The children of one's father's sister or one's mother's brother – chiefly of interest because they are close relatives who

yet may fall outside the *unilineal descent group* or tribe, organized
in terms of male or female descent alone. They may, therefore, be
persons of lesser honour (or greater honour) than *parallel cousins*.
Of some interest for marriage alliances in tribal societies with a
developing economic or political hierarchy, since they maintain
exogamy but encourage dependence.

Donatio propter nuptias 'A gift in consideration of the marriage'
from the groom to his bride; typical of Mediterranean societies,
where it was arranged as a counterpart to, and in proportion to,
the *dowry*. Often confused with the *arras*.

Dower Provision for the bride in widowhood out of her husband's
property, either as a customary proportion, or as fixed in the
wedding contract. Typical of English customary law, evolving out
of the old Germanic *bridewealth*, where the wife did not receive or
did not control her own *dowry*.

Dowry Endowment of the bride by her own family of origin. Distinguished from the *dower* not only by its origin, but also by the
fact that the wife retained control during the marriage itself,
though the property was administered by her husband, and by the
fact that her family of origin kept a lively interest in it, weakening
the autonomy of the conjugal family. A very Mediterranean institution in this sense.

Endogamy Marriage within the group, properly within the group of
consanguines, but also loosely applied, according to the context, to
the neighbourhood, the village or the social class (*homogamy*).

Exogamy Marriage outside the group, a basic rule of tribal
societies, where it is used to define the boundaries of the *unilineal
descent group* or *clan*. Tends to give way to *endogamy* when daughters are allowed to inherit with sons.

Extended family household Household grouping any relative addi-
tional to the husband, wife and children. Typical enough of pre-
industrial western Europe through informal arrangements for taking in 'demographic casualties' – orphaned sisters or nephews, a
widowed and incapacitated grandparent. Unlike the 'joint' or
'stem' family, is compatible with a proletariat and a market-
orientated economy.

Gens The Roman clan, tracing descent in the male line only from a
common ancestor.

Joint family household Where two or more married couples live
under the same roof (sometimes loosely known as 'patriarchal').
Typical until recently of parts of Russia and the Balkans. A system

which maximizes labour in an economic setting where land is not yet scarce or a marketable commodity. Also to be found among share-cropping families in more developed economies.

Lineage   A *unilineal descent group* or clan, distinguished by some students from the latter because of its focus on the transmission of a patrimony, which ensures greater control and awareness of the line of descent, restricting marriages and the proliferation of collateral branches thereby. Akin to a 'stem family'.

Matrilineal   Descent traced through the mother.

Multiple family household   see Joint family household

Parallel cousins   The children of one's father's brother, or one's mother's sister. The opposite of the 'cross-cousins', in the sense that they are often full members of the *unilineal descent group* and enjoy an equivalence of honour. They are usually forbidden as marriage partners in tribal societies, but in Arab, and more informally in Christian Mediterranean countries, marriage with the father's brother's child seems to be an interesting way of reconciling female inheritance with maintenance of 'tribal' honour.

Patriarchal   Fundamentally a loose way of describing a *joint family household*, where the older male exercises a hegemony over his married sons and their children.

Patrilineal   Descent traced through the father

Prestation   In family studies, usually applied to endowment at marriage.

Segmentary   The branching system of clans, each of whose parts stands in an identical relationship with the next one, the solidarity or rivalry of brothers, for example, being a microcosm of that of cousins or more distant kinsmen.

Sib, Sippe   The *cognates*, or descendants in both the father's and the mother's line, on whom a man could count for blood vengeance among the ancient Germans. Less clearly defined and stable than a clan, since it does not 'segment' naturally, but has to be legally defined afresh for each new generation (otherwise numbers would have multiplied out of all control). Among the Franks, possibly the descendants of the first cousins of one's four grandparents.

Stem family   A patrimonial grouping, keeping property together (as far as possible) in the 'stem', or (usually) eldest child, for the good of the whole. Can take the concrete form of co-residence of the single married child with his parents, pending their death and the transfer of the inheritance.

Unilineal descent group   A grouping defined by its descent from a common ancestor 'in one line only', that is, either through the father or the mother, but not both. The technical definition of a *clan*.

Verba de futuro The form of words by which, in canon law, a man and a woman contract a binding betrothal, which can only in exceptional circumstances be broken.

Verba de praesenti The form of words by which, in canon law, a man and women contract a valid and binding marriage.

Index